# Was America a Mistake?

## An Eighteenth-Century Controversy

Frontispiece depicting a Sachem of the Mohawks, from *Ouabi, or the Virtues of Nature,* by Philenia, a Lady of Boston (Sarah Wentworth Morton), Boston, 1790. Courtesy of the New York Historical Society, New York City. The original caption reads: Then amidst yon Chiefs retire / Seated round the sacred fire, / Waiting for the warrior-feast, / Let them hail thee as their guest.

# Was America a Mistake?

## An Eighteenth-Century Controversy

by

Henry Steele Commager

and

Elmo Giordanetti

HARPER TORCHBOOKS

*Harper & Row, Publishers*

*New York, Evanston, and London*

*To*

*Evan*

*who makes the question ridiculous*

WAS AMERICA A MISTAKE?



Printed in the United States of America.

First edition: HARPER TORCHBOOKS, 1967,
Harper & Row, Publishers, Incorporated,
49 East 33rd Street, New York,
N.Y. 10016.

Library of Congress Catalog Card Number: 67-21563.

*Designed by Darlene Starr Carbone*

## Contents

## Illustrations

*(Illustrations 1–10 will be found in a group following page 64.)*

# Preface

ONE OF THE GREAT, but forgotten, controversies of the eighteenth century had to do with the meaning of America. Was the discovery of America a mistake? Would mankind have been better and happier had the New World never been discovered by the Old? Did America add anything to civilization or to the happiness and well-being of mankind? Scientists like the Comte de Buffon, *philosophes* like the Abbé Raynal, asserted that Man and Nature degenerated in the New World and predicted that Europeans, too, would degenerate there. More, they charged that the discovery of America had led to the extermination of the native races, centuries of imperialist wars, the extension of slavery, and the spread of deadly diseases. Champions of America on both sides of the water repudiated these accusations, contending that the discovery of America has been not a curse but a blessing to mankind, and predicting that in the New World man would advance to ever greater glory and happiness. Not surprisingly Americans themselves had a good deal to say about the matter; they offered not only arguments but evidence to prove the superiority of the New World to the Old. *Was America a Mistake?* recounts something of the history of this famous Old World controversy and provides a selection of leading documents in the argument.

# Part One: The Debate

# 1.

# "America Is Degraded and Degenerated"

IT IS A TYPICAL eighteenth-century question, this. For the Enlightenment addressed itself only to the great questions, and contemplated these incessantly. What a din of controversy and debate; what a clashing of minds, and of philosophies; what a febrile interchange from country to country. What is the nature of the universe and of the celestial mechanics which God, or Nature, has imposed upon it? How does man fit into the cosmic system? Is primitive man happier than civilized man? Were the Greeks or the Romans superior to modern man? Is civilization itself a mistake? What is the origin of government? What is the end of government? Are wars ever justified? Are colonies worth their cost? What are the Rights of Man? What is virtue, what is happiness?

These are the importunate questions which launched a thousand controversies, sent pens scratching across an infinity of pages, exploded into encyclopedias and histories and discourses and treatises by the hundred. . . . How they speculated, how they argued, how they wrote! They studied the past, they surveyed the present, they imagined the future. Nothing trivial commanded their concern, nothing parochial; always the great universal questions. They were all cosmic philosophers, even the meanest of them. They read history, confident that they could wrest from it great moral lessons. They analyzed government to learn the spirit—and the substance—of the laws. With extensive view, they surveyed mankind from China to Peru. They sought the good and the true and considered the sublime and the beautiful.

No question more importunate, none more fascinating, than this: was America a mistake? Was it a mistake to have discovered this strange new world? a mistake to have conquered it, if she was indeed conquered; a mistake to plant colonies on those alien shores? Everywhere the philosophers debated that, but nowhere more insistently than in France. And not the philosophers only, but scientists and statesmen and churchmen as well—they were all philosophers, to be sure; who in that day was not a philosopher?

It was the Abbé Raynal who brought it all to a head for Europe, and perhaps for us as well, and we will do well to begin with him.

What an extraordinary figure he was, this Guillaume Raynal, prancing across the stage of Europe at mid-century, yet another of those abbés who are so ubiquitous, another child of the Jesuits in revolt against that order. He was a preacher, for a time; a teacher, a man of letters. He was an economist, though whether a physiocrat or a mercantilist it was hard to say. He was a philosopher, he was an historian, the first, it is said, to use the term "Enlightened Despot"; he was even a patron of the arts, for somewhere along the way (his critics said it was in the slave trade!) he had picked up a fortune, and he dispensed it with a free hand, here a literary prize, there a subsidy to one of the Academies that had honored him with membership; here support to the young Provençals who flocked about him in Paris, there—it happened to be on an island in the Lake of Lucerne—a statue to Liberty which figured no other than the Abbé Raynal! He was not a great man, far from it, but he wrote one of the great books of the age: *A Philosophical and Political History of the Settlements and Trade of Europeans in the Two Indies.* That history was, in its day, like the *Encyclopédie* itself; it was like Buffon's *Histoire naturelle;* it was more than a work of history or of literature. It was a weapon, it was a force, it was an institution.

Never was there such a history, really a work of philosophy, just as the title promised. It appeared first in 1770 (or was it 1772?—there is some confusion even here), in four large volumes, then in eight and eventually in twelve, and it went through edition after edition, twenty authorized and forty or fifty more that were pirated. Franklin read it and was amused by it and provided materials that would modify its excesses; Jefferson read it, and was moved to reply in his *Notes on Virginia.* Crèvecoeur read it, the American Farmer, and dedicated his wonderful *Letters* to its author, not a very logical gesture.

Gibbon read it and admired it, and so did his rival, William Robertson up in Edinburgh. Frederick the Great read it with enthusiasm until he came to that outrageous criticism of his Wars, and then he threw it in the fire; the Duke of Gotha read it and when he prepared to flee to the New World he was careful to pack it in his trunks. Samuel Romilly read it, and it filled him with hatred for slavery; and Toussaint L'Ouverture read it in his hut in Haiti, spelling out the burning words, "Where is he, that great man, whom Nature owes to the honor of the human race? Where is he, that new Spartacus, who will find no Crassus. Then the Black Code will vanish; how terrible will the White Code be." How terrible, indeed; did Toussaint remember that, languishing in his island prison on the Lake of Geneva? The Baron Grimm read it; he read everything, it was his business to read everything, for six sovereigns waited breathless for his Reports. "Since Montesquieu," he wrote, "our literature has produced no monument that is worthier to pass to the remotest posterity," and—mark this—"to consecrate the progress of the Enlightenment." That was it, Raynal's great book was to consecrate the progress of the Enlightenment!

And what a history it was with its nineteen grand divisions, a magnificent pot-pourri of history, economics, politics, anthropology, and morality, written every which way, and by half a dozen contributors, too, though Raynal saw to it that he got all the credit. It was the first history to deal with the expansion of Europe as a single grand theme, the first to do justice to the colored races, the first to fit together politics and economics and religion and society in a single pattern. It preached the immorality of war and the iniquity of colonies and the betrayal of religion by the Church and the right of revolution, and the virtue of simplicity in contrast to the wickedness of sophistication.

If it was not "against all governments and all religions" as Horace Walpole wrote, it was certainly against the governments of those powers which had so wickedly exploited the Two Indies; if it was not against all religion, it was certainly against the religion preached by the Jesuits to the Chinese and the Paraguayans and the Hurons. No wonder the book was anathema to the authorities of France; no wonder it was put on the Index, banned, burned; no wonder it was read with rapture in every country in Europe.

And what was the message that Europe read in this flaming history? It was this, that wherever Europeans had gone, in the East or in the West, they had carried death, disease, and destruction. They had created empires—but at the price of ceaseless wars and of the lives of millions of innocent natives. Not since the Deluge had there been such a holocaust. They had added undreamed-of luxuries to life—and had enervated those who indulged in them: how much happier the natives, without luxury or vice! They had spread commerce but inflamed speculation and substituted the love of gold for the love of honor. They had spread Christianity, and with it superstition and fanaticism. Worst of all, it had fastened slavery on one half of the globe.

Was that the fault of the New World? Was it right to blame America for all of this misery and tragedy?

How futile to speak of fault! The discovery of America was worse than a sin; it was a mistake. How much better for mankind had America remained hidden in that oblivion to which a kind nature had consigned her.

For the American continents were primitive, degenerate, and irremediable. So the great Buffon had made clear; so the great Raynal reaffirmed:

> Everything [in the New World] exhibits the vestiges of a malady of which the human race still feels the effects. The ruin of that world is still imprinted on its inhabitants, they are a species of men degraded and degenerated in their natural constitution, in their stature, in their way of life, and in their understanding, which is but little advanced in all the arts of civilization. A damper air and a more marshy ground must necessarily have infected the very roots and seeds both of the subsistence and the multiplication of mankind.

Nature was corrupt, animal life feeble, and as for the savages who roamed the jungles and swamps and deserts:

> The men had less strength and less courage, no beard and no hair; they have less appearances of manhood, and are but little susceptible of the lively and powerful sentiment of love.

Inevitably

> Men who have little more hair than eunuchs cannot abound in generating principles. The blood of these people is watery and cold.

The males have sometimes milk in their breasts. Hence arises their tardy inclination to the sex . . . hence hath proceeded that want of population which hath always been observed in them.

It was not just the savages of America who were doomed by nature to inferiority, it was the Europeans as well. Clearly Spain was on the decline, in the Old World and in the New alike. The Creoles of Louisiana were enervated in mind as in body. Even the English—this was in the earlier editions—"had visibly degenerated." Has nature punished them for colonizing in this unwelcoming world? "Are they a people degenerated by transplanting," asked the Abbé, "by mixture?"

The conclusion of this elaborate investigation was harsh but inescapable: the discovery of America had been a mistake. Far better had Columbus never lifted the veil that had so long hidden this world from the greedy eyes of the East; far better had the Conquistadores failed in their campaigns against the Aztecs and the Incas; far better had Cabot and Verrazzano and Henry Hudson and all the other intrepid navigators found a watery grave in those oceans that had so long guarded the Western world and "served it in the office of a wall."

That was certainly the conclusion of Raynal's first edition, in 1770, and of the second as well, published the year of American independence. Then came the French alliance and the triumph of the Americans, Lafayette and Rochambeau, Benjamin Franklin and George Washington. Did all that persuade the Abbé to change his tune? In part, yes, but only in part, only for the English settlements in the New World. Otherwise Raynal stuck by his guns. More, as if to flaunt his independence of the vicissitudes of history, he now, in the very year of Yorktown, made explicit what before had been implicit.

"Let us stop here," he wrote in his concluding chapter, "and consider ourselves as existing at the time when America and India were unknown. Let me suppose that I address myself to the most cruel of the Europeans in the following terms. There exist regions which will furnish thee with rich metals, agreeable clothing, and delicious food. But read this history, and behold at what price the discovery is promised to thee. Dost thou wish or not that it should be made? Is it to be imagined that there exists a being infernal enough to answer this question in the affirmative! Let it be remembered, that there will not be a single instant in futurity, when my question will not have the same force."

Surely that verdict was both clear and final. But no, not for the Abbé Raynal, who was never quite sure where he stood. Even as he was penning this final chapter of his history he decided to reopen the whole question. The Academy down at Lyon had honored him with membership, and now he rewarded it by establishing a prize for an essay on precisely the question he already answered so conclusively. "Was the discovery of America a blessing or a curse to mankind? If it was a blessing, by what means are we to conserve and enhance its benefits? If it was a curse, by what means are we to repair the damage?"

This was not really a new question, though Raynal, who believed that he had discovered both the Indies, thought that it was. In reality Raynal's prize essay contest was not so much the opening as the closing chapter of the debate, for after this the problem took on a new form, and even those who participated in the contest found themselves discussing not so much the question of the discovery of America as its history. It was not a new question; it was not even a wholly honest question, for there was more here than met the eye, more than an inquiry about America. There is no evidence that Raynal himself cared a fig about America, and as for those who answered his question, what they cared about was quite clearly not the New World, hardly even the Old World, but quite simply their own world. America was merely a kind of stalking-horse for their own domestic problems. There is nothing surprising about this. Half a century later the magisterial Tocqueville was to admit that "in America I saw more than America," and the phrase might serve for almost the whole body of European commentary on the New World over a period of two centuries.

# 2.

# The Problem of America Is Really the Problem of Europe

DOUBTLESS AT THE BEGINNING the problem of America had been genuine enough. In the sixteenth and seventeenth centuries with what wonder, what astonishment, what incredulity did Europe look upon this strange new world. Where had it been all these centuries? Why had Providence seen fit to set it apart from the other quarters of the globe, and conceal it from the rest of mankind? Whence came its people, strange of color and of tongue and strange of faith or, stranger still, wholly lacking in faith? They were all descendants of Adam, they were all children of Noah; how then had they come to these distant shores, and how explain their differences from the peoples of other continents? Were they descendants of the Canaanites fleeing before Joshua? Were they Phoenicians who had sailed westward from Tyre and Sidon through the Gates of Hercules? Were they descendants of the Greeks?—Père Lafiteau was prepared to prove that on scientific grounds. Were they Egyptians, were they Ethiopians, were they the remnants of the lost tribes of Israel? Had they come from Asia, perhaps, making their way across Siberia to western America, or drifting across the Pacific from China? Were they refugees from the lost Atlantis which had been swallowed up in some prehistoric catastrophe, or from the mythical island of Antillia? Or perhaps Noah himself had planted a colony on the shores of Brazil? Perhaps—audacious thought—they were pre-Adamites, a special creation; that would explain much otherwise enveloped in mystery.

How explain this new world of monsters and of wonders? How explain the Patagonian giants who were eight feet tall and could sweep aside seven Spaniards with a single swing of their arms? How explain the hermaphrodites of the jungles and the

Amazons, the men with one leg, the men with their heads on their chests, and the men with faces of dogs? How explain the albinos of the Isthmus and the pygmies of the far north? How explain the poisonous snakes that swung from tree to tree, the swarms of venomous insects that attacked you like an army, the frogs that bellowed like bulls? How explain the prodigies of geography: deserts that stretched for two thousand miles into infinity, no doubt; mountains that soared fifty miles into the clouds, the vast swamps and marshes with their noxious fumes, the soil frozen fifty feet into the earth for most of the year? How explain a world that was unlike any world man had ever known, people unlike any of recorded history?

In time—by the eighteenth century anyway—Europe came to terms with America. The Patagonians were cut down to size—you could thank Admiral Bougainville for that—and the pygmies given new stature. The hermaphrodites, the Amazons, the men with heads like dogs, the albinos disappeared from most accounts, though some were stubborn enough to linger on. In time the conquistadors and the settlers even accepted the notion that the Indians might have souls, though they were reluctant to accept the implications of that notion. Indeed that process of transforming degenerate natives into noble savages was already under way in the seventeenth century, and so too that shift in the center of interest from Spanish to English America. But these things took time. Of over six hundred articles in the great *Encyclopédie* dealing with America, less than forty touched on British America, and when the Comte de Buffon wrote of the New World in his *Histoire naturelle* he confined himself almost entirely to the America that lay west and south of the Caribbean.

No scientist more distinguished than the Comte de Buffon, and none so imperial, not even Linnaeus, the monarch of the North. Others had explained one aspect of Nature, or another; all Nature, the earth, the skies, the seas, the animal kingdom and the mineral, yielded their secrets to Buffon. He was so great that when he and Nature differed, Nature gave way. When he walked in his garden he could contemplate a statue of himself, and when he considered the history of science, he concluded that he, and he alone, ranked with Bacon and Newton, and Catherine the Great agreed with him on this! Princes made pilgrimages to his château at Montbard, in Burgundy;

Jean-Jacques worshiped him as the very incarnation of Nature, and the exiled Clavigero, who took issue with him about his native Mexico, nevertheless wrote that "there never was in the world one who made such progress in the knowledge of animals" as this Keeper of the King's gardens.

Now Buffon set himself to account for the backwardness of America.

We can summarize his findings briefly, but we shall not be done with them for a long time.

America is in very truth a new world, for it emerged later from the flood than did the other continents; perhaps it experienced a series of floods. Only now are the waters draining away from the marshes, only now is the sun breaking through the dense forests to the sorry earth below.

In these melancholy regions nature remains concealed under her old garment and never exhibits herself in fresh attire. Being neither cherished nor cultivated by man she never opens her fruitful and beneficent womb. . . . In this abandoned condition everything languishes, corrupts, and proves abortive. The air and the earth, overloaded with humid and noxious vapors, are unable to purify themselves, or to profit by the influence of the sun, who darts in vain his most enlivening rays upon this frigid mass.[1]

All is miserable, nature is wretched; the new world is taken over by reptiles and insects; animal life is feeble; man himself is no exception.

"Man is no exception." That was the principle at which this greatest of naturalists had arrived. Listen to his verdict on the American Indian:

Though the American savage be nearly of the same stature with men in polished societies, yet this is not a sufficient exception to the general contraction of animated nature throughout the whole continent. In the savage the organs of generation are small and feeble. He has no hair, no beard, no ardor for the female. Though nimbler than the European because more accustomed to running, his strength is not so great. His sensations are less acute, and yet he is more cowardly and timid. He has no vivacity, no activity of mind. It is easy to discover the cause of the scattered life of savages, and of their estrangement from society. They have been refused the most precious spark of nature's fire . . . their heart is frozen, their society cold, their

[1] Quoted in Gilbert Chinard, "America as a Human Habitat," 91 *American Philosophical Society Proceedings* (1947), 27 ff, p. 32.

empire cruel. They regard their females as servants destined to labor, or as beasts of burden whom they load unmercifully with the product of their hunting . . . they have few children, and pay little attention to them. Everything must be referred to the first cause. They are indifferent because they are weak, and this indifference to the sex is the original stain which disgraces nature, prevents her from expanding, and by destroying the germs of life, cuts the root of society.[2]

Did these animadversions apply to Europeans as well: were they, too, condemned by nature to feebleness, futility, and degeneration? Buffon was not prepared to be dogmatic about this question; some centuries hence, he predicted, when the marshes had been drained and the forests felled and the land brought under cultivation, things might be very different.

There was no animus in all this. When, in a few years, Buffon learned (from Franklin, of course) that the English colonists in America had drained the swamps and felled the trees, when he studied the flora and fauna which the Americans shipped over for his inspection, when he contemplated that elk which General Sullivan had sent over from the forests of Maine, and the beaver and the panther and the eagle which Jefferson had found for him, he confessed himself mistaken, and, what was more, wrote a supplement to his *Histoire naturelle* just to make amends.[3]

Not so with the Abbé Corneille de Pauw. He was full of malice, and he did indeed mean to attack America, though the motives of this animus remain a mystery. The amiable Franklin said he was "ill-informed and malignant": the Italian Giovanni Carli called his *Philosophical Investigations* a "dream book," and Francisco Javier Clavijero charged that he "sheds malevolence and invective from his pen." There may be some exaggeration in all this. Certainly de Pauw did write without fear and without research, but who did not in that day when history was philosophy teaching by examples? Aside from that he appears to have been amiable enough, enough of a scholar to attract the patronage of Frederick the Great, independent enough to break away from that monarch and take refuge in the

[2] Buffon, *Natural History*, London, 1791. Translation by William Smellie, quoted in Chinard, *op. cit.*, p. 31.

[3] "*Dans un pays où les Européans multiplient si promptement, où la vie des naturels du pays est plus longue qu'ailleurs, il n'est guère possible que les hommes dégénèrent.*" *L'Histoire naturelle de l'Homme,* Paris, 1778, p. 531. English translation by the editors, p. 74.

little town of Xanten where he devoted his life to philosophy and history and to his nephew, the self-styled orator of the human race, Anacharsis Cloots. He wrote about the Chinese; he wrote about the Egyptians; he wrote about the Greeks; none of these books commanded any interest. But his two-volume (eventually three) *Philosophical Investigations of the Americans* (1768 and 1769) did. With its ready gullibility, its mixture of fancy and fable, its animus, it marks the outer boundaries of the attack upon America. More important, for reasons that elude explanation, it appealed strongly to the Encyclopedists who invited the infatuated author to write the article on "America" for the Supplement to the *Encyclopédie*—where he repeated everything he had said six years earlier in his *Recherches Philosophiques.*

America, De Pauw contended, was a recent creation, and only now emerging from the pangs of its creation. Unlike the other continents, it had not yet achieved its final form. No wonder it was, as yet, unfit for human habitation; no wonder its miserable denizens, spread thin over this immense and forbidding territory, were primitive and degenerate. Everything about America itself is primitive. The air is unwholesome; the soil poisonous, and the vegetation infected; the surface of the earth is overrun with serpents and lizards, toads and rats; the air is filled with monstrous bats and insects that spread disease and death. The men, climbing down from those elevations where they had taken refuge from the flood into "vast prairies still covered with slough and slime" were enervated by the vapors of the earth and the humidity of the air. No wonder they were

> destitute of that physical strength which characterizes Europeans. The least vigorous European is more than a match for the strongest American. Their constitution is weak, they succumb to the lightest burden. Their stature is smaller than that of Europeans. At first they were taken not for men, but for orang-outangs, or big monkeys, that could be destroyed without remorse or reproach. Then, to add ridicule to calamity, a Pope issued a Bull in which he declared that, as he wished to establish Bishoprics in the richest countries of America, it pleased Him and the Holy Spirit to declare the natives men.[4]

The inhabitants of these wretched continents were, indeed, as degenerate as the animals. Feeble, indolent, insensitive alike

[4] Quoted in Church, PMLA, Vol. LI, p. 186.

to pain or to pleasure, sluggish of mind and of body, cruel without courage, dependent without gratitude, they do not deserve the name of men. They lacked, indeed, the insignia of manhood: they had no beards, they had no hair; they had not even eyebrows. "They are cold in love and utterly indifferent toward women. So lacking are they in virility that many men have milk in their breasts, and in Brazil there are tribes where the fathers nurse the children instead of the mothers." [5]

So much for the natives. The same climate and soil which condemned them to degeneracy condemned the luckless Europeans who had the ill-fortune to sail to the New World. "The Creoles, though educated at the Universities of Mexico, of Lima, and the College of Santa Fe, have never produced a single book." Indeed, "through the whole extent of America, from Cape Horn to Hudson's Bay, there has never appeared a philosopher, an artist, a man of learning, whose name has found a place in the history of science or whose talents have been of any use to others." And in his diatribe in the Supplement to the *Encyclopédie* the Abbé found room for a gratuitous fling at Harvard University where "the professors have not as yet produced a single scholar capable of adding anything whatever to the literature of the world." [6]

You could ignore De Pauw—John Adams and Jefferson thought him merely despicable—and as for Raynal, you never knew where he stood. But what are you to say to Dr. William Robertson, Rector of the University of Edinburgh, and the greatest historian since David Hume; that was an article of faith with all Scotsmen. Alas, Dr. Robertson had picked up the Buffon-Raynal thesis and incorporated it into his monumental *History of America,* which was published just the year of Saratoga: The soil was thin and sterile; vast swamps covered millions of acres of the interior; animals in the New World were visibly inferior, and so, too, men: the very principle of life was less active and vigorous in the New World than in the Old. How odd that so many of Dr. Robertson's countrymen were crossing the ocean to that unfortunate land. "The same qualities in the climate of America which stunted the growth and enfeebled the spirits of its native animals," wrote the learned doctor, "proved pernicious to such as have migrated into it voluntarily."

[5] *Ibid.,* p. 186.
[6] Supplement to the *Encyclopédie,* I, p. 351.

He meant the Spaniards, of course, but he did not make that clear, nor did the logic of his argument exempt the British colonists from the malign impact of the climate. Certainly all this would have interested the Scots-Irish along the frontiers of Pennsylvania and Virginia, but perhaps they were too busy fighting Indians and founding commonwealths to read Dr. Robertson.

So much for the naturalists and the historians. Now a group of philosophers took up the refrain. Their interest was not scientific; it was not historical. It was philosophical, it was economic, it was political. They took from Buffon their inspiration, or perhaps only their point of departure, not their standards of scientific inquiry, nor their readiness to square interpretation with fact. They took from Raynal their point of departure, their enthusiasms, their prejudices, and perhaps something of his and their confusion. They were not interested in science; they were not interested in philosophy, though they thought of themselves as *philosophes;* they were scarcely even interested in America, though they were fascinated by it. They were interested in their own problems, their own concerns, their own societies. And that is what they proceeded to write about.

With every argument, with every pamphlet, with every book, it became clear that the debate on America was really part of a series of debates which had long agitated European philosophers, clear that those who had been discussing the New World had been thinking, all along, of the Old—not Buffon, of course, but then he was a person apart. With each passing year it became increasingly clear that those who took sides on the Problem of America were really using America as a kind of stalking horse for their own battles, campaigns, and crusades.

For that is what the great debate over America was about. It was about America, no doubt, but it was really about Europe.

What were the great controversies in which America found herself involved?

First, then, America was inextricably involved in the controversy between the champions of Nature and Civilization. Rousseau had announced that Nature was good and Society evil; that man is born free, in a state of Nature, and is everywhere—in civilization of course—in chains. Natural man was virtuous, innocent, and wise; he was even noble. But civilization, ah, that was another matter. Civilization meant great cities, wretched and miserable, and a countryside going to waste, luxury and poverty side by side; it meant tyrannical government, vast armies and navies and colonies and perpetual wars; it meant the Church, the priestcraft, the Inquisition: *that* was civilization.

Yet how confusing it all was. It was Voltaire, after all, who had launched the campaign *Écrasez l'Infâme;* it was Voltaire, too, whose *Candide* was one of the heaviest literary blows struck against the pretensions of society. Yet clearly Voltaire was on the side of civilization rather than of Nature. The Encyclopedists as a group were on the side of civilization, D'Alembert and Diderot and the Baron d'Holbach; Goethe was on the side of civilization and Herder and Lessing. Horace Walpole was never happy away from the Court and the salons, and Dr. Johnson never happy away from London. And how interesting that few of them had any real interest in America. Voltaire, to be sure, celebrated an imaginary Quaker paradise in Pennsylvania, and forty years later Goethe could affirm that *Amerika du hast es besser.* But mostly they regarded the New World as something of a bore.

But Nature was coming into its own, at last. Even Voltaire could not resist her: did not *Candide* end with the observation "we must cultivate our garden"? Now romanticism was challenging the claims of rationalism, and with America as a prize exhibit. How that generation rejoiced in Émile, that child of Nature educated by Nature to innocence and wisdom. How it admired Paoli who fought for freedom against the tyranny of the French: the English almost went to war for him, the Americans named a town after him, and Mrs. Macaulay tried to adopt him! How it adored Omai, child of Tahiti, who strutted across the stage of England, alas so briefly; George III gave him a sword and all the great ladies swooned for love of him. How it was fascinated by the Vikings, rescued by the Swiss Mallet from the mists and fogs which had so long enshrouded them. How it venerated Benjamin Franklin, Solon and Lycurgus rolled into one, a child of Nature and a philosopher, at once the wisest and the most virtuous of men. The tide of romanticism was to swell into turbulence and to engulf America, and the controversy over America was part of the larger issue dividing romanticism and rationalism. The Enlightenment, which exalted order, classification, and common sense, looked with suspicion on an America that was wild, impetuous, and disorderly, on animals that were strange and exotic and did not fit into the great chain of being, on vast shaggy forests, and rivers that were like lakes and lakes that were like oceans, on savages who were primitive but claimed to be noble, on societies that did not acknowledge order and degree.

But the romantics saw a different America, an America where the savage was indeed noble, where the landscape was no longer savage or primitive but had been tamed into a pastoral stage setting, where the inhabitants were simple and virtuous and wise. They were ready, like the dashing Irish exile Lord Fitzgerald, to cast their lot in with the Indians; like Filippo Mazzei, to give up all the pleasures of London for Jefferson's Virginia; like Albert Gallatin to abandon Geneva for the wilds of Pennsylvania; like Crèvecoeur to find happiness in tilling the soil of some frontier farm; like the Dutch patriot Van der Kemp to flee tyranny for the freedom of rural New York. There were so many of these refugees from civilization; you found them in the woods of Maine, or wandering along the Ohio frontier, painting the hundreds of birds of that rich country, or setting up a Utopia in some American wilderness.

For America was involved in still another controversy besides those between Nature and civilization, romanticism and rationalism. It was deeply involved in the controversy between the physiocrats and the mercantilists. Mercantilism was irretrievably committed to world-wide trade, commerce, cities, manufactures, colonies, empire and—unavoidably—war. It drained the New World of precious metals which played hob with the economy of the Old. It caught up thousands of virtuous young men and sent them off to some distant continent to waste away their lives, fighting for trivial causes in futile wars, trading in some obscure factory for useless luxuries, joined in unholy union with some dark-hued stranger while maidens languished into spinsterhood back home in France or Holland.

How much better to stay home and cultivate the soil, the only source of wealth, the only seat of virtue and happiness. So said the famous Dr. Quesnay, who was physician to the Queen and doomed to enjoy all the luxuries of Versailles, which he despised. So said the elder Mirabeau, who was happily known as *l'Ami des Hommes.* So said Gaspar Jovellanos, down in Spain —how hopeless it was to preach agrarianism there—and Filangieri in Naples, and—at times, at least—the great Antonio

Genovesi who held the first chair ever established in Political Economy. So said the forgotten Pierre André Roubaud who wrote a ponderous five-volume *History of Asia, Africa, and America,* with America as a kind of prize exhibit of all the virtues of agrarianism. So said Turgot, the greatest of them all, who looked upon America as "the hope of the human race"; and his disciple Dupont de Nemours, who served as editor of the magazine *Les Ephémérides,* which was at once the organ of the *Economistes*—for so they called themselves—and of the American cause, and who cast his lot, eventually, with the New World and with Jefferson. So, too, said the Abbé Raynal, now and then; he was not precisely a physiocrat, but he gave aid and comfort to the physiocrats, what with his detestation of luxury and his suspicion of commerce and his hostility to imperialism and colonies.

True happiness was not to be found in colonies, or in trade, in wealth or in luxury; true happiness was to be found in cultivating the soil, and true wealth as well. And where do you find such happiness but in America? Europeans, wrote Brissot de Warville, "will see here [he was writing of Pennsylvania] a country where the desires of their hearts will be realized, a land which speaks to them in their own language. The happiness for which they have longed does in truth exist."

There was still another thread in this tangled skein of argument about America and doubtless it was the most important of them all. To attack or to defend America were methods of criticizing the evils of government and economy and society in the Old World. It was a risky business, in that century of censorship and the Bastille and the Inquisition, to attack King or Law or Church head-on; even a Buffon, even a Voltaire, even a Diderot had to watch himself. But what could not be done directly might be done by indirection, by innuendo, and by contrast. So Montesquieu wrote his *Persian Letters* and Goldsmith his *Letters from a Citizen of the World,* and Diderot his *Supplement to Bougainville,* and Voltaire *Candide* and Ludwig Holberg *Nils Klim's Visit to the Underworld* (oddly enough, it was named Utopia and all the customary arrangements were reversed). But America was far better than any of these. It was not imaginary but real and, what was more, real for European purposes. If you wanted to attack the slave trade you could attack slavery in America; if you wanted to hold religion or the Church or the Inquisition up to scorn, how better than to recite the history of their misdeeds in America; if you wanted to prove that trade and commerce and colonies were all part of a violation of the natural order of things, there was America to prove your point: what good had all the gold and silver, all the colonies, done Spain and Portugal? With America you could prove almost anything: how much happier is natural man than civilized man; how much happier the farmer than the tradesman; how much happier a people who worship simply and freely, like the Quakers, than a people who groan under the tyranny of an established Church—like the French or the Spaniards.

By now the confusion was almost inextricable. By now it was clear that those who asked "Was America a Mistake?" were not really talking about America, they were talking about the Old World, about Nature and Civilization, Mercantilism and Physiocracy, about the corruptions and misfortunes that afflicted their own societies. And when they did turn to America they could never quite make up their minds what America it was they were writing about. Was it America before the coming of Columbus, an America abandoned—all except the Incas of course—to savagery? Was it America south of the Caribbean, or perhaps north of the Great Lakes, an America of jungle and desert and mountain and frozen lakes? Was it Spanish America, or Portuguese, or French, or English? Or was it perhaps an imaginary America, a lost Atlantis, a Utopia, a second India, destined never to satisfy the hopes and longings of its inventors and its interpreters?

# 3.

## The Degeneracy of the New World Rebounded on the Old

BUT LET US LISTEN to the debate as it enters a new and more acrimonious phase, listen to it as it shifts from the broad argument of degeneracy to the specific arguments of corruption, from impotence to guilt, from Nature to Man. Alas, most of those who competed for the Abbé Raynal's prize, or for the similar prize offered by the Académie des Jeux Floraux down in Toulouse, did not quite realize the implications of this shift. Buffon, after all, had said all there was to say about Nature in the New World, and Raynal had said pretty much all there was to say about the sins of omission and of commission of its native inhabitants and its conquerors. What was left for the critics and the malcontents but variations on familiar themes? No wonder an air of monotony broods over all the arguments, and enervates them.

Here they are, pamphlet after pamphlet; almost all of them intone the same litanies, and there is no need for us to indulge them in their repetitiousness. Let us rather organize and summarize their arguments.

The conclusion, as it turned out, was usually the point of departure. The discovery of America was a mistake, and a tragedy. Inevitably discovery was followed by conquest: how awesome the sins of the conquistadors, how obsessive the Black Legend. Consider the price of the conquest. Twenty million dead—that was the figure most commonly given—whole islands and countries depopulated by conquest, by murder, by starvation, by disease; great civilizations wiped out, the civilizations of the Incas and the Aztecs.

But it was not only the New World that suffered. The conquest of America depopulated the Old World as well, draining away the boldest and most enterprising of the young men, thousands lost every year in watery graves, or in the miasmal swamps and the jungles of the New World, other thousands scattered to distant colonies in the Two Indies, lost themselves, and their progeny lost, lost to civilization and to Christianity. No wonder the population of Spain and Portugal barely held its own throughout the eighteenth century!

And it was not only the colonizing enterprises which drained Europe of her population and her strength, but the interminable wars into which the contest for the New World plunged almost every European nation, not the great nations alone, but the smaller as well. For two centuries now Spain and England and France had fought for the wealth of the Indies, and they had dragged into the conflict almost every other nation of Europe, Prussia and Holland and Austria and Denmark; all that could safely be put down in the American debit column.

And all to what purpose? It was gold and silver that had lured the conquistadors into Mexico and Peru, and wherever rumor told of the Seven Cities of Cibola. They found the gold and silver, but the result was not wealth, but inflation and impoverishment: there was something to the legend of King Midas after all. More, the New World—the world of the East as well as of the West Indies—flooded the Old with articles that were useless or pernicious. What use that noxious weed, tobacco? what use the furs and silks, the precious stones and precious metals, and all the luxuries which in the end but weakened the moral fiber and enervated the will, which distracted Christian men and women from the simple life enjoined alike by moralists and economists?

Ah, but there was worse to come. The New World took revenge upon the conquerors by afflicting them with the most terrible of diseases, and thus spreading it throughout the Old World. For it was America that infected Europe with venereal disease—that was an article of faith, and of science, of course, to which all of the critics and the moralists subscribed. Such was the price of conquest: misery, tragedy, shame, and death, for millions of Europeans, generation after generation.

But we are not yet through with the indictment: the worst is yet to come, the worst and the most indisputable: slavery. How the critics rang the changes on that evil! First the conquistadors had killed off the gentle natives of the Islands; then they had stolen hapless Negroes from the coasts of Africa and sold them into slavery in the New World, and once this evil was planted it grew to prodigious dimensions. You could search in vain through all the darkest pages of history for any infamy, any abomination, to compare with this. And remember that slavery was dying out in the Old World when America revived it; in the eyes of history it was America that must bear the responsibility.

And finally, "Suppose these speculations to be ill-founded," as Simon Linguet put it when he so carefully hedged his bets, there was always this further argument, that if America did succeed, if somehow the American colonies should survive and flourish and become prosperous and powerful states, they would inevitably turn on the Old World; they would drain her of her best stock, they would steal her commerce, they would subvert her governments, they would rend her and destroy her.

A formidable indictment, this, and what was more an irrefutable one: could even the most infatuated champion of the New World deny any of these charges? And all to what end? Certainly the Indians had been happier, by far, before the coming of the white man. And Europeans had been happier, too, when they lived out their days bound each to each in natural piety, unstained by wickedness, unscathed by war, unflawed by loss of faith!

There were many variations on these themes, to be sure. Here, for example was Pierre Poivre, who had been a soldier, writing as a *philosophe* on "the customs and manners of the peoples of Asia, Africa, and America." He belonged to the pre-Adamite school: as the Americans were a separate creation they had no share either in original sin or in Redemption, and he cited with approval the sage observation of a Spanish priest that as God had not given the Americans grapes from which to make sacramental wine, it was clear that He had not intended that they should be Christians! The savages were inferior to Europeans, but they were not therefore less happy; on the whole they were happier than their conquerors.

Or here was Simon Linguet, a distinguished figure, in his way, and an odd one; a friend of the *philosophes,* he had been exiled to London where he edited a magazine, *Annales politiques du 18e Siècle,* dedicated in part to defending the British and attacking the American cause. Whether America was a mistake or not, it was certain that the United States was; and Linguet's arguments, if you did not analyze them too closely, were irrefutable. The United States was a mistake because it would inevitably attract to its shores the dregs of Europe who, instead of working, would engage in perpetual discord. At the same time, by draining away the young and able-bodied from the Old World, the United States would do irreparable harm to Europe. Then again, if with all her immense resources the United States does succeed, that will be equally disastrous. Then she will manufacture all the goods, her ships will carry all the cargoes; she may in time turn upon Europe and destroy it. How is that for having it both ways!

Or here was Joseph Mandrillon, a merchant from Amsterdam, who presents us with something of a puzzle. Under his own name he wrote a *Recherches philosophiques* (all of them made sure they would appear as philosophers), which demonstrated that America would, in the end, bring ruin to Europe. But under the pseudonym of "A merchant of Amsterdam" he produced "The American Spectator," which said just the opposite. "People of Europe," he apostrophized there (if it was indeed he), "stop looking at America as a savage society. Learn that civilization has reached the same standard there as in the Old World, and that it may well surpass yours." What was one to make of that?

Or there was the Reverend Niels Clausen of Fredericia, in Denmark, one of the few who spoke in Latin in the voice of religious orthodoxy. No one more vindictive than this Lutheran priest. America, he charged, far from spreading true faith had corrupted it. The conquest had killed off millions of potential Christians, and had not truly converted those who survived. It had spread not only disease but immorality. Altogether, Dr. Clausen concluded triumphantly, "no calamity in history, not even the Deluge itself, had given rise to so many and such lasting misfortunes to mankind" as the discovery of the New World.

So much, then, for the critics and the malcontents. But even as they wrote, history had passed them by; some recognition of this creeps into their complaints and diatribes, from time to time, and explains the shrillness of their style. How few of them had the good sense to hold their hand when the situation changed, the good sense to recognize what the sagacious Dr. Robertson acknowledged when, in the fateful year 1775, he abandoned his plan to bring up to date his *History of America.*

"It is lucky," he wrote, "that my American History was finished before this event. How many plausible theories, that I should have been entitled to form, are contracted by what has now happened." How many by 1775, how many more by 1783!

Even before all this, to be sure, the New World had had its defenders. Buffon had issued a supplementary volume of the great *Histoire naturelle,* withdrawing most of his original impeachment of America after Franklin had taught him the true scientific facts, and Jefferson had showered him with specimens. The Abbé Raynal, too, had handsomely retracted most of his animadversions in so far as they applied to English North America: listen to the Abbé writing now about a people joined, so surprisingly, with France in a common cause.

> The inhabitants [of the English settlements of North America] were universally thought to be less robust in labor, less powerful in war, and less adapted to the arts than their ancestors. . . . It was concluded that they were degenerated, and unable to elevate their minds to any complicated speculations.
>
> In order to dispel this fatal prejudice it became necessary that a Franklin should teach the philosophers of our continent the art of governing the thunder. . . . It was necessary that eloquence should renew, in that part of the New World, those strong and rapid impressions which it had made in the proudest republics of antiquity. It was necessary that the rights of mankind and the rights of nations should be firmly established there, in original writings, which will be the delight and consolation of the most distant ages.[1]

And Pierre Roubaud, that historian of Asia, Africa, and America, had devoted an entire volume of his ample history to a meticulous refutation of all the abominations of De Pauw, and, more, had predicted that the American colonies were already on the way to becoming *"le chef-lieu de l'humanité."*

As for the English, they had never really subscribed to the degeneracy theory, nor could they, as long as their own colonies were loyal and flourishing, accept the notion that the whole enterprise of discovery and colonization had been a mistake. Indeed, because they had had the good fortune to plant their colonies in the most temperate zone, on the most fruitful soil, of the New World, they had celebrated rather the beauty, the richness, the abundance of the America they knew: it was a note

[1] *History of the Two Indies,* 1783 edition, Vol. VIII, p. 407.

which was sounded pretty consistently and harmoniously from John Smith to Crèvecoeur! Nor did ingratitude and rebellion persuade them to repudiate their judgment or their commitments. The English *philosophes,* if we may use that word for men like Tom Paine and Benjamin Vaughan, Dr. Price and the Rev. Joseph Priestley, transferred their loyalty to America herself, while the stalwarts—the supporters of George III, Lord North and the Empire; such men as Lord Sheffield, and Dr. James Anderson and Dean Josiah Tucker, for example—had the decency to concede that they had raised up in America not a weak and degenerate offshoot of the British race, but a formidable rival.

For now the swift rush of events was to vindicate the champions of the New World. As long as the discussion had centered on Spanish or Portuguese America it had been hard to make out a case for the New World, for even if you reject all the nonsense about degeneracy, how could it plausibly be argued that this New World was really an improvement on the Old? Why, it was merely all the worst features of the Old World transplanted, and to unpropitious soil, at that. Even its apologists had to admit that so far, at least, more had been lost than gained in the transplanting.

But turn your gaze from the south to the north, from the Spanish and Portuguese to the English settlements, and it is truly a New World that greets you, a new people, a new nation, a new civilization. Now the defenders entered the fray, armored with the arguments of philosophy and of history, and armored with facts, too—that was more to the point.

# 4.

## The New World Finds Defenders: It Is the Hope of the Human Race

NOW THE DEFENDERS OF America enter the fray.

Chronologically the defenders overlap the critics. Raynal, who had formally launched the controversy over America with his *History of the Indies,* still, in a sense, presided over it; a good many of the champions of the New World were competitors for that prize which he had set up at the Academy in Lyon, and some of them were very conscious of the debt they owed him. Crèvecoeur, it will be remembered, dedicated his American *Letters* to Raynal, and General Chastellux paid the most lavish tribute to his inspiration.[1]

Whether they were really champions of the New World or merely critics of the Old, enthusiasts for the American Revolution or precursors of the French, is not important; doubtless they were a bit of both. It was not, in any event, the whole of the New World which they now undertook to defend against the calumnies and slanders of De Pauw and Raynal; these were all but forgotten now, or pushed aside as irrelevant. Gone, now, were the speculations about Patagonian giants and pygmies, Amazons and hermaphrodites; gone the solemn investigations of flora and fauna; gone, too, the anguished protests against the iniquities of the conquistadors, the wickedness of slavery, the affliction of the venereal diseases, and all that was summed up in the Black Legend. Now they were writing about the new United States rather than the New World; now they were writing economics and history rather than philosophy. Now

[1] He was "one of the most illustrious writers of the century . . . as expert as he is profound," he wrote in the preface to his Prize Essay. "His bold and infatigable thought covered two continents; he scrutinized all laws, and learned the secrets of all Councils." *Discours sur les avantages, etc.,* London, 1787.

they all but abandoned speculation and took refuge in facts: something new in this controversy! Granted the facts did not always turn out to be true—one Poncelin de la Roche Tilhac, who edited the *Almanach américain,* asserted that New Hampshire produced cocoa, coffee, and cotton—and much the same might have been said of the earlier speculations. A good many of the champions knew America at first hand: Clavijero, certainly, who was an American; and Crèvecoeur, who called himself an American farmer; Mazzei who had lived under the shadow of Monticello; and the Marquis de Chastellux who was one of Rochambeau's generals; and those two abbés, the Abbé Robin and the Abbé Bandole; and those staunch democrats Brissot de Warville and François Barbé-Marbois; and the Amsterdam merchant Joseph Mandrillon; and the German scientist David Schöpf who had served with the Hessians; and a handful of others as well, for these were the years when soldiers from half a dozen countries fought on American soil and when refugees from almost as many countries found asylum there. Oddly enough the most learned of the champions, Condorcet in France, Christopher Ebeling and Friedrich von Gentz in Germany, saw America only through the eyes of history: perhaps that is why they saw more deeply than most of the others.

A formidable group, these; if there was no one quite as great as Buffon was, or as Raynal thought *he* was, the general level of distinction was high. They were men who had moved out of the misty realms of speculation and into the tumultuous arena of history. Several of them—Condorcet and Brissot and Gentz come to mind—played an active role in public affairs. They represented, too, something of a cross-section of western Europe; not surprising, this, for by now the whole of Europe was an interested party. There was the exiled Jesuit, Father Francisco Clavijero, who had taken refuge in the exquisite Spanish College in Bologna, and there wrote his compendious *History of Mexico* to refute Buffon and Raynal: the Spanish authorities would not permit him to publish his *History* in that language, so he wrote it in Italian. From Italy, too, came the romantic Filippo Mazzei, one of those familiar eighteenth-century figures, a kind of respectable Casanova, flitting from career to career, and from country to country: a physician in Smyrna, a wine merchant in London, a farmer in Jefferson's Virginia, and a soldier too, a diplomat in Poland and in Russia, an historian and philosopher, trying his hand at half a dozen tasks and not doing any of them very well, but full of enthusiasm and of good will. Jefferson put him up to writing a Defense of America against the canards of Raynal and the Abbé Mably, though Mably was harmless enough, and while he was at it he covered the whole ground of American history and economy, three volumes of his own, and a fourth by no other than the Marquis de Condorcet. There was the Mennonite preacher Adrian van der Kemp in Leyden, a follower of the nobleman van der Capellen, who had blocked the proposal to send the famous "Scotch" Brigade to fight the Americans, and had called for a revolution along American lines. Van der Kemp had made the acquaintance of Minister John Adams, and published a collection of American State Papers; tried for a mixture of heresy and subversion, he was acquitted, joined the patriot ranks in the abortive revolution of 1787, and then fled to the American wilderness where he lived in Arcadian simplicity on the shores of Lake Oneida. There was Johann Schöpf of Ansbach, in Franconia. A tireless scientist, a student of botany, zoology, geology, mineralogy, and a practicing physician, Schöpf had come to America with one of the regiments of mercenaries, and after almost seven years of service was finally free to conduct those scientific observations which resulted in an American *Materia Medica,* and a score of other scientific papers, and in that masterpiece of description translated simply as *Travels in the Confederation*; it was mostly flora and fauna, but the social commentary was there, in the interstices, and almost all of it was favorable. Finally, of the "Amsterdam Merchant," Joseph Mandrillon, we must speak with hesitation. He was, no doubt, the author of *Recherches philosophiques* which made clear that the discovery of America had indeed been a mistake. But was he not also that *Spectateur américain* who came to precisely the opposite conclusion: that the people of the United States had "raised the standard of liberty in the New World," and that civilization there was quite up to the level of European and would inevitably surpass it? Poor Mandrillon; like Brissot he had come to America, like Brissot he was drawn irresistibly back to Revolutionary France, and like Brissot, too, he died a victim of his misguided enthusiasm.

As the French had, in a sense, launched the whole controversy (even the Dutchman, De Pauw, chose to write in French), it was proper that they should now conclude it. None wrote with greater authority than the Marquis de Chastellux. A soldier, an economist, a philosopher, he was bold and audacious, he was curious and perspicacious, he was learned and sagacious, he was a man of sentiment and a man of the world; he could write not only on great questions of economy and philosophy but on The Union of Poetry and of Music, and his Inaugural Address as member of the Academy was on *Taste*. He was, above all, an expert on happiness. He had written two volumes on this subject which made it irresistibly clear that the present age was the veritable Golden Age, and he proved his devotion to that subject by providing *Romeo and Juliet* with a happy ending. He had been a major-general under Rochambeau and cut a great figure in the French expeditionary force. He knew America as well, perhaps, as any visitor, for he had an inquiring mind, one trained to the study of national character, and after the war he had traveled the length and breadth of the United States, with all doors open to him, the doors of farm houses and inns, of Mt. Vernon and Monticello. All this went into the volumes of his *Travels,* which described the American as the most enviable of societies, at once pastoral and sophisticated. The pastoral note was insistent and pervasive, but clearly what pleased the Marquis was the sophistication, for he was a cosmopolite, never really happy away from the Court, the Army, the theater, the salons, and the Spa. He traversed the virgin forest, and what delighted him was a girl at a wayside inn "whom Greuze would have been happy to have taken as a model," and the discovery that his landlord read Newton's *Principia.* He rejoiced in the sturdy independence of the American farmer, but he was happiest in the company of American philosophers, like Bishop Madison of Virginia or Thomas Jefferson, and though he pronounced the customary warning against luxury, it was no rural Utopia that he foresaw but a nation whose trade and cities and wealth would in time create a flourishing civilization. No one gave more attention to the problem of arts and letters in the New World, and no one was more encouraging; the measure of his infatuation with this theme was his enthusiasm for David Humphreys' dreadful poem on *The Happiness of America.*

In the light of his volumes on happiness, it was not surprising that Chastellux should think the discovery of America a blessing. His argument, too, was very much that of these earlier volumes.

Civilization, he insisted, is the product of commerce, and the discovery of the New World had immensely stimulated commerce. What a cornucopia of blessings from that activity: commerce brought new wealth, and distributed wealth anew and thus leveled ancient inequalities. It introduced luxuries, and luxuries were a mark of a high civilization. It expanded horizons, intellectual as well as geographical. It provided new areas of expansion and, at the same time, assured new resources for the Old World, thus banishing forever the specter of famine and want; even trade in slaves was not wholly to the bad, for it ameliorated the lot of the Negro, and who could doubt that, in time, the Americans would put an end to this pernicious institution of slavery!

What a change from the gay and worldly Chastellux, to Condorcet, whom d'Alembert called a volcano covered with snow. Of all those who participated in Raynal's prize contest, the Marquis de Condorcet—he confessed to the resounding name of Marie Jean Antoine Nicholas de Caritat—was easily the most distinguished, the one who made the strongest impression on his own time, the one whose fame, and fate, still affects us most deeply. He was a mathematician and Perpetual Secretary to the Academy of Sciences; he was an economist, a disciple of Turgot, whose biography he subsequently wrote, and of that other quasi-physiocrat, Adam Smith, and his wife had translated the *Wealth of Nations* into French. He was the only true Philosopher who was permitted to play a significant role in that Revolution whose coming he had foreseen: he drew up the "Address to the European Powers"; he formulated the most elaborate of all programs for public education, never, alas, adopted; he helped frame the ill-starred Constitution of 1793. And, like his friend Brissot, he was not merely a precursor of the Revolution, but a victim.

It was as a physiocrat, humanitarian, and a prophet of progress, that Condorcet considered America, first in that Essay which Mazzei levied upon to fill out the fourth of his volumes, then in his projected contribution to the Raynal prize contest, and finally in the ninth section of that *Sketch of an Historical Pageant of the Progress of the Human Mind* which he wrote while hiding in the garret of the good Madame Vernet, staring at death every day and in the end embracing it.

"It is not enough," wrote Condorcet, "that the rights of men be written in the tomes of philosophers and in the hearts of virtuous men. The weak and the ignorant must be able to read them in the example of a great nation. America has given us that example." This was the theme to which the Marquis returned throughout his long argument. America gave to the Old World, and to the future, the example of a people who had won their independence by arms, but who were dedicated to peace. She gave an example of religious toleration, indeed "the most universal tolerance any people has ever enjoyed." She provided an example of freedom—freedom of religion, freedom of the press, freedom from tyranny and oppression. She furnished, too, a sample of the working of equality, and now "we need no longer suppose that Nature divided the human race into three or four orders, and that one of these orders was condemned to work hard and to eat little." With her vast extent of land, and her inexhaustible resources, America would long maintain an agricultural economy, exchanging her products for the manufactures of Europe; that would not only bring happiness to the Americans but prosperity to the French as well. And finally, America spelled progress:

> America is a country of vast extent, with millions of men preserved by their education from prejudice, and disposed towards study and reflection. There exist no social distinctions, no lure of ambition, that can turn them away from their natural desire to improve their minds, to apply themselves to useful studies, to aspire to that glory which rewards great enterprises and discoveries. And nothing there holds down a portion of humanity to that abject condition which condemns it to ignorance and poverty. There is reason, then, to hope that, by producing almost as many men who contribute to knowledge as all Europe, America will, in a few generations, double the progress of Mankind and make that progress doubly swift. That progress will embrace both the useful arts and the speculative sciences.[2]

Now should we include Brissot? No aristocrat like Chastellux and Condorcet, but the son of an innkeeper, an ardent democrat, who took the name De Warville to sound more aristocratic! He adored Voltaire, and dedicated a book to him; he adored Rousseau who hated Voltaire; he adored Dr. Franklin, and Mr. Jefferson, who wrote that he was "truly estimable and a great

[2] "De l'influence de la Révolution de l'Amérique sur l'Europe," in *Oeuvres complètes de Condorcet*, ed. Garat & Cabanis, Paris, An IX [1800–1801], Vol. XI, pp. 249–294. English translation by the editors, p. 195.

enthusiast for liberty." Inevitably, therefore, he adored America, or thought he did. Chastellux was kind enough to America—but not kind enough to suit Brissot; in between editing the *Courrier d'Europe*, and the *Journal du Lycée de Londres*, and the *Bibliothèque philosophique de Jurisprudence*, he wrote an *Examen critique* exposing the General's errors. He founded a "Society of the Friends of the Blacks," to do away with slavery, and a "Gallo-American Society" to cement friendship with the United States. He longed for "a radical and entire reform" and found it in America. "Hundred-times happy America," he exulted, "where this reform can be executed to the foundations, in every part." [3] As the hart panteth for water-brooks, so he longed for America, and in 1787 his longing was gratified, and he sailed for the United States to speculate in western lands, and to see for himself the moral and physical regeneration of the human race which was going on there. "The first building the Americans build," he wrote, "is for the minister. The second is for the school; and the third is for a printing press." [4] He would have cast his lot in with the New World, but Revolution called him back to the Old, and to the guillotine.

Before that happened, however, he found time to record in three volumes his *Travels* in the New World:

> O Frenchmen! . . . study the Americans of the present day. Open this book: you will here see to which degree of prosperity the lessons of freedom can elevate the industry of man; how they dignify his nature, and dispose him to universal fraternity; you will here learn by what means liberty is preserved; that the great secret of its duration is in good morals. It is a truth that the observation of the present state of America demonstrates at every step. Thus you will see the prodigious effects of liberty on morals, on industry, and on the amelioration of men. . . . You will see [the Americans] invigorating their minds, and cultivating their virtues; reforming their government, employing only the language of Reason to convince the refractory; multiplying everywhere moral institutions and patriotic establishments; and, above all, never separating the idea of public from private virtues.[5]

[3] Quoted in Palmer, *New Cambridge Modern History,* Vol. VIII, p. 441.
[4] Quoted in Echeverria, *Mirage in the West,* Princeton, 1957, p. 160, from *Nouveau Voyage*, I, 175.
[5] Preface to *New Travels,* 1792 edition.

The German response to America was curiously late and, in a sense, marginal to the Enlightenment and to the questions raised by the Philosophers. The Germans, for all their interest in the New World and for all their propensity for philosophical speculation, had little philosophical or speculative interest in America. Odd, this, for there were more Germans, by far, than French in America: the German contingent was much the largest from the Continent, and it was greatly augmented during the war by the addition of thousands of Hessians and Brunswickers who chose to stay in that country to which they had been so violently transported. Yet, on the question of the value of the discovery of America—just the kind of question you might expect the German mind to seize upon—they had little to say.

Easily the most learned of the German commentators was the historian Christoph Ebeling of Hamburg; no other scholar possessed his intimate and intricate knowledge of America. He edited an *Amerikanisches Magazin*; he edited an *Amerikanisches Bibliothek*; he collected, there at his academy in Hamburg, what was in all likelihood the most comprehensive library of American history and geography to be found anywhere on the globe. He knew everyone, he corresponded with everyone. All through the last years of the century and far into the next, the letters and packages of books, newspapers, and maps flowed across the Atlantic, from the Reverend William Bentley, from Jeremy Belknap, from Dr. Prince, from President Ezra Stiles, from Noah Webster, from Dr. Benjamin Smith Barton, from Mr. Jefferson. What came out of it, in the end, was the seven stout volumes (there were to have been thirteen) of a *Geographical History of the American States*, accurate, compendious, but innocent alike of interpretation or of philosophy. Ebeling was a friend to America; he wished her well; but he took her for granted.

Among the German interpreters perhaps only Friedrich von Gentz had some claim to philosophical mind. An extraordinary creature, this Von Gentz. Madame de Staël thought him "the most interesting man in Germany," and no one knew Germany better than the author of *De l'Allemagne*; and Henrietta Herz, whose salon rivaled those of Paris, said somewhat wildly that his "love of liberty was forever memorable." In his youth he had, no doubt, engaged in a fleeting flirtation with liberty, and he confessed to an enthusiasm for the American Revolution which he was never able to transfer to the French. He had studied under Kant at Königsberg; he had read Montesquieu and Rousseau; he proposed to vindicate freedom of the press; and his first book was an essay on *The Origin and Principles of Right,* which was designed to vindicate natural right as a "deduction from experience." The excesses of the French Revolution changed all that. Soon he was translating Burke's *Reflections,* and he became the most ardent of Burkeans. Was it a coincidence that the change came, and the translation, just as Prussia decided to go to war with France, and that he dedicated his translation to Frederick William II with a letter condemning "French sophistry" and promising a companion volume which would "develop on philosophical grounds a complete theory of the anti-revolutionary system." Soon, too, he was comfortably in the pay of the British government—one thousand pounds a year, no less—and, just to be on the safe side, of the Russian and the Prussian as well. Soon he was down in Vienna, where he became, eventually, an aide to Metternich, and the philosopher of reaction.

It was during the transition years, when he was turning from Mirabeau to Burke, that Gentz wrote that essay with the mouth-filling title "Concerning the Influence of the Discovery of America on the Well-being and the Culture of the Human Race," an essay which (like all the others on that subject) failed conspicuously to live up to the promise of the title. Like Chastellux and Condorcet, he focused the whole thing on the benign influence of trade. Trade stimulated industry; it fostered the growth of cities; it created wealth and a middle class; it widened horizons and brought new ideas. It was the new ideas which were important—the Enlightenment, wrote this intransigent enemy of the Enlightenment, and the discovery of America, were more important here than the invention of the printing press or the Reformation. Freedom, that is what the New World meant: freedom from feudalism, freedom from superstition, freedom from tyranny. And Gentz ended on a note that might have been transposed straight into Condorcet.

A penetrating look at the history of the last three centuries, and especially at the present century, must console everyone who contemplates the future state of our race. Obstacles and disturbances there will continue to be, perhaps for all time, but the prospects are on the whole heartening. As we approach the third millennium, we can look forward with reassurance to a radiant condition for mankind on the path towards ultimate perfection if there is no interruption to the progress which began with the discovery of America.[6]

These were the men who played the leading roles, as it were; behind them a vast supporting cast, each with his own contributions, but blending harmoniously enough with the grand chorus. If they did not all say quite the same thing, they all sang variations on the same theme: the example that America offered to the Old World, the path it opened to the human race.

Let us listen, briefly, to some of these variations on a theme by taking them as they come.

Here is that precursor of romanticism, Gaspar de Beaurieu, dedicating to The Inhabitants of Virginia (why Virginia? we may well ask) his fantastic tale of a child of nature cast naked upon an island and growing to virtue and wisdom:

In that land which you inhabit and which you cultivate, there are to be found neither cities nor luxuries nor crowns nor infirmities. Every day of your lives is serene, for the purity of your souls is communicated to the stars above you.[7]

Here is that indefatigable physiocrat, the Abbé Roubaud, asserting that "the Inhabitants of the English Colonies of North America are both physically and morally perhaps the healthiest of all the peoples in the world." [8]

Regnier, who in 1778 edited a Collection of American Constitutions and Laws, asserted that these were "the finest monuments of human wisdom. They constitute the purest democracy which has ever existed; they already appear to be achieving the happiness of the people who have adopted them and they will forever constitute the glory of the virtuous men who conceived them." [9]

That was the year, too, when the greatest of statesmen, Jacques Turgot, wrote that famous letter to his friend Dr. Price over in London:

[6] "On the Influence of the Discovery of America on the Prosperity and Culture of the Human Race," in *Gesammelte Werke* (1795), Vol. V, pp. 175 ff. English translation by the editors, p. 231.

[7] Quoted in Echeverria, *op. cit.*, pp. 32–33.

[8] *Ibid.*, p. 30.

[9] *Ibid.*, p. 72.

This people is the hope of the human race. It may become the model. It ought to show the world by facts that men can be free, and peaceful, and may dispense with the chains in which tyrants and knaves . . . have presumed to bind them. . . . The Americans should be the example of political, religious, commercial, and industrial liberty. The asylum they offer to the oppressed of every nation, the avenue of escape they open, will compel governments to be just and enlightened.[10]

After the victory at Yorktown the Abbé Bandole, chaplain to the French Embassy at Philadelphia, assured Americans that

You offer the universe the admirable spectacle of a society which, founded on the principles of equality and justice, and now arriving at perfection, can insure to the individuals who compose it, all the happiness of which human institutions are capable.[11]

Just a few months later the heroic Van der Kemp delivered in Leyden an oration on freedom:

In America the sun has risen brightly, a promise to us if we will accept it . . . America can lift us up, if we but dare look up. It is a land of justice, we are a land of sin. America can teach us to reverse the degradation of the national character, check the corruption of morals, stop bribery, smother the beginnings of tyranny and restore dying freedom to health.[12]

And the Amsterdam merchant, Joseph Mandrillon, asserted that

doubtless the natives of America are not without vice, but their corruption falls far short of that of Europeans. Their virtues, drawn from Nature and from the simplicity of their lives, are not, as ours so often are, the products of hypocrisy or of pride. Theirs is an unsullied virtue, such as flourished in the halcyon time when man's primitive innocence did not need to combat the incessant tyranny of the passions or the seductions of bad examples.[13]

[10] Quoted in Morison and Commager, *Growth of the American Republic*, I, p. 314.
[11] Quoted in Faÿ, *The Revolutionary Spirit in France and America in the Second Half of the 18th Century*, New York, 1927, p. 134.
[12] Harry Jackson, *Scholar in the Wilderness*, pp. 42–43, quoted from J. Hartog, *Uit de Dagen der Patriotten*, p. 78.
[13] *Le Spectateur américain*, Amsterdam, 1784. English translation by the editors, p. 183.

The author of the *Fragment de Zénophon*, the Abbé Gabriel Brizard, rejoiced that

> The golden age, sung by the poets, seems to be realized in that happy land. Dissension and war, which rule the rest of the globe, have respected these climes which are protected by the surrounding seas, and by the innocence of the inhabitants.[14]

And one L. G. Bourdon, who traversed America through two volumes of verse, asked his rapt readers to

> Behold a refuge where the never-changing law
> Is to be just and kind, without intolerance. . . .
> Where, of their sacred rights, by our Sages made aware,
> A people lifts the prayers of Truth and of Mankind
> Before the holy shrine of Joy and Liberty
> Unto Philosophy, the Priestess of their God.[15]

Surely this is enough.

May we then say that Chastellux and Condorcet, Brissot and Gentz, and all the lesser figures concluded the debate which had been raging for a generation, concluded it triumphantly by confuting and confounding the critics and detractors of the New World? No, say rather that even as the battle raged, the battleground trembled and quivered beneath the contestants, and the old landmarks came tumbling down, and, as with so many debates, the issue of the debate itself was drained of meaning and took on a faintly archaic air.

Yet the debate was not wholly irrelevant, not even after it had been antiquated by events. For, oddly enough, the contestants had almost wholly ignored one part of the problem submitted to them by the zealous Abbé Raynal. They had mightily debated the central question which the Abbé had asked: was America a mistake? But they had signally failed to answer Raynal's further question: If the discovery of America was a blessing, what could be done to conserve and enhance its benefits; if a curse, what could be done to repair its damages?

Now after all the din of controversy, the libraries of argument,

[14] Quoted in Echeverria, *op. cit.*, p. 73.
[15] Quoted in Faÿ, *op. cit.*, p. 236.

the torrents of debate, these questions remained unanswered. How, indeed, could they be answered: the answers lay in the womb of time. And, these were the questions which, for generations to come, would confront not only the philosophers of Europe and of America, but of continents and peoples and nations not yet dreamed of by the eighteenth century.

# Part Two: The Debaters

# 1.

## The Comte de Buffon

*"In America, nature is weaker, less active, and more circumscribed in the variety of her productions."*

THE COUNT DE BUFFON was born Georges-Louis Leclerc, in Montbar (Burgundy) in 1707. His father, a wealthy man prominent in the region as a judge at the *Parlement* (high court) of Dijon, held liberal views on education, and after supervising a sound early training for his children, allowed each of them to prepare for whatever occupation or profession he wished. Georges-Louis' direction was profoundly influenced by his meeting, in Dijon, the young Duke of Kingston and his tutor. The two youths became friends and traveled together in France and Italy in company with the tutor, who stimulated in Georges-Louis a strong interest in the sciences. After a sojourn of some months in England, he began the translations into French of scientific works as, in part, a means of improving his knowledge of English. The result of these efforts was the publication, with introductions by the translater, of Hale's *Statistique des végétaux et analyse de l'air* (*Vegetable Statistics*) in 1735, and Newton's *Méthode des fluxions et des suites infinies* (*Fluxions*) in 1740.

His other scientific studies of this period were concerned with physics, mathematics, and even agriculture, though he seemed especially interested in mathematics. Elected to the Academy of Sciences in 1733, Buffon gave many papers before the Academy on a variety of scientific topics.

Appointed Keeper of the Royal Gardens in 1739, Buffon

recognized all that still needed to be done in the field of natural history. There existed no comprehensive work in this area, and the plan he conceived in those early years was of a dimension never before attempted. He planned, simply, a thorough study of all aspects of natural history, an investigation into all the divisions of the animal, vegetable, and mineral realms, which should combine precise observation and description of the most minute detail with broad theory and a unified view of the whole of creation. It was inevitable that in addition to being a scientific work of impressive proportion, the *Histoire naturelle* should also be a historical and philosophical treatise; it is fortunate that Buffon was not only a scientist but a philosopher and a man of letters with a style notable for lucidity, harmony, variety, and grace. The work was truly a great literary, and a great scientific, achievement.

Ten years after its inception, in 1749, the first three volumes of the *Histoire naturelle* appeared; subsequent volumes appeared with regularity thereafter. Buffon had indeed some notable collaborators—altogether over thirty—and these continued the great study even after his death. Yet after fifty years of his own untiring labors, and all the contributions of his collaborators and continuers, the resultant publications made up only a part of the grand scheme Buffon had outlined for himself in 1739.

The success of the work was instantaneous, and the fame of its author universal. Tribute came from scientists and from sovereigns in France and abroad. Louis XIV created Buffon a count; election to the Académie Française followed in 1753. His speech upon being seated among the Immortals reflected the importance he placed upon literary considerations: it was entitled *Discours sur le Style*. Buffon thought enough of it to attempt, toward the end of his life, to develop and write it as a separate work, but it remained unfinished at his death.

It is nevertheless true that the *Histoire naturelle* did not go uncriticized—some errors of detail, perhaps inevitable given the magnitude of the work; the vagueness and even contradictions of some of his philosophical ideas and theories—but Buffon himself never deigned to answer any criticisms. His life remained tranquil and secure; his work demanded much of him and his devotion to it allowed no interference or distraction. The philosophical, political, and social turmoils of the eighteenth century swirled around him without his seeming to notice them. Rather late in life, in 1762, he was married to a Mademoiselle de Saint-Bélin; the only child of this marriage, a son, was guillotined during the Revolution. Buffon died in Paris on April 16, 1788.

The first three volumes of the *Histoire naturelle* were published in 1749, and at this time, Buffon's principal collaborator for ten years had been Daubenton. Between 1749 and 1767, fifteen volumes were published by the two men. These volumes included *Théorie de la Terre, Histoire naturelle de l'Homme,* and *Histoire des Quadrupèdes.* Between 1770 and 1783 appeared the nine volumes of the *Histoire des Oiseaux,* with the collaboration of Guéneau de Montbéliard and the Abbé Bexon. Five volumes on minerals, published by Buffon alone, appeared between 1783 and 1788. There were in addition seven supplementary volumes, the first of which appeared as early as 1774 and the last in 1789, the year following Buffon's death. Of these, the most important is clearly the fifth volume, *Époques de la Nature* (1778), in which he contradicts his earlier theories of the earth published in his first volume.

## FROM NATURAL HISTORY, GENERAL AND PARTICULAR[1]

### *Of Animals Peculiar to the New World*

THE ANIMALS of the New World were equally unknown to the Europeans, as ours were to the natives of America. In the New Continent, the only half-civilized people were the Peruvians and Mexicans. The latter had no domestic animals; but the former had reduced to slavery the llama, the pacos, and the alco, a small creature resembling a little dog. The pacos and the llama, to which Fernandes gives the name of *peruichcatl,* or *Peruvian cattle,* like the chamois goat, frequent the highest mountains only, as those of Peru, Chile, and New Spain. Though they had become domestic in Peru, and, of course, had been spread over the adjacent countries; yet, instead of multiplying in the place of their nativity, their number has diminished since the European cattle, which have succeeded wonderfully in all the southern regions of America, were transported thither.

[1] Translated by William Smellie, London, 1812.

It is singular that, in a world almost totally occupied by savages, whose manners approached to those of the brute creation, there should have been no society or correspondence between these savage men and the animals which surrounded them; for no domestic animals appear without some degree of civilization. Does it not follow, that man, in the savage state, is only a species of animal, incapable of governing others, and, possessing nothing but his individual faculties, employs them for procuring subsistence, and providing for his safety by attacking the weak and avoiding the strong animals, without any desire of reducing them to subordination? In every nation, though half-civilized only, we meet with domestic animals. In France, the horse, the ass, the ox, the sheep, the goat, the hog, the dog, and the cat; in Italy, the buffalo; in Lapland, the reindeer; in Peru, the llama, the pacos [alpaca], and the alco; in the eastern countries, the dromedary, the camel, other species of the ox, the sheep, and the goat; in the southern regions, the elephant; all these have been reduced to servitude, or rather admitted into society; while the savage, who hardly wishes for the society of his female, either fears or disdains that of other animals. It is true, none of the species we have rendered domestic existed in America. But if the savages with whom it was peopled had anciently united, and diffused the mutual knowledge and resources of society, they would have subjugated almost all the animals of that country, most of them being of gentle, tractable, and timid dispositions, very few ferocious, and none formidable. Hence these animals have avoided the slavery of a domestic state neither by the fierceness of their nature, nor by the indocility of their dispositions. Their liberty has resulted solely from the weakness of man, whose powers are extremely circumscribed without the aid of society, upon which even the multiplication of his species depends. The immense territories of the New World contained not, upon its first discovery, a greater number of inhabitants than what are to be found in one half of Europe. This scarcity of the human species allowed the other animals to multiply prodigiously. They had fewer enemies and more space: every circumstance was favorable to their increase; and each species, accordingly, consisted of a vast number of individuals. But the number of the species, when compared with those of the Old Continent, was not above one-fourth or one-third. If we reckon that two hundred species of quadrupeds exist in the whole known quarters of the globe, we shall find above 130 of them in the Old Continent, and less than seventy in the New; and if we subtract the species common to both continents, or those which by their constitution were able to endure the rigors of the North, and passed by land from the one continent to the other, the New World cannot claim above forty native species. In America, therefore, animated Nature is weaker, less active, and more circumscribed in the variety of her productions; for we perceive, from the enumeration of the American animals, that the number of species is not only fewer, but in general that all the animals are much smaller than those of the Old Continent. No American animal can be compared with the elephant, the rhinoceros, the hippopotamus, the dromedary, the camelopard, the buffalo, the lion, the tiger, etc. The tapir or *tapiierete* of Brazil is the largest quadruped of South America. This animal, the elephant of the New World, exceeds not the size of a calf of six months old, or of a very small mule; for he has been compared to both of these animals, though he has no resemblance to either, having neither a whole nor a cloven hoof, but feet irregularly digitated, namely, four toes on the forefeet and three on the hind feet. His body is shaped nearly like that of the hog. His head, however, is proportionally much larger: he has no tusks or canine teeth; and the upper lip is very long and moveable at pleasure. The llama is not so large as the tapir, and he appears to be large only by the length of his neck and legs. The pacos is still a much smaller animal.

The cabiai [capybara], which, next to the tapir, is the largest animal of South America, exceeds not the size of an ordinary hog. He differs as much as any of the former from all the animals of the Old Continent; for though he has been called the *marsh* or *river hog*, he differs from that animal by conspicuous and essential characters. He is digitated, having, like the tapir, four toes on the forefeet and three on the hind feet. His eyes are large, his muzzle gross and obtuse, his ears small, his hair short, and he has no tail.

The tajacou is smaller than the cabiai, and has a greater resemblance to the hog, from which he differs greatly in the structure of his internal parts, as in the form of the stomach and lungs, etc. He has also an open gland on the lower part of his back, which discharges a fetid liquor. He is, therefore, a species different from that of the hog; and neither the tajacou, the cabiai, nor the tapir are found in any part of the Old Continent. The same thing may be said of the *tamandua-guacu* or *ouariri,* and of the *ouati, riou,* which we have called *ant-eaters.* These animals, the largest of which is below mediocrity, seem to be peculiar to South America. Their structure is very singular; they have no teeth; their tongue is long and cylindrical, like that of the birds called woodpeckers; the opening of the mouth is so small that they can neither bite nor hardly lay hold of anything, but extend their long tongue and, putting it in the way of the ants, retract it when loaded with these insects, which is the only method they have of procuring nourishment.

The sloth, which the natives of Brazil call *ai,* or *hai,* on account of the plaintive cry, *ai,* which it perpetually utters, seems likewise to be peculiar to the New Continent. He is still smaller than any of the former, being only about two feet long. He is remarkable for walking slower than the turtle, for having three toes both on the fore- and hind feet, the forelegs much longer than the hind ones, a very short tail, and no external ears. Besides, the sloth and the armadillo are the only quadrupeds which have no cutting and canine teeth but cylindrical grinders only, which are rounded at the extremities, nearly like those of some of the cetaceous animals.

The cariacou [deer] of Guiana is an animal of the nature and size of our largest roebucks. The male has horns which fall off annually, and the female has none. At Cayenne he is called the *wood hind.* There is another species called *the little cariacou,* or *marsh hind,* which is considerably smaller than the former, and the male has no horns. From the resemblance of the name, I suspected that the cariacou of Cayenne might be the *cuguacu,* or *cougouacou-apara* of Brazil; and, having compared the descriptions given by Pison and Margrave of the cougouacou, with the characters of the cariacou, which I had alive, it appeared to be the same animal but at the same time so different from our roebuck that it ought to be regarded as a distinct species.

The tapir, the cabiai, the tajacou, the ant-eater, the sloth, the cariacou, the llama, the pacos, the bison, the puma, the jaguar, the cougar, the juguarete, the mountain cat, etc., are the largest animals of the New Continent. The middle-sized and smaller kinds are the gouandous, or cuandus, the agoutis, the coatis, the pacos, the opossum, the Indian hogs, the cavies, and the armadillos, which, I believe, are all peculiar to America, though our latest nomenclators mention a species of armadillo in the East Indies and another in Africa. For the existence of these, we have only the testimony of the describer of the cabinet of Seba, which is not an authority that merits credit, for errors arising from the names of countries are very common in collections of natural objects. An animal is purchased under the name of the *Ternate*, or *American bat*, another under that of the *East India armadillo*. They are immediately announced under these apellations in the description of this collection, and are adopted into the lists of our nomenclators. But when examined more closely, these Ternate, or American bats, are found to be French bats, and the Indian or African armadillos may likewise belong to America.

We have not hitherto mentioned the ape tribes, because their history demands a particular discussion. The word *ape* is a generic name, applied to a great number of species; it is not therefore surprising that many of them are said to be found in the southern regions of both continents. But we must now inquire whether the apes of Asia and Africa are the same with the American animals to which that name has been applied, and whether, out of more than thirty species which we have examined alive, there be a single one of them common to both continents.

The satyr, or man of the wood, whose figure differs less from that of a man than of an ape, is peculiar to Africa and the south of Asia, and exists not in America.

The gibbon, whose forelegs, or hands, are as long as the whole body, including the hind legs, is found in the East Indies but not in America. These two apes have no tails.

The ape, properly so called, whose hair is of a greenish color mixed with a little yellow, and has no tail, is a native of Africa and some other parts of the Old Continent, but not of the New. The same thing may be said of the *cynocephali*, or dog-headed apes, of which there are two or three species. Their muzzle is not so short as that of the former; but they have no tail, or it is so short as scarcely to be visible. All the apes which have no tail, particularly those with short muzzles, and whose face, of course, greatly resembles that of man, are the genuine apes; and the five or six species we have mentioned are all natives of the warm climates of the Old Continent and are found in no part of the New. Hence we are authorized to affirm that there are no true apes in America.

The baboon, an animal larger than a dog, and whose body is contracted like that of the hyena, is very different from the apes formerly mentioned. His tail is very short, and always erect; his muzzle is long, and broad at the extremity; his buttocks are naked, and of a blood color; his legs are very short, and his nails strong and sharp. This animal, which has great strength and is very mischievous, is found only in the southern deserts of the Old Continent, and not in America.

Hence all the apes which have no tails, and all those whose tails are remarkably short, belong solely to the Old Continent; and of those with long tails, almost all the large kinds are found in Africa. There are a few of a middle size in America; but the animals called *little monkeys, with long tails,* are very numerous in the New World. These little monkeys are the *sapajous* [monkeys with prehensile tails], the *sagouins* [monkeys with straight, but not prehensile tails], the *tamarins,* etc. When we give the particular history of these animals, it shall be shown that all the American monkeys are different from those of Africa and Asia.

The makis, of which we know three or four species or varieties, make a near approach to the monkeys with long tails, having, like them, hands, but longer and sharper muzzles, and are also peculiar to the Old Continent. Thus all the animals of Africa and the south of Asia which have received the names of *apes* or *monkeys* are not to be found in America, any more than the elephant, rhinoceros, or tiger.

The more minutely we inquire into this subject, the more shall we be convinced that the animals of the southern regions of the one continent existed not in the other, and that the few which are now found there, were transported by man, as the Guinea sheep which has been carried to Brazil; the guinea pig, which was brought from Brazil into Guinea, and perhaps some other small animals, the transportation of which was facilitated by the commerce and small distance of these two parts of the globe. Between the coast of Guinea and that of Brazil, there are about 500 leagues of sea; and there are more than 2,000 between the coast of Peru and the East Indies. All those animals which, from their nature, cannot endure cold climates, and even those which, though they could subsist, cannot produce in such climates, are confined on two or three sides by seas which they are unable to traverse, and on the other by countries so cold that they cannot live in them. Hence we ought not to wonder at this general fact, which at first appeared singular, and was never before so much as suspected, namely, that none of the animals which are natives of the Torrid Zone of the one continent are to be found in the other.

### *Of Animals Common to Both Continents*

From the preceding enumeration, it appears that not only the quadrupeds in the warmest climates of Africa and Asia, but most of those in the temperate regions of Europe, are wanting in America. But several of our animals, which can endure cold and multiply in the northern climates, are found in North America: and though they differ considerably, we are obliged to acknowledge them to be the same, and to believe that they formerly passed from the one continent to the other by lands which are still unknown, or rather have long since been swallowed up by the ocean. This proof, drawn from natural history, is a stronger demonstration of the almost continued contiguity of these two continents than all the conjectures of speculative geographers.

The bears of the Illinois, of Louisiana, etc., appear to be the same as ours, only the former are smaller and blacker.

The stag of Canada, though smaller than ours, differs from him only by the greater height of his horns, more numerous antlers, and a longer tail.

The roebuck, which is found in the south of Canada and in Louisiana, is likewise smaller, and has a longer tail than the European kind. The original is the same animal as the elk, though it is not as large.

The reindeer of Lapland, the fallow deer of Greenland, and the caribou of Canada appear to be the same animal. The fallow deer or stag of Greenland, described and painted by Edwards, has too great a resemblance to the reindeer to be regarded as a different species. As to the caribou, though there is no exact description of it, yet from the marks we have been able to collect it seems to be the same animal with the reindeer. M. Brisson has made the caribou a different species, and refers it to the *Cervus burgundicus* of Johnston. But this *Cervus burgundicus* is an unknown animal, and certainly never existed either in Burgundy or in Europe: it is a simple name that has been given to some uncommon horns of the stag or fallow deer; or rather, M. Brisson may have seen the head of the caribou, whose horns consisted of one straight stem on each side, about ten inches long, with an antler or branch near the base, turned forward; or the head of a female reindeer; or a head of the first or second year; for the female reindeer bears horns as well as the male, though much smaller, and in both, the direction of the first antlers is forward; and lastly, in this animal as well as in all others of the deer kind, the ramifications of the horns are exactly proportioned to the number of years they have lived.

The hares, the squirrels, the hedgehogs, the otters, the marmots, the rats, the shrew-mice, and the moles are also species common to the two continents, though in all these kinds there is not an American species perfectly similar to those of Europe; and it is extremely difficult, if not impossible, to pronounce with certainty whether they are really different species or only varieties of the same, changed by the influence of the climate.

The beavers of Europe appear to be the same with those of Canada. Though these animals prefer cold countries, they can subsist and even multiply in temperate climates. There are still some of them in France, upon the islands of the Rhone. Their number was formerly much greater, and they seem to avoid populous countries more than very warm climates. They never establish their societies but in deserts remote from the habitations of men: and even in Canada, which may be considered as a vast desert, they have retired far from any of our settlements.

The wolf and fox are also common to both continents. They are found, but with some varieties, in all parts of North America, where there are black foxes and wolves; but all of them are smaller than those of Europe, which is the case with every animal, whether native or transported.

Though the weasel and ermine frequent the cold countries of Europe, they are at least very rare in America; but the pine-weasel, the martin, and the polecat, are more numerous.

The pine-weasel of North America appears to be the same with ours. The vison, or pekan weasel of Canada, has a great resemblance to the martin; and the striped polecat of North America is perhaps only a variety of the European kind.

The American lynx seems to be the same with the European. He prefers cold countries; but he likewise lives and multiplies in temperate climates, and generally frequents the forests and high mountains.

The seal, or sea-calf, seems to be confined to northern countries, and is found equally on the coasts of Europe and of North America.

These are nearly all the animals which are common to the Old and New Worlds; and from this number, which is not considerable, we ought perhaps to retrench more than a third part, whose species, though apparently the same, may be different in reality. But, admitting the identity of all these species with those of Europe, the number common to the two continents is very small when compared with that of the species peculiar to each. It is further apparent that, of all these animals, it is those only which frequent the northern countries that are common to both continents; and that none of those which cannot multiply but in warm or temperate climates are found in both worlds.

It is therefore no longer a doubtful point that the two continents either are, or have formerly been, contiguous toward the north, and that the animals common to both have passed from the one to the other by lands with which we have now no acquaintance. We are led to believe, especially since the discoveries made by the Russians to the north of Kamchatka, that the lands of Asia are contiguous to those of America; for the north of Europe seems to have been always separated from the New World by seas too considerable to permit the passage of any quadruped. These animals, however, of North America, are not precisely the same as those of the north of Asia, but have a stronger resemblance to the quadrupeds of the north of Europe. It is the same with the animals which belong to the temperate climates. The argali, or Siberian goat, the sable, the Siberian mole, and the Chinese musk appear not in Hudson's Bay, nor in any other northwest part of the New Continent; but on the contrary we find, in the northeast parts of it, not only the animals common to the north of Europe and Asia but likewise those which appear to be peculiar to Europe, as the elk, the reindeer, etc. It must, however, be acknowledged, that the northeast parts of Asia are so little known that we can have no certainty whether the animals of the north of Europe exist there or not.

We formerly remarked, as a singular phenomenon, that the animals in the southern provinces of the New Continent are small in proportion to those in the warm regions of the Old. There is no comparison between the size of the elephant, the rhinoceros, the hippopotamus, the camelopard, the camel, the lion, the tiger, etc., and the tapir, the cabiai, the ant-eater, the llama, the puma, the jaguar, etc., which are the largest quadrupeds of the New World: the former are four, six, eight, and ten times larger than the latter. Another observation brings additional strength to this general fact: all the animals which have been transported from Europe to America, as the horse, the ass, the ox, the sheep, the goat, the hog, the dog, etc., have become smaller; and those which were not transported, but went thither spontaneously, those, in a word, which are common to both continents, as the wolf, the fox, the stag, the roebuck, the elk, etc., are also considerably smaller than those of Europe.

In this New World, therefore, there is some combination of elements and other physical causes, something that opposes the amplification of animated Nature: there are obstacles to the development, and perhaps to the formation of large germs. Even those which, from the kindly influences of another climate, have acquired their complete form and expansion, shrink and diminish under a niggardly sky and an unprolific land, thinly peopled with wandering savages, who, instead of using this territory as a master, had no property or empire; and, having subjected neither the animals nor the elements, nor conquered the seas, nor directed the motions of rivers, nor cultivated the earth, held only the first rank among animated beings, and existed as creatures of no consideration in Nature, a kind of weak automatons, incapable of improving or seconding her intentions. She treated them rather like a stepmother than a parent, by denying them the invigorating sentiment of love and the strong desire of multiplying their species. For, though the American savage be nearly of the same stature with men in polished societies, yet this is not a sufficient exception to the general contraction of animated Nature throughout the whole continent. In the savage, the organs of generation are small and feeble. He has no hair, no beard, no ardor for the female. Though nimbler than the European, because more accustomed to running, his strength is not so great. His sensations are less acute; and yet he is more timid and cowardly. He has no vivacity, no activity of mind. The activity of the body is not so much an exercise or spontaneous motion as a necessary action produced by want. Destroy his appetite for victuals and drink and you will at once annihilate the active principle of all his movements; he remains, in stupid repose, on his limbs or couch for whole days. It is easy to discover the cause of the scattered life of savages, and of their estrangement from society. They have been refused the most precious spark of Nature's fire. They have no ardour for women, and, of course, no love to mankind. Unacquainted with the most lively and most tender of all attachments, their other sensations of this nature are cold and languid. Their love to parents and children is extremely weak. The bonds of the most intimate of all societies, that of the same family, are feeble; and one family has no attachment to another. Hence no union, no republic, no social state can take place among them. The physical cause of love gives rise to the morality of their manners. Their heart is frozen, their society cold, and their empire cruel. They regard their females as servants destined to labor, or as beasts of burden, whom they load unmercifully with the produce of their hunting, and oblige, without pity or gratitude, to perform labors which often exceed their strength. They have few children, and pay little attention to them. Everything must be referred to the first cause: they are indifferent because they are weak; and this indifference to the sex is the original stain which disgraces Nature, prevents her from expanding, and, by destroying the germs of life, cuts the root of society.

Hence man makes no exception to what has been advanced. Nature, by denying him the faculty of love, has abused and contracted him more than any other animal. But, before examining the causes of this general effect, it must be allowed, that, if Nature has diminished all the quadrupeds in the New World, she seems to have cherished the reptile, and enlarged the insect tribes; for, though at Senegal there are longer serpents and larger lizards than in South America, yet the difference between these animals is not near so great as that which subsists between the quadrupeds. The largest serpent of Senegal is not double the size of the Cayenne serpent. But the elephant is perhaps ten times the bulk of the tapir, which is the largest quadruped of South America. With regard, however, to insects, they are nowhere so large as in South America. The largest spiders, beetles, caterpillars, and butterflies are found in Cayenne and other neighboring provinces: here almost all insects exceed those of the Old World, not in size only, but in richness of coloring, delicacy of shades, variety of forms, number of species, and the prodigious multiplication of individuals. The toads, the frogs, and other animals of this kind, are likewise very large in America. We shall take no notice of birds and fishes because, as Nature has enabled them to pass from the one continent to the other, it is hardly possible to distinguish those which are proper to each. But reptiles and insects, like the quadrupeds, are confined to their respective continents.

Let us now examine why the reptiles and insects are so large, the quadrupeds so small, and the men so cold, in the New World. These effects must be referred to the quality of the earth and atmosphere, to the degree of heat and moisture, to the situation and height of mountains, to the quantity of running and stagnant waters, to the extent of forests, and above all, to the inert condition of Nature in that country. In this part of the globe the heat in general is much less, and the humidity much greater. If we compare the heat and cold of every degree of latitude, we shall find very considerable differences: at Quebec, for example, which is under the same degree of latitude with Paris, the rivers freeze every year some feet thick; a coat of snow still thicker covers the land for several months; the air is so cold that the birds fly off and disappear during the winter, etc. This difference of heat, under the same latitude in the Temperate Zone, though very considerable, is perhaps still less than the difference of heat under the Torrid Zone. In Senegal, the sun is perfectly scorching; while in Peru, which lies under the same line, an agreeable temperature prevails. The same remark applies to all the other latitudes. The continent of America is so formed and situated that every circumstance concurs in diminishing the action of heat. America contains the highest mountains and, of course, the largest rivers of the world. These mountains form a chain which seems to bound the continent towards the west, through its whole extent. The plains and low grounds are all situated on this side of the mountains, and run from their bottoms to the sea, which separates the continents on this side. Thus the east wind, which blows perpetually between the Tropics, arrives not in America till it has traversed a vast ocean, by which it is greatly cooled. Hence this wind is much cooler in Brazil, Cayenne, etc., than at Senegal, Guinea, etc., where it arrives impregnated with the accumulated heat acquired from all the lands and burning sands in its passage through Asia and Africa. Let us recollect what was remarked concerning the different colors of men, and particularly of the Negroes. It seemed to be demonstrated, that the greater or less degree of a tawny, brown, or black color, depends entirely on the situation of the climate; that the Negroes of Nigritia [Sudan], and those of the west coast of Africa, are blackest, because their countries are situated in such a manner that the heat is always greater than in any other part of the globe, the east wind before its arrival having traversed vast tracts of land; that, on the contrary, the American Indians under the Line are only tawny, and the Brazilians brown, though under the same latitude with the Negroes; because the heat of their climate is neither so great nor so constant, the east wind arriving not till after being cooled by the waters and loaded with moist vapors. The clouds which intercept the light and heat of the sun, and the rains which refresh the air and the surface of the earth, are periodic, and continue several months in Cayenne and other regions of South America. This first cause renders all the east coasts of America much more temperate than Africa or Asia: and after the east wind has arrived in a cool state, in traversing the plains of America, it begins to assume a greater degree of heat, when it is suddenly stopped and cooled by that enormous chain of mountains of which the western part of the New Continent is composed; so that it is still colder under the Line at Peru than at Brazil, Cayenne, etc., on account of the prodigious elevation of the land. Hence the natives of Peru, Chile, etc., are less brown, red, or tawny than those of Brazil. If these mountains were reduced to a level with the adjacent plains, the heat on the western coasts would become excessive, and we would soon find Negroes at Peru and Chile, as well as upon the west coasts of Africa.

Thus, from the situation of the land alone in the New Continent, the heat must be greatly inferior to that of the Old; and I shall now show that there is likewise a greater degree of moisture in America. The mountains, which are the highest upon the globe, and are opposed to the direction of the east wind, stop and condense all the aerial vapors and of course give rise to an infinite number of springs, which, by uniting, soon form the greatest rivers in the world. Hence in the New Continent, there are more running waters in proportion to the extent of territory than in the old; and this quantity of water is greatly increased for want of proper drains or outlets. The natives having neither stopped the torrents, nor directed the rivers, nor drained the marshes, the stagnating waters cover immense tracts of land, augment the moisture of the air, and diminish its heat. Besides, as the earth is every where covered with trees, shrubs, and gross herbage, it never dries. The transpiration of so many vegetables, pressed close together, produces immense quantities of moist and noxious exhalations. In these melancholy regions, Nature remains concealed under her old garments and never exhibits herself in fresh attire; being neither cherished nor cultivated by man, she never opens her fruitful and beneficent womb. Here the Earth never saw her surface adorned with those rich crops, which demonstrate her fecundity and constitute the opulence of polished nations. In this abandoned condition, everything languishes, corrupts, and proves abortive. The air and the earth, overloaded with humid and noxious vapors, are unable either to purify themselves, or to profit by the influences of the sun, who darts in vain his most enlivening rays upon this frigid mass, which is not in a condition to make suitable returns to his ardor. Its powers are limited to the production of moist plants, reptiles, and insects, and can afford nourishment only to cold men and feeble animals.

The scarcity of men, therefore, in America, and most of them living like the brutes, is the chief cause why the earth remains in a frigid state, and is incapable of producing the active principles of Nature. To expand the germs of the largest quadrupeds, and to enable them to grow and multiply, requires all the activity which the sun can give to a fertile earth. It is for the opposite reason, that insects, reptiles, and all the animals which wallow in the mire, whose blood is watery, and which multiply in corruption, are larger and more numerous in the low, moist, and marshy lands of the New Continent.

When we reflect on these remarkable differences between the Old and New World, we are inclined to believe that the latter is actually more recent, and has continued longer than the rest of the globe under the waters of the ocean; for if we except the enormous western mountains, which appear to be monuments of the highest antiquity which this globe affords, all the low parts of this continent seem to be new lands, elevated and formed by the sediments of waters. In many places, immediately under the vegetable stratum, we find sea shells and madrepores already forming large masses of limestone, but which are commonly softer than our freestone. If this continent be really as ancient as the other, why was it so thinly peopled? Why were

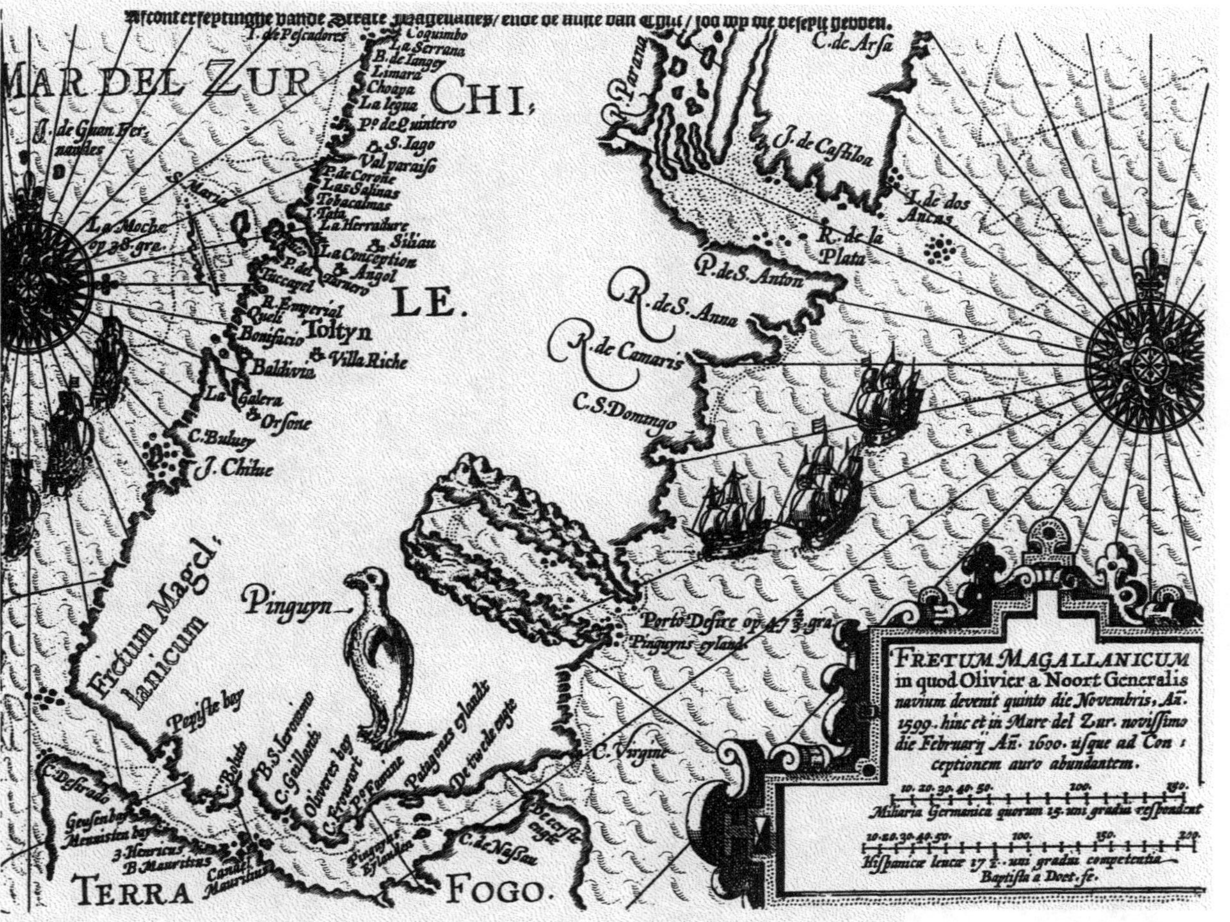


1. Map of Spanish America, from *Voyage of Van Noort*, 1601.

2 and 3. Frontispiece of the French translation of St. John de Crèvecoeur's *Letters from an American Farmer* . . . , Paris, 1787 (see page 35), and an engraving of Koohassen, a warrior of the Oneida nation, from de Crèvecoeur's *Voyage*, 1801 (see pages 73, 74). Both illustrations courtesy of the Rare Book Room, the New York Public Library.

4. An allegorical representation of America by Adriaen Collaert (1550-1618) after Martin de Vos. Courtesy of the Metropolitan Museum of Art (Estate of James Hazen Hyde, 1959). See page 87 where DePauw discusses cannibalism, warfare, monstrous men, and America herself.

5. A ritual sacrifice or dance of the Canadian Indians to Quitchi-Manitou, the Great Spirit. From Bernard Picart, *Ceremonies et coutumes religieuses de tous les peuples du monde*, Amsterdam, 1723. Courtesy of the Library of Congress. See page 98.

6. Drawing from Charles Becard de Granville, *Codex Canadiensis,* c. 1700, depicting an Iroquois who had undergone tortures to show that he could withstand them should he be taken prisoner by enemy tribesmen. Courtesy of the American History Room, the New York Public Library.

7. Tee Yee Neen Ho Ga Row, Emperor of the Six Nations (Mohawk). Note the European clothing. Courtesy of the Library of Congress.

8. Indian slaves in the mines. From de Bry, *Grand Voyage,* 1590. See page 172. Courtesy of the Folger Library.

9. America, an imaginary interpretation. Engraving by Carel van Mallery (Antwerp, 1576-1631), after a drawing by Joan van der Straet. Courtesy of the New York Historical Society, New York City.

10. An allegorical representation of America in a ceiling painting by Tiepolo in the Residenz, Würzburg. Courtesy Art Reference Bureau, from Foto-Swicker, Würtzburg.

almost its whole inhabitants wandering savages? Why did the Peruvians and Mexicans, who had united into society, reckon only two or three hundred years since the existence of the first man who taught them to associate? Why are they still ignorant of the art of transmitting facts to posterity by permanent signs, since they had already discovered a method of conveying their ideas at a distance by tying knots upon cords? Why did they not reduce the llama, the pacos, and other animals into a domestic state? Their arts, like their society, were in embryo; their talents were imperfect, their ideas locked up, their organs rude, and their language barbarous. . . .

Hence every circumstance indicates that the Americans are new men, or rather men who had been so long separated from their original country, that they had lost every idea of the part of the world from which they had issued; that the greatest part of the continent of America was new land, still untouched by the hand of man, and in which Nature had not time sufficient to accomplish her plans, or to unfold the whole extent of her productions; that the men are cold and the animals small because the ardor of the former and the magnitude of the latter depend upon the salubrity and heat of the air; and that some centuries hence, when the lands are cultivated, the forests cut down, the courses of the rivers properly directed, and the marshes drained, this same country will become the most fertile, the most wholesome, and the richest in the whole world, as it is already in all the parts which have experienced the industry and skill of man. We mean not, however, to conclude, that large animals would then be produced. The tapir and cabiai will never acquire the magnitude of the elephant or hippopotamus. But the animals transported thither will no longer diminish as they have formerly done. Man will gradually fill up the vacuities in these immense territories, which were perfect deserts when first discovered.

The first historians of the Spanish conquest, to augment the glory of their arms, have exaggerated prodigiously the number of the enemies they had to encounter. Can these historians persuade any man of sense, that there were millions of inhabitants in Cuba and Santo Domingo, when, at the same time, there was neither a monarchy, a republic, nor hardly any society among them; and that in these two large adjacent islands, and at no great distance from the continent, there were only five species of quadrupeds, the largest of which exceeded not the size of a squirrel or a rabbit? Nothing can be a stronger proof of the empty and desert state of Nature in these new lands. "We found," says Laet, "in the island of Santo Domingo, but few species of quadrupeds, as the *hutias,* which differs not much from our rabbit, but is only a little smaller, with short erect ears, and a tail like that of a mole; the *chemi,* which is nearly of the same form with the *hutias,* but somewhat larger; the *molui,* which is smaller than the *hutias;* the *cori,* of equal size with the rabbit; its mouth resembles that of the mole; it has no tail, and its legs are short; some of them are black, but oftener a mixture of black and white; it is a domestic animal, and very tame; besides a small kind of *dogs,* which were absolutely mute; their number is now much diminished, because the European dogs have destroyed them."

"In the islands of Santo Domingo, Cuba, and the Antilles," says Acosta, "there were hardly any of the animals belonging to the continent of America, and not one that resembled those of Europe." "All the sheep, goats, horses, oxen, and asses," remarks Father du Terte, "In the Antilles, in Guadaloupe, and in all the French islands, have been brought there by the people of that nation; for none were carried there by the Spaniards, because the Antilles were then so thickly covered with wood, that the cattle could find no herbage for their subsistence." M. Fabry, who traversed, during fifteen months, the western territories of America, beyond the Mississippi, assured me that he often traveled three or four hundred leagues without seeing a single man. All our military gentlemen, who went from Quebec to the Ohio River, and from the Ohio to Louisiana, agree that a person may frequently travel one or two hundred leagues, in the depth of the forests, and not meet with a single family of savages. All these testimonies show the desert and melancholy state of the New Continent, even where the temperature of the climate is most agreeable. But, what is more directly to our present purpose, they destroy the posterior evidence of our nomenclators, and describers of cabinets, who people the New World with the animals peculiar to the Old, and mark others as natives of particular countries where they never existed. For example, it is certain, that, in Santo Domingo, there were originally no quadrupeds larger than a rabbit; and though there had, they would have been devoured by the European dogs, which soon became as wild and ferocious as wolves: however, to the *marac* or *maracai* of Brazil, they have given the name of the tigercat of

Santo Domingo, though it is no where found but on the continent. They have made the scaly lizard, or long-tailed manis of Java, an American animal, called *tatoe* by the Brazilians, which is peculiar to the East Indies: they maintain, that the civet, which is a native of the southern parts of the Old Continent, is found also in New Spain, without considering that a creature so useful, which is reared in several parts of Africa, of the Levant, and the Indies as a domestic animal for the purposes of collecting the musk, an important article of commerce, would not have been neglected by the Spaniards if the civets really existed in New Spain.

But our nomenclators have likewise denied to America some animals to which she has an original title. They have placed the opossum in the East Indies and the sloth in Ceylon, though these animals belong solely to the New World, and are so remarkable, the one for a sac under its belly, in which it carries its young, the other for the extreme slowness of all its movements, that, if they existed in the East Indies, travelers could never have passed them over in silence. Seba relies on the authority of Francis Valantine for the East Indian possum. But this authority can have no weight; for Francis Valantine was so ignorant of the quadrupeds and fishes of Amboyna, and his descriptions are so bad, that Artedi declares no use can be made of his information.

We pretend not, however to affirm absolutely that none of the quadrupeds in the warm climates are common to both continents. Of this we can have no physical certainty, till the whole of them be accurately examined. But it is evident that none of the large, and very few of the small American animals, exist in the Old Continent. Besides, though there should be some exceptions, which I hardly imagine, they must be limited to a very small number of animals, and could have no influence on the general law which I mean to establish, and which seems to be the only rule for enabling us to acquire a proper knowledge of the animal kingdom. This law which leads us to judge as much by the climate and dispositions of animals as by their figure and structure will seldom deceive, and will enable us to avoid or detect a multiplicity of errors. Suppose the question, for example, to be concerning an Arabian animal, as the hyena, we may safely pronounce that it exists not in Lapland; but we will never maintain, with some naturalists, that the hyena and glutton are the same animal, nor with Kolbe, that the cross fox, which inhabits the most northern regions of the New Continent, is found at the Cape of Good Hope; and we will find that this animal is not a fox but a jackal: neither should the animal, called by the same author the *earth-hog,* which feeds upon ants, be confounded with the ant-eaters of America: this Cape animal is probably the manis or scaly lizard, which has no other resemblance to the ant-eater than that of using the same food. In the same manner, if it had been considered, that the reindeer is a northern animal, this name would have never been applied to an African antelope. The phoca, or seal, which frequents the seas of the north, ought not to be found at the Cape of Good Hope. The genet, which is a native of Spain, Asia Minor, etc., and peculiar to the Old Continent, is ranked by Klein under the name of *coati,* which is an American animal. The *ysquiepatl* of Mexico, an animal which exhales an offensive odour, and for that reason we shall rank it with the polecats, should never be considered as a small fox or badger. The *coatimondi* of America should not be confounded, as has been done by Aldrovandus, with the badger-hog, which is always mentioned as an European animal. But I mean not to exhibit all the errors of nomenclators. My aim is to prove that their blunders would not have been so numerous if they had attended to the difference of climates; if they had studied the histories of animals, and discovered, as I have done, that those of the southern parts of each continent are never found in both; and lastly, if they had abstained from generic names, by which numbers of species, not only different, but very remote from each other, are blended together.

Thus the genuine object of a nomenclator is not to lengthen, but to contract his list, by making impartial inquiries and comparisons. No task can be easier than to peruse all the writers on animals, and to form a table of their names and phrases, which will always be longer in proportion as the labor bestowed in investigations is less: but nothing is more difficult than to examine and compare animals with that judgement and discernment, which are necessary to reduce this table to its just dimensions. I again repeat, that there are not in the whole habitable earth above two hundred species of quadrupeds, even including forty different species of monkeys. To each of these, therefore, we have only to allot a proper name; and a very indifferent memory is able to retain two hundred names. For what purpose, then, are quadrupeds arranged into classes, orders, and genera? Methodical distributions are only a kind of scaffolds invented to aid the memory in the recollection of plants, the number of which is so great, their distinctions so minute, and their species so liable to variation that it is necessary to consider them in bundles or genera, by putting together such as have the greatest similarity to each other. As in all works of genius, what is absolutely useless is always ill imagined, and often becomes hurtful; instead of giving names to two hundred quadrupeds, we have dictionaries loaded with such a variety of terms and phrases that it would require more labor to explain than was spent in composing them. Why employ a phraseological jargon when we can speak plain language, by pronouncing simple names? Why change all the acceptation of terms, under the pretext of making classes and genera? When a genus is composed of a dozen of animals, under the name, for example, of the *rabbit,* why is not the rabbit itself to be found there, but must be sought for under the genus of *hare?* Is it not absurd, and even ridiculous, to fabricate classes, where genera the most remote are assembled together; for example, to unite in the first, *man* and the *bat;* in the second, the *elephant* and *scaly lizard;* in the third, the *lion* and the *ferret;* in the fourth, the *hog* and the *mole;* in the fifth, the *rhinoceros* and the *rat,* etc. Such heterogeneous and ill-conceived ideas cannot be supported. The works, accordingly, which contain fancies so crude, have been successively destroyed by their own authors. One edition contradicts another, and the whole receives no applause but from tyros and children, who are uniformly the dupes of mystery, to whom the fopperies of method appear to be scientific, and, in fine, who respect their master in proportion to the talent he possesses of representing the clearest and most perspicuous objects under the most abstruse and dark points of view.

By comparing the fourth edition of Linnaeus's work with the tenth, we find, that man is no longer ranked with the bat but with the scaly lizard; that the elephant, the hog, and the rhinoceros, instead of being ranked, the first with the scaly lizard, the second with the mole, and the third with the rat, are all associated with the shrew-mouse. Instead of the five orders or classes of *anthropomorpha, ferae glires, jumenta,* and *pecora,* to which he had reduced all quadrupeds, the author, in this last edition, has split them into seven, *viz., primates, bruta, ferae, bestiae, glires, pecora, belluae.* From these general changes, we may conceive the many alterations introduced among the genera and species, which last alone have any real existence. He says, that there are two species of men, the *day-man,* and the *night-man, homo diurnus sapiens; homo nocturnus troglodites;* and that these distinct species should not be regarded as varieties only. Is not this to add fable to absurdity, to represent the ravings of old women, or the falsehoods of credulous travelers, as constituting a principal part in the system of Nature? Is it not better to be silent with regard to matters of which we are ignorant than to establish essential characters and general distinctions upon the grossest errors, such as, for example, that of all animals which give suck, woman alone has a clitoris? This is so opposite to the truth that, of above a hundred different animals which we have dissected, not a single one wanted that organ. But I have dwelt perhaps too long on criticisms of this kind, especially as they are not my principal object. I have said enough to guard the reader against errors both of a general and particular kind, which are no where so numerous as in the works of nomenclators; because, being solicitous to comprehend every thing within the limits of their systems, they are obliged to associate all that they are ignorant of with the little that they know.

From what has been advanced, the following general conclusions may be drawn: that man is the only animated being on whom Nature has bestowed sufficient strength, genius, and ductility, to enable him to subsist and to multiply in every climate of the earth. No other animal, it is evident, has obtained this great privilege; for instead of multiplying everywhere, most of them are limited to certain climates, and even to particular countries. Man is totally a production of heaven: but the animals, in many respects, are creatures of the earth only. Those of one continent are not found in another; or, if there are a few exceptions, the animals are so changed and contracted that they are hardly to be recognised. Is any further argument necessary to convince us that the model of their form is not unalterable; that their nature, less fixed than that of man, may be varied, and even absolutely changed in a succession of ages; that for the same reason the least perfect, the least active, and the worst defended, as well as the most delicate and heavy species, have already, or will soon disappear; for their very existence depends on the form which man gives or allows to the surface of the earth?

The prodigious *mammoth,* whose enormous bones I have often viewed with astonishment, and which were, as least, six times larger than those of the largest elephant, has now no existence; yet the remains of him have been found in many places remote from each other, as in Ireland, Siberia, Louisiana, etc. This species was unquestionably the largest and strongest of all quadrupeds; and, since it has disappeared, how many smaller, weaker, and less remarkable species must likewise have perished without leaving any evidence of their past existence? How many others have undergone such changes, either from degeneration or improvement, occasioned by the great vicissitudes of the earth and waters, the neglect or cultivation of Nature, the continued influence of favorable or hostile climates, that they are now no longer the same creatures? Yet the quadrupeds, next to man, are beings whose nature and form are the most permanent. Birds and fishes are subject to greater variations: the insect tribes are liable to still greater vicissitudes: and, if we descend to vegetables, which ought not to be excluded from animated Nature, our wonder will be excited by the quickness and facility with which they assume new forms.

Hence, it is not impossible that without inverting the order of Nature, all the animals of the New World were originally the same as those of the Old, from whom they derived their existence; but that, being afterwards separated by immense seas, or impassable lands, they would, in the progress of time, suffer all the effects of a climate that had become new to them, and must have had its qualities changed by the very causes which produced the separation, and, consequently, degenerate, etc. But these circumstances should not prevent them from being now regarded as different species of animals. From whatever cause these changes, produced by the operation of time and the influence of climate, have originated, and though we should date them from the creation itself, they are not the less real. Nature, I allow, is in a perpetual state of fluctuation: but it is enough for man to seize her in his own age, and to look backward and forward, in order to discover her former condition, and what future appearances she may probably assume.

## FROM THE NATURAL HISTORY OF MAN

### *On The Americans*

Concerning other nations inhabiting the interior of the new continent, it seems to me that M. DePauw claims and affirms without any basis that in general all Americans, although fleet and agile, are destitute of strength, that they succumb under the slightest burden, that the humidity of their constitutions is the reason they have no beards, and that they are bald only because their temperament is cold. Further on, he says it is because Americans are beardless that they have long hair like that of women, that no American with kinky or curly hair has ever been seen, that they rarely turn grey and *never lose their hair at any age*. Yet he earlier advanced the theory that the humidity of their temperament makes them bald. Surely he must also have known that the Caribes, the Iroquois, the Hurons, the Floridians, the Mexicans, the Peruvians, etc. were vigorous, robust, and far more courageous than the inferiority of their weapons to European arms would allow us to believe. . . .

M. DePauw appears to support his statements with facts, but in reality he chooses these facts to agree with his opinions. I am disturbed that a man of talent, who seems also to be well-educated, should indulge in such excessive partiality in his judgments, and use such doubtful facts as confirmation. How wrong he is to criticize so bitterly those travelers and naturalists who advanced facts which might have been suspect, since he himself offers so many others which are more than suspect! He accepts and uses any such arguments as long as they favor his opinion. He wants us to believe him on his word only, without citing any other authority. Consider, for example, what he tells us about the frogs that bellow like bulls, the flesh of the iguana which gives venereal disease to those who taste of it, the ground which freezes to depths of two feet, and so on.

He claims Americans in general are degenerate; that it is difficult to conceive that newly-created beings should be in a state of decrepitude or decay, yet that such is the state of Americans; that no shells or other relics from the sea are to be found on high mountains, nor even on mountains of moderate height; that there were no oxen in America before its discovery; that only those who have not seriously studied the American climate could believe that the natives of this continent are a new race; that beyond the 24th degree of latitude, humans constituted like ourselves could not breathe during the entire year's twelve months because of the density of the atmosphere; that Patagonians are of the same height as Europeans, etc. But it is useless to set forth a longer catalogue of the false or doubtful assertions that this author advances with a confidence that must antagonize every reader who seeks the truth.

The imperfection of nature, which he fortuitously attributes to America in general, is applicable only in the case of animals of the southern part of this continent, and these are much smaller than, and quite different from, those of the north.

"This imperfection," as the judicious and eloquent author of the *History of the Two Indies* so well states it, "does not prove the newness of this hemisphere, but rather its renaissance. It must have been peopled at the same time as the Old World, but was perhaps flooded at a later time. The skeletons of elephants and rhinoceroses found in America prove that these animals formerly inhabited that continent."

It is true that there are some regions of South America where the natives appear to be less robust than Europeans; but this is due only to local and particular causes. In Cartagena, the inhabitants, both Indian and foreign, live in what amounts to a hot steam bath during the six summer months; their heavy and continuous perspiration gives them their livid and sickly complexions. Their movements are affected by the softness of the climate, which weakens the muscles. This is evident even in the words that come out of their mouths, in low voices and with long and frequent interruptions.

In that part of America on the banks of the Amazon and the Napo, women are not fertile, and their sterility increases when they are made to change climate; they are nevertheless frequently aborted. The men are feeble and bathe too frequently to acquire any strength. The climate is unhealthy and contagious diseases are common.

But these examples should be considered exceptions, or rather as differences common to the two continents, for even in the Old World, the inhabitants of mountains and elevated regions are noticeably stronger than those of the coasts and low lands. In general, all the inhabitants of North America, and those of elevated lands in South America, such as in Peru and Chile, are men perhaps less active but certainly just as strong as Europeans.

We know from a respectable witness, the famous Mr. Franklin, that in twenty-eight years, the population of Philadelphia was doubled without the help of any foreign immigration. I therefore find it very difficult to accept M. Kalm's charge against this country. He tells us, in his *Voyage en Amérique*, that the men of Philadelphia seem not even to be of the same nature as Europeans.

According to him,

> their bodies and minds are very early formed; consequently they age earlier. It is not unusual to find children who speak with mature good sense, but it is no less rare to find octogenarians. This last observation applies only to the colonists, for the former inhabitants reach extreme old age, though much less now that they have begun to drink strong liquors. Europeans there degenerate noticeably. In the last war, it was observed that the American-born children of Europeans were unable to endure the fatigues of war and changes of climate as well as those children who had been brought up in Europe. At the age of thirty, women are no longer fertile.

In a country in which Europeans multiply so readily, where the natives live longer than elsewhere, it is hardly possible that men degenerate, and I fear these observations of M. Kalm are as ill-grounded in fact as the serpents he claims enchant squirrels and by virtue of this spell cause them to come and fall right into their mouths. In Canada and in all the other regions of North America, only strong and vigorous men were found, and all accounts agree on this point. . . .

# 2.

## The Abbé Corneille de Pauw

*"Americans, a degenerate species of the human race, cowardly, impotent, without physical strength, without vitality, without elevation of mind. . . ."*

THE AUTHOR OF THE strongest attack on America, the *Philosophical Investigations on the Americans,* lived a quiet and withdrawn life, dedicated to study and to writing large comprehensive philosophical and historical works on ancient and modern civilizations. THE ABBÉ CORNEILLE DE PAUW was born in Amsterdam in 1739. His parents died when he was a child, and he was sent to live with relatives in Liège. A canon of the cathedral there took an interest in the intelligent young man and obtained for him the means to study at the University of Göttigen. In gratitude to this benefactor, De Pauw eventually returned to Liège and took minor orders.

The Bishop of Liège perhaps quite naturally selected him to serve as his legate to the court of Berlin, and there De Pauw attracted the attention and patronage of Frederick the Great. Desirous of keeping him at Potsdam, Frederick made him many offers, including an important place in his Academy, a pension of 3,000 francs, and the Bishopric of Breslau. But after only eight months, De Pauw returned to the small town of Xanten, and there devoted himself entirely to a life of study and isolation.

In 1768, his *Recherches philosophiques sur les Américains* were published in two volumes in Berlin. The work was attacked by Pernety in 1770, and a subsequent three-volume edition in 1772 included both Pernety's critique and De Pauw's *Défense* in answer.

De Pauw's other works attracted far less attention. He published his *Recherches philosophiques sur les Egyptiens et les Chinois* in 1774, and in 1778 appeared his *Recherches philosophiques sur les Grecs*. For a decade he worked assiduously on a study to be entitled *Recherches philosophiques sur les anciens Germains*, but became discouraged when another work appeared on the same subject before his own was completed. He intended to keep his manuscript, however, though in a moment of depression during the Revolution he burned it in its entirety.

Though spent in near isolation, the last years of his life were far from tranquil. He was a man of some reputation and could not remain apart from the Revolution and its agitations. He tried almost desperately to remain neutral, but events forced themselves upon him. The Directory in Paris asked him to serve as its commissioner in Cleves, but he refused and was therefore suspect; he was suspected by all parties, even by his neighbors; his nephew, the young baron Clootz, was executed in Paris. These events depressed and demoralized him sorely; his health declined, and he died in Xanten in July 1799.

## FROM THE PHILOSOPHICAL INVESTIGATIONS OF THE AMERICANS

### *Preliminary Discourse*

SINCE AMERICANS constitute the most curious and the least known chapter in the history of mankind, it is our purpose to make them the principal object of these investigations. We shall consider the peculiarities of their physical constitution, and at times the peculiarities of their moral nature.

No event is more memorable for the human race than the discovery of America. Looking back from the present to the most remote ages, we see no event that can be compared with it; and indeed it is an impressive and terrible spectacle to see one-half of this globe so ill-favored by nature that all it contains is either degenerate or monstrous.

Would any physicist of Antiquity ever have suspected that this same planet had two hemispheres so different one from the other, one of which would be conquered, subjugated and devoured by the other just as soon as it was discovered, after having been lost for centuries in the dark abyss of time?

This astonishing revolution that has altered the face of the earth and the fortunes of nations was an absolutely instantaneous phenomenon, for by an almost unbelievable fatality, there was no balance between attack and defense. All strength and all injustice were on the side of the Europeans. Americans had only weaknesses; they were therefore bound to be exterminated, and exterminated in an instant's time.

Whether this was due to a fatal combination of our destinies, or whether it was instead the necessary consequence of so many crimes and errors, it is nevertheless certain that the conquest of the New World, so celebrated and so unjust, has been the greatest of all misfortunes to befall mankind.

After the rapid massacre of some millions of savages, the heinous conqueror found himself attacked in turn by an epidemic disease which, attacking both the origins of life and the source of propagation, quickly became the most horrible scourge of the civilized world. Already crushed under the burdens of existence, man encountered, as his crowning misfortune, the germs of death in the arms of pleasure and in the very bosom of enjoyment. Easily could he believe that an irate Nature had vowed his ruin.

The annals of the universe reveal no other similar period, nor perhaps will there ever be another. If such disasters could occur more than once, the earth would be a dangerous abode where our species, succumbing under all these evils or exhausted from resisting its destiny, would become extinct, abandoning this planet to happier or less afflicted beings.

Yet scheming politicians continue, by their treasonable writings, to encourage princes to invade more austral lands. It is unfortunate that certain philosophers have exploited their talent for inconsistency to the point of expressing their own wishes for the success of this guilty enterprise. Already they have in theory traced the route to be followed by the first vessel leaving our shores to carry chains of servitude to the peaceful inhabitants of an unknown land. Arousing the greed of men with false needs and imaginary wealth is tantamount to provoking tigers that should be feared and kept enchained. Those distant peoples already have too many grievances against Europe. Toward them, Europe already has strangely abused her superiority. And now prudence, if not a sense of fairness, should tell Europe to leave these distant lands in peace, and to cultivate her own lands instead.

If the spirit of devastation and torrents of blood always precede our conquerors, let us not buy enlightenment on a few points of Geography at the cost of the destruction of a portion of the globe. Let us not massacre the Papuans just so that we might read on Réaumur's thermometer the climate of New Guinea.

After having been so daring, we have no more glory to acquire except through the moderation we lack. Let us put an end to this rage for invading everything for the sake of knowing everything.

It is fine and it is noble to uproot these barbarous hordes from the depths of their forests and to make men of them. But the philosophers who should themselves assume this task often find too much pleasure in boring us with their writings to bring themselves to travel to these far regions. If those who preach virtue in civilized nations are themselves too depraved to instruct savages without tyrannizing them, we should allow these savages to vegetate in peace. Let us pity them, if their misfortunes surpass ours; and if we cannot contribute to their happiness, let us at least not increase their misery.

In the historical portion of this work, we have followed, as much as has been possible, contemporary authors on the discovery of the New World, those who were able to observe it before it was ruined by the cruelty, the avarice, and the insatiability of Europeans. Almost nothing is left of this former America but its sky, its land, and its memories of those fearful calamities.

Already in his day, Oviedo complained that Europeans were in such haste to slaughter Americans that naturalists scarcely had the time to study them. In undertaking this work, therefore, we despaired at first of being able to find some light among so much obscurity. Finally we were obliged to fortify ourselves with sheer tenacity in order to clear our way through the contradictions and faulty observations of those voyagers whose exaggerations were excessive, beyond compare, even more pernicious than those of other writers. Their preconceptions, traveling with them, acquired a certain authority in crossing the Equator. In spite of a severely critical approach to these many witnesses, it is still a matter of chance to be able to recognize and seize upon the truth, so often misrepresented by their imbecility or violated by their malice.

The edifying letters of missionaries are particularly full of absurdities and prodigies. It is astonishing to find so many untruths in the writings of those who, according to what they tell us, preach truth in all the corners of the world. If these Apostles, dazzled by their own enthusiasm, observed so inaccurately, they ought, through respect for reason, to have abstained from describing. We did not need from them these accounts in which miracles are so profuse that one can hardly discern two or three facts among them, and these only more or less probable.

When, after laborious and thankless research, we start to establish our conclusions, contradictions appear on all sides. We are overwhelmed by them, and that which we took to be true in one sense ceases to be so in another, because our most rational judgments can never coincide so precisely as to form the perfect circle that will take in the immensity of phenomena. There will always remain openings for errors and even great errors, so that the human mind is constantly reminded of its impotence, and the philosopher, in spite of his tendency to make pronouncements, is led to doubt in spite of himself.

More than any other land, America offers numerous and singular phenomena, but up to now these have been so poorly observed, so inaccurately described, and assembled with such confusion, that they offer no more than a hideous chaos. The Spaniards, those indolent and fanatical possessors of a land they have devastated as brigands and barbarians, have never shown the least curiosity for reassembling the debris of this prodigious edifice. Content with having demolished it with their greedy hands, they have neglected its ruins partly hidden under brambles, partly dispersed over an immense area. We do not flatter ourselves that we have trod with surer step on this prickly path. This would be excessive temerity, whereas what we need is excessive indulgence.

If we have depicted Americans as being a race of men who

have all the faults of children, as a degenerate species of the human race, cowardly, impotent, without physical strength, without vitality, without elevation of mind, we offer nothing in such a portrait that would surprise the imagination by its novelty, for the history of man in his natural state has been more neglected than one might think. This essay will at least demonstrate what one might accomplish in this area, if great teachers encouraged its emulation.

Since we have had to consider subjects that are isolated and very diverse one from the other, we have not attempted to relate them by the thread of our narrative for fear of losing our study of facts in the study of style. We can even, in this instance, reproach our modern naturalists for having shown too much predeliction for an ornate and mannered style. In strewing too many flowers about their works, they betray their weakness. They try to charm the reader in order to compensate him for being neither instructed nor convinced. This sacrifice of eloquence, or this game of declamation that is so futile when one is right, is more than ridiculous when one is wrong. . . .

Since full knowledge of physical man is the primary object of our studies, it would be extremely odd not to allow us certain freedoms that every day are permitted those who describe insects and who compose entire volumes on the copulation of snails.

Equally removed from a cynical licentiousness as from a too scrupulous restraint, we have not hesitated to turn our gaze upon all the mysteries and all the aberrations of animal nature. But in the exposition of our findings, we have considered words only in their philosophical nature. These words, therefore, will not, or should not, be offensive to modesty. . . .

### *Of the Climate of America, of the Faded Complexion of Its Inhabitants, of the Discovery of the New World, etc.*

At the outset of this work, I will make some striking and conclusive observations that will give a precise notion of the climate of the New World. I will then describe its inhabitants, their physical constitution and their temperament, with all the exactitude of which I am capable. Whatever the extent of my plan, I will bear testimony to the fact that I nowhere gave way to my own preconceptions or conjectures at the expense of the verity of facts whose causes and origins I found in nature itself and not in my own ideas.

The subjects to be discussed, although all of equal interest, will nevertheless be very disparate and, of course, some more attractive than others. My reader should imagine that he is going to traverse, successively, barren and unpopulated areas, and other lands that are delightful and picturesque. This variety is not a disorder that could confuse objects or blur the composition of this tableau. Indeed it is far more a consequence imposed by the subject itself than by the arbitrary arrangement of the author.

At the time of the discovery of America, its climate was unfavorable to most quadruped animals, which in fact are one-sixth smaller in the New World than their counterparts on the old continent. In particular, the climate was injurious to the natives who, to an astonishing degree, were stupefied, enervated, and vitiated in all the parts of their organism.

The land itself, either bristling with mountain peaks or covered with forests and marshlands, presented the aspect of an immense and sterile desert. The first adventurers to settle there all underwent the horrors of famine or the great sufferings of thirst.

The Spaniards, from time to time, were forced to eat Americans and even other Spaniards for lack of nourishment. The Floridians, observing these horrible repasts, understood immediately the ferocity of such a conqueror for whom hunger held no fears.

The first French colonists sent into this hapless world also ended by eating each other. The English who conquered Virginia returned home famished on the ships of Commodore Drake; in London, they were taken for ghosts and for many years thereafter no one was found in all of England who would embark for such a land. But when it was learned that the earth there held inexhaustible treasures in its depths, the thirst for gold affronted all dangers, overcame all obstacles, and conquered nature itself.

In spite of the progress brought about by the efforts and industry of tradesmen and planters, there still remain, in the West Indies, several secondary colonies absolutely incapable of supporting themselves by means of their own produce. These would disappear, if the nations of Europe did not assume the burden of providing them with food.

In the southern sections and in most of the islands, the earth was covered with impure water, noxious, and even fatal. When the sun's heat caused a sort of evaporation of this water, there arose thick fogs, heavy with sea salt, although the physicists of the Old World had denied that sea salt had this property of evaporation. Facts proved them wrong. Even today in America, we find on mangrove trees and other plants a salt that constantly reappears, for it rises in the form of a vapor and then becomes crystallized on each leaf wet with this brine.

In this fetid and marshy terrain grew more poisonous trees than there are in the remaining three parts of the known world. The much-feared sap of these trees was extracted by savages who dipped the points of their arrows into it, and if it as much as scratched the skin of men and animals, it caused immediate death.

The principal food of Americans living on the eastern coast was a poisonous plant made edible only by their skill and knowledge. I refer to the many species of Yucca and of manioc which are almost all poisonous when eaten raw and in their natural state.[1] Nevertheless, for Americans, this manioc replaced the rye or wheat they had no knowledge of. It must be admitted that the history of the Old World offers no similar example, and whatever our other misfortunes may be, we have no instance of an entire nation forced to obtain its staple food from a poisonous tree, except perhaps in times of extraordinary famine when people resorted to eating the arum root, which of all European plants most closely resembles the manioc by its caustic and nutritive qualities after it has been treated.

Most plants which are tender and herbaceous in our climate are found in America in the form of woody shrubs. This results from the great quantity of niter in the soil they feed upon. In New France, the first time one tried to use wood ash for bleaching laundry, one was astonished to see this lye cut the cloth into shreds in an instant, then reduce it to a pulp, and this was rightfully attributed to the violence of the sharp and copious salt these ashes contained.

[1] The true antidote for this manioc sap is absinthe salt diluted in mint water. In some islands, roucou dregs are also used, but with less success.

The surface of the earth, full of putrefaction, was flooded with lizards, snakes, serpents, reptiles, and insects that were monstrous by their size and the power of their poison extracted from the juice of this earth, so barren, so vitiated, so abandoned, where the nutritive sap became sour like milk in the breasts of animals that do not propagate.

There, caterpillars, butterflies, centipedes, scarabs, spiders, frogs, and toads were found in gigantic size for their species, and multiplied beyond imagining. Glancing at the excellent drawings made in Surinam by Mademoiselle Merian, we are struck by the prodigious growth of butterflies that equal our birds in size.

Even today, the oldest European colonies in America are not yet cleansed of filthy or poisonous animals whose propagation is encouraged by the atmosphere. Panama is afflicted with serpents, Cartagena by clouds of enormous bats, Portobello by toads, Surinam by albinos, Guadaloupe and other island colonies by scarabs, Quito by mosquitoes, Lima by lice and bedbugs. The ancient kings of Mexico and emperors of Peru learned that the best way to rid their subjects of the vermin that devoured them was to impose tributes of a certain quantity of lice, that they were obliged to offer yearly. Hernando Cortés found sackfuls in Montezuma's palace. Garcilasso tells us that Peruvians were also obliged to offer a hornful yearly to the Incas, which is somewhat similar to that tribute of sparrow heads imposed upon the peasants in the Palatinate.

M. Dumont tells us in his memoirs that in Louisiana grow frogs weighing up to thirty-seven pounds, whose croaking is like the bellowing of young bulls. Monsters like this exist nowhere else in the world.

Ants so ravage the regions in the south of the Americas that this insect was named the king of Brazil: *il rey di Brasil.*[2] In the time when, by a singular contrast, American leopards, tigers, and lions were completely degenerate, small, pusillanimous, and a thousand times less dangerous than those of Asia or Africa, whose ferocity and power are limitless, Canada nourished a sort of tiger so cowardly that it became known as *le tigre poltron,* the timid tiger. That was the cougar. Wolves and wolverines

[2] When the Dutch were in possession of Brazil, the India Company was offered a plan for freeing this province of the ants that were destroying it. This plan has never been made public. It seems that the best method would be to encourage the multiplication of the large and small ant-eaters.

and bears, in this land, were also of smaller size and less ferocious than those of their species in the Old World. It even appears, according to the observations of M. du Pratz and others, that American caymans and crocodiles have neither the impulsiveness nor the fury of those of Africa. In short, a general deterioration and degeneracy had impaired, in this part of the world, all quadrupeds even unto the origins of life and propagation.

As soon as American soil was penetrated to a depth of six or seven inches, it was found to be very cold, even in the Torrid Zone. Tender grain planted a bit too deeply froze and did not germinate; thus it has been observed that most trees native to America, instead of sinking down their roots perpendicularly, instinctively thrust them out horizontally, just under the surface, to avoid the cold of the earth's interior. Pison, Margrave, and Oviedo made this same observation both on the islands and on the mainland. At the same time, the trunks and tufts of these trees nourished a multitude of parasitic plants—polypods, mistletoe, toadstools and mushrooms, dodders, moss and lichen, originating in the sediment from impure sap, sucked up by the vegetation from this land which had never been cared for and where nature, for want of direction at the hand of man, would succumb under its own efforts. An inconceivable number of worms bred there, from which the human body and all members of the animal and vegetable kingdoms suffered endlessly. All sores and wounds neglected for two or three days would swarm with vermin.

The cankerworms on dikes and vessels were brought[3] from America by a French squadron to Europe, where they were unknown, sixty years ago. Their multiplying has been so prodigious and so rapid in our seas that they have by now infected all our ports and added new perils to the dangers of navigation, causing the hulls of ships to crumble under the sailors' feet. Those insects that made Zeeland tremble also probably came from America, where Europeans in turn brought their rats and mice which had not existed there before the discovery, and which afterwards pullulated so that they became a veritable plague for the colonies. In certain islands, if the mice had not found

[3] See a *mémoire de M. des Landes, commissaire de la marine;* he names the vessels and the officers in command of the squadron which carried the first shipworms from the American islands to France.

serpents to be dangerous enemies, they would have populated these islands to the point of committing the same devastations that rabbits did in the past on the Balearic Isles and in Spain.[4]

In comparing experiments made with thermometers by Messrs. de la Condamine and Juan d'Ulloa in Peru, and the indefatigable M. Adamson in Senegal, we can easily note that the air is cooler in the New World than in the Old. In evaluating the differences of temperatures as accurately as possible, I believe this difference will correspond to 12° of latitude, that is to say, that it is as hot in Africa at 30° from the Equator as it is at only 18° from the Equator in America. In Peru, in the center of the Torrid Zone, the thermometers rise no higher than they do in France in the heat of summer. Quebec, which is approximately as far north as Paris, has a climate that is incomparably sharper and colder than that of Paris. The difference is equally perceptible between the Thames and Hudson Bay which are on the same latitude.

No large quadruped animal existed in the tropics of the New World. Naturalists who observed this peculiarity for a long time have suspected that large sperms cannot develop in this climate so unfavorable to the propagation of the animal kingdom and favorable only to insects and serpents. It rather appears, however, that an upheaval of the elements had long ago destroyed in America all the large animals of the Torrid Zone. The prodigious skeletons dug up there make this theory very probable, and we shall stop longer on this subject later in this work when we shall consider the nature of these fossils.

As for animals native to the New World, they were for the most part of a very inelegant size, and sometimes so badly formed that the first people to draw them had much difficulty in discerning their contours and in making clear their character. It was observed that most species lacked tails and that there was a certain irregularity between the division of toes on their front and rear paws, very striking indeed in the tapir, the anteater, the sloth, and other rodents.

[4] In 1524, a vessel from the squadron sent by the Bishop of Plaisance to discover new southern lands, having passed the Straits of Magellan, reached the port of the city of Los Reyes. In this ship were the first rats ever to be seen in Peru, and since that time they have multiplied furiously. It is believed that some baby rats must have gone unnoticed in cases and bales of merchandise. The Indians called them *ococha,* which means something from the sea. *Zarate conq. du Pérou,* p. 155.

The ostrich, with only two toes joined by a membrane in our continent, had four separated toes in America.

The animals of European or Asiatic origin that were transported to America immediately after the discovery became stunted; their height shrank and their instinct and character were diminished by half. The cartilage and fiber of their flesh became more rigid and leathery; the flesh of oxen is so fibrous that in Santo Domingo it can be chewed only with difficulty.

Only hogs there have acquired a corpulence that is astonishing, for they thrive in swampy lands that abound in aquatic food, insects, and reptiles. The quality of their flesh has improved and doctors prescribe this meat to their patients in preference to all others. Herrera speaks of the island of Cuba, where hogs brought from Castile changed their form in so short a time and to such an extent that they were unrecognizable. Their nails grew so, that they reached a half-palm in length.

European sheep also undergo a great deterioration in Barbados, and it is well known that dogs brought to the New World from the Old lose their faculty of barking.

Certainly the camel has been the least successful among all the animals brought to the New World. In the early sixteenth century, some were brought to Peru from Africa, but the cold weather affected their reproductive organs and they did not multiply.

The Portuguese have often considered taking elephants to Brazil, but it seems that these animals would suffer in the same manner as the camels in Peru. They would not procreate even if left free in the forests there, for more than any other large quadruped, the elephant is especially sensitive to changes of diet and climate.

Among exotic plants brought to America, almond, plum, cherry, and walnut trees have flourished little if at all. Peach and apricot trees have grown on the island of Juan Fernandez, but deteriorated elsewhere, whereas aquatic and succulent plants that require a humid and even muddy soil, such as sugar cane, melons, pumpkins, cabbages and turnips, have surpassed all expectations of the planters. Our rye and wheat have not succeeded, save in some sections of the north. Rice, which needs to be submerged, and *féveroles*, a type of bean, planted in swamps, have given plentiful harvests.

The nature of a climate can be judged better by animal and

vegetable products than by any other; this is why we have given more attention to these particular observations than to those which seemed to us less decisive or more vague.

Iguana lizards and fighting cocks, eaten by so many Americans, hastened, unbeknown to them, the progress of the disease to which all men and many animals are subject from the Straits of Magellan to Labrador, where venereal disease stops to make way for the muriatic scurvy which appears to be only a variation of the same disease.

It must be pointed out, however, that the same species of iguana lizard is prevalent in southern Asia, where its flesh has always been eaten without ever having produced the slightest symptom of the American disease. Thus it develops this virus wherever it encounters it, without however spreading it to the blood of those immune to it. (I, 1–12)

. . .

The flesh of this animal (*i.e.*, the iguana) is harmful to those who taste of it when they are infected with venereal disease. Not only does this food irritate this indisposition to an unbelievable degree; it also revives it when it seems to be dormant. Negroes, who in general have a marked preference for the flesh of serpents and lizards over every other meat, are also extremely fond of iguana. But if they be the slightest bit infected, their members become putrefied, and to save them from death, very powerful remedies must be administered, especially tortoise broths. Europeans also eat the flesh and eggs of this animal, but with more restraint and precaution now than in the first years following the discovery of America, when their harmful properties were not yet known nor even suspected.

Some authors insist that the Negroes brought this malady from Africa to the West Indies; but this opinion, refuted a hundred times, is all the more ridiculous since these self-styled authors have never known the exact moment of the arrival of the first Negro in the New World. Although it is difficult to establish such a date, we nevertheless know with assurance that it is after the time when the companions of Christopher Columbus, in particular a certain Margarita and a monk named Buellio, brought venereal disease back from Santo Domingo. In Ferreras' general history, this ardent missionary is called Boil, a head of the Benedictine order. As soon as he landed on

Santo Domingo, he excommunicated Christopher Columbus, who as a result became the first European to be excommunicated in America. But Buellio was not satisfied with such a base and spiteful act. He returned to Spain, where he infected his compatriots and so schemed at court that he succeeded in having Columbus put in irons. This great man, finding himself prey to the rage of such a vile fanatic, repented for having discovered a new world.

The inhabitants of the Antilles, where venereal disease was more prevalent than anywhere else, claimed it had come to them from the American continent; those of the continent insisted it had come to them from the Antilles. No one wanted his country to be its source. But they all agreed that since time immemorial they had been afflicted by this plague, which the Europeans received in exchange for the smallpox they brought to the New World. The first American of note to die of this transplanted smallpox was the brother of the timid and unfortunate Montezuma, emperor of Mexico. The first distinguished European carried off by the American disease was King Francis I. But even before his death in 1547, the disease had already made immense ravages on our continent. The rapidity of its spread was astonishing. The Moors expelled from Spain infected Asiatics and Africans with it. In less than two years, it spread from Barcelona to northern France. In 1496, the Parlement of Paris, in full session, pronounced its famous edict prohibiting all citizens afflicted with the American disease from appearing in the streets, under penalty of hanging, and ordering all infected foreigners to leave the capital within twenty-four hours under the same penalty.

Two years later, this same contagion appeared in Saxony. At least the Scholastics of Leipzig, as early as 1498, defended theses on the venereal disease supposedly unknown to them. On this occasion, they hurled violent insults at each other in their barbarous Latin, presented many formal arguments, and cured no patients.

The first poem written on this great evil was by a Flemish poet named Le Maire. Reading his poem, we realize that the principal symptoms accompanying the disease at that time have since completely disappeared. We might almost dare believe that becoming less virulent from one century to the next, this disease will eventually exhaust itself just as leprosy did when its germs disintegrated and destroyed themselves for having, so to speak, spread over too wide an area. One of Europe's greatest doctors, in fact, has predicted that the blood of our tenth generation will finally be entirely purefied of it, and that we shall then see nature and love regain all their original rights. Doubtless it is to be hoped that this prediction be more accurate than that of Maynard, who announced the extinction of the venereal virus by 1584, and never was there a higher mortality from the disease than in that very year.

The Guinean disease, called *yaws* and *erabyaws,* is so different an indisposition from the American disease, that mercury is absolutely harmful to Negroes afflicted with yaws. Furthermore, the characters and the consequences of these diseases have nothing in common with each other.

The ultimate proof, without possible contradiction, that venereal disease came from America is the quantity of remedies used by its natives to combat its fatal progress. They used more than sixty different elements that urgent danger had forced them to discover. It would be supremely absurd to say that Americans had sought so many cures for a malady unknown to them. Oviedo, who, according to Fallopio had become infected in Naples, was ingenious enough to guess that since his disease came from the East Indies, he would also find in the Indies the most potent specific or the best prescription. The voyage he then undertook proved him to be right. The Santo Domingo natives, by no more than a glance at his forehead, recognized that he was gangrenous and showed him the guaiacum tree. Ovideo's calamity turned out to be auspicious. He gained an immense fortune in Spain where he brought the gum, the bark, and the sap-wood of the guaiacum, with the prescription used by the Americans. Carpi, who in Italy discovered the virtues of mercury in treating the disease, became the wealthiest individual of his century, and the opulence of his style of living eclipsed that of all the ultramontane princes. (I, 14–20)

. . .

Americans, though light and agile in racing, were deprived of the lively physical force that comes from the tension and resistance of muscles and nerves. The weakest European overcame them easily in any combat. What a difference between them and the ancient savages of Gaul and Germany who became so famous for the strength of their limbs and their massive and indefatigable bodies!

The constitution of Americans, so little defective in appearance, is fundamentally weak. They collapse under the slightest burden. In transporting the belongings of the Spaniards, more than two hundred thousand of them died in less than one year under the weight of these loads, even though ten times more men were used for these transports than would have been required in Europe.

In general, they were shorter than Castilians, though the difference was slight. Ancient authors have said that their height decreased as one approached the Equator, but this observation was ill-founded. The inhabitants of the Torrid Zone are not commonly as tall as the natives of the Temperate Zone, nor are they as small as the polar peoples. It is true that among the survivors of the ancient Peruvians, according to Ulloa, there are many individuals who in Europe would be considered dwarfs.

At first Americans were not thought to be men, but rather orang-utangs, or large monkeys, that could be destroyed without remorse and without reproach. Finally, to add the ridiculous to the calamities of that era, a certain pope issued a bull in which he decreed that, as he wished to establish dioceses in the richest regions of America, it pleased him and the Holy Spirit to recognize Americans as true men. Thus, without this decision made by an Italian, the inhabitants of the New World would still today be, in the eyes of the faithful, a race of dubious animals. There has never been another example of such a decision since the world was first inhabited by both monkeys and men. . . .

Americans were particularly distinguished by the fact that most of them had no eyebrows and none had beards. We cannot infer from this defect alone that they were debilitated in their reproductive organs, since the Tartars and the Chinese have more or less the same characteristics. Nevertheless, these peoples are far from fecund, and are not inclined to love. And yet it is not true that the Chinese and the Tartars are absolutely beardless. When they are about thirty years old, a thin mustache grows on their upper lip and a few tufts grow on their chin.

In addition to being beardless, Americans also completely lacked hair on any part of their bodies and on their genitals, and this distinguished them from all other peoples of the earth. It is from this fact that we can draw some conclusions about the weakness and the deterioration of these very members, although nothing unusual or irregular was noted about them save the smallness of the organ and the length of the scrotum, which in some was excessive. (I, 31–34)

. . .

The little inclination, the little warmth of Americans toward women, unquestionably demonstrated their lack of virility and the deterioration of their reproductive organs. Love exerted over them hardly half its usual power. They experienced neither the torments nor the delights of this passion, because the most ardent and the most precious spark of nature died out in their tepid and phlegmatic souls.

The blood was certainly poorly constituted, for in certain places, fully grown men had milk in their breasts. This gave rise, in some old travel accounts, to the legend that in South American provinces only the men breast fed the children. This exaggeration was entirely gratuitous for a phenomenon that needs no elaboration and which in fact deserves to be discussed in a special treatise wherein the author, at his ease, could consider all the details and develop all the causes of such a surprising effect. But to forestall boredom and cut short this physiological study, I will say in a few words what I believe to be sufficient to explain this difficulty.

I am persuaded that humidity of temperament in the inhabitants of the New World caused this defect which, as one can easily understand, necessarily influenced their physical and moral faculties. We can therefore say that in the New World, men were more like women, more cowardly, more timid, and more afraid of the dark, than we can possibly conceive.

As far as I know, no naturalist has ever tried to discover why male children everywhere are born with milk in their breasts. It seems this must be brought about by the humidity in which the embryo is enveloped in the uterus, which prevents the bile from turning sour and from extravasating enough to render the chyle sanguineous. (I, 38–40)

. . .

After having considered the impotence of the inhabitants of the New World, for such do I call the weakness of their temperament, we are no less surprised when we consider their general physical insensitivity.

The savages of the New World have always subjected their prisoners, and still do today, to horrible tortures, without being able to move these unfortunate victims, without being able to draw from them either sighs or tears. Crushed under the curses of the victors, pierced a thousand times by their torturers, they seem to lose all consciousness, and even those who tear open their entrails show no sign of any sensitivity or emotion. Travelers who have witnessed these inhuman spectacles and were able to observe over a length of time the attitude and the untroubled countenance of those being cut to pieces, thought that these peoples must be far more cold-blooded than we, and that this deadened their pain. They were unable to give any other explanation for the phenomena. I know this explanation has been considered false and ridiculous; yet it is nonetheless true that there must exist in the physical constitution of Americans some cause that stupefies their sensitivity and their mind. The climate, the coarseness of their humors, the basic defects of their blood, the nature of their excessively phlegmatic temperament, could have diminished the tone and sharpness of the nerves in these stupefied and brutish men. (I, 66, 67)

. . .

It is a great problem to know whether Europe would not have been truly happier if two Italians had not, in the fifteenth century, shown it the way to the New World. Without speaking here of that cruel malady that poisoned the reproductive organs of mankind, a malady that could not be compensated by all the treasures of Potosí and Brazil, it is certain that we have not gained from America all the benefits we think. If eight times all the gold and silver that existed in Europe in 1490 have been extracted from its mines, and if the price of all commodities has multiplied eight times, it is easy to see that in spite of the great mass of metals imported, Europeans are neither richer nor poorer for it, and he who has 8,000 *livres* today is no more wealthy than the man who had 1,000 *livres* in the fourteenth century.

It is commonly believed that the wealth of the West Indies prevented the downfall to which the spice trade, in the hands of the Venetians, was about to drag Europe by draining it forever of its gold and silver; but this ruination was not as likely as was thought.

The few food plants that Europe obtained from America and that flourished extraordinarily in our climate constitute a real advantage that we never take into account, that we never even think of. Yet these plants could ward off misfortunes that all the gold in the world could not prevent; I refer to times of famine.

It was not until the treasures of the Indies became a practical source of trade that any real advantage was realized; yet nations also thereby saw their own interests multiply and reasons for attacking each other have consequently become more frequent and more universal. A spark of discord over some acres of land in Canada arouses and inflames Europe; and when Europe is at war, all the world is at war. All points of the globe are shaken in turn, as though by some electric power. Scenes of massacre and of carnage have spread from Canton to Archangel, from Buenos Aires to Quebec. The commerce of Europeans having closely bound all the parts of the world by the same chain, these parts are also dragged into revolutions and the vicissitudes of attack and defense. Asia can no longer remain neutral when a few merchants have a dispute in America over a few beaver skins or some logwood.

As for the commerce of the West Indian colonies, as soon as it excludes foreigners and is limited to the parent state, its advantages and profits are not as great as one would think, as the author of the *Philosophie rurale* so exactly demonstrated. If smuggling and illegal trade in the colonies are successfully eradicated, the colonies themselves are ruined. If, in the balance of profits and gains, the colonies get the better of the mother country, it is easy to foresee that the colonists who have become enriched will one day tire of the yoke imposed upon them. They will want to be free of this tutelage, and whenever they so wish, they assuredly will have the means to bring it about, and to affirm their liberty. (I, 85–87)

### *On the Stupefied Intelligence of Americans*

Up to this point we have considered the American peoples only in terms of their physical faculties which, being basically corrupt, had caused the loss of moral faculties. Degeneracy had affected their senses and their organs, and their moral character had suffered to the same extent as their bodies. Nature, having deprived one hemisphere of the globe for the benefit of the other, placed in America only children who have not yet become men. When Europeans arrived in the West Indies in the fifteenth century, they found not one single American who could read or write; even today there is not one who can think.

If the reader has quickly passed over the multitude of facts reported so far in this work, he should pay careful attention to this chapter, for at this point we can determine whether our reasoning has been logical, and if our conclusions all concur to prove in general what they prove in particular.

Intelligence has not been equally distributed among the peoples of our own continent. Negroes in the Torrid Zone, and Lapps within the Arctic Circle, have never written a single philosophical treatise, and never will. But in the entirety of the New World, in spite of its great diversity of climates, no one has ever found one man with greater intellectual capacity than any other.

A brutish insensibility forms the basis of the character of all Americans; their indolence prevents them from being attentive to any instruction; they know no passion strong enough to move their souls, to transcend their nature. Superior to animals in the use they make of their hands and their tongue, they are nevertheless truly inferior to the lowest Europeans. Deprived of both intelligence and perfectability, they can only obey the impulse of their instincts. No incentive for fame can enter their heart; their unpardonable weakness forces them either into a state of servitude where it keeps them, or into a savage existence they are too cowardly to quit. America was discovered nearly three centuries ago; since that time, Americans have constantly been brought to Europe. Attempts have been made to give them all sorts of education and culture, and never has one of them succeeded in making a name for himself in the sciences, in the arts, or in the trades.

Garcilaso de la Vega, usually taken for an American, was only a half-breed, born in Cuzco of a Spanish father and Peruvian mother. Wishing to write the history of his country, he produced a work so indigestible, so pitiful, fundamentally so illogical, that the three French authors who attempted to edit it and give it some sort of order were incapable of doing so. In the last history of the Incas, published in Paris in 1744 and attributed to Garcilaso, not one sentence was retained from the original text. In short, we can judge his lack of ability by the very fact that he could not even write a bad book, which is usually so easy in all countries, for anyone who wants to try. Yet, however limited this half-breed may have been, it is certain that a true American would never have been able to compose a page in the style and the taste of this Garcilaso, who himself would never have written at all had he not had a European father. The true western Indians cannot connect their ideas, for they do not think upon what they have said nor what they will say next. They do not think, and they have no memory. This defect is also common to Negroes who often are obliged to cover their eyes with their hands, to shut out all light, in order to remember in the morning what they did the night before. They have to think very hard to recall ideas, for ideas make little impression on their minds and vanish almost as soon as they are conceived. This should be attributed to the coarse viscous humors that circulate in their brain, for it has been proved that the faculty of memory can be restored or helped by strong sneezing agents, such as euphorbia and tobacco oil, which cause considerable evacuations of phlegm. Patients suffering from loss of memory, to whom these drugs were administered, agree that they dispel a sort of fog that absorbs the images of past things the patient tries to recall. Spiritous and fermented liquors produce analogous effects in certain men, and restore ideas they had thought lost.

As it was thought that transporting Americans to Europe was harmful to their temperament, attempts were made to educate some in their own country. These attempts were no more successful than the others, but the results of observations made on this occasion are very curious: it is admitted that the children of this race show some glimmer of intelligence until the age of sixteen or seventeen. During this period, they learn to read and write a little and give some promise to their teachers that their labors will not be lost if they continue to study. But towards the twentieth year, a stupor suddenly overcomes them. At that point, the harm is done. They regress instead of developing, and so completely forget what they have learned that one is obliged to give up all attempts at educating them, and to abandon them to their fate.

I have not attempted to discover with all possible exactitude the secret causes of such an astonishing effect. I only note the stupidity that overcomes them around the age of puberty. To be sure, it is true that even in Europe we see many young people whose intelligence declines at that age. That period of life is a terrible and critical moment that destroys or consumes all one had hoped for from the child's alertness. It is possible that in some cases the first effusions of the prolific fluid obstructs some passages and dulls their vital spirits. And yet it has been proved by experience that even immoderate enjoyment of women is not harmful to the development of the mind, whereas castration performed in early childhood is manifestly harmful and produces only men who are pusillanimous, indolent, without vivacity, and whose souls are as degraded as their bodies, for the violence of this operation turns back the seminal matter and diverts the fibers. On the other hand, the degree of intelligence depends upon the regular flow of blood and the subtlety of fluids that flow into the interior parts of the head where are situated the ends of the nerves and the beginnings of ideas. In young folk before the age of puberty, the blood flows too impetuously for their intellect to have any consistency; in old people, intelligence weakens as their blood becomes cold and stagnant. We therefore have an intermediate period between puberty and old age, a true period of vigor and force of imagination. If, in adolescence, impure and superfluous humors mix with vital fluids and benumb the fibers, intelligence diminishes or entirely disappears. If the temperament of Americans is constituted as we have described it, if it is corrupted by the causes we have indicated, weakness of understanding must be natural to Americans; they are condemned to it. This transient lucidity observed in their children lasts as long as their blood circulates rapidly; when it slows down as they approach the age of virility, it stupefies them and deprives their mind of the activity the fire of youth had given it.

As there are no means of making them attentive to instruction, it is impossible to make them retain any connection of abstract ideas. They have already forgotten the principles by the time one wants to demonstrate the results. In the mechanical arts, where each piece and each instrument leads to an ensemble, they lack the patience required to copy a model. It is a prodigious accomplishment that a Peruvian native succeeded in making a very poor copy of a very good original, even though he had devoted several years to making this painting. Whatever excessively presumptuous idea these barbarians might have of themselves, they secretly recognize the superiority of Europeans and fear all men with beards. When the first Americans were brought to France, during the minority of Charles IX, it was evident that they thought little of the King, whom they took for an Indian because he had no beard, whereas they trembled before the Swiss guards who wore enormous mustaches. This error was far less excusable than that of the Dutchman who took the fabulist LaFontaine for the King's preacher, and Pierre Corneille for his Secretary of State because he made princes speak so nobly in his tragedies.

I have already mentioned how the first Synod at Lima argued heatedly over whether American natives could be admitted to the sacraments of the Church, because of their stupidity. Many priests were obstinate in their refusal and this attitude has prevailed to this day, for the number of Peruvian Indians receiving communion is very small compared with those refused it. They have so little intelligence and memory that they lack all adroitness in confession. The penitentiary priest is obliged to ask if they have not committed such and such a sin, and they answer very simply, Yes or No. Others protest that they remember nothing, and it has to be proved to them, for instance, that they are guilty of adultery, otherwise they persist in denying it.

I am far from supposing that the zeal of our missionaries has not always been as fervent as they tell us it is, but I flatter myself to think that most of them, if they are sincere, will not contradict me if I state as a fact that no American native has ever understood a word of the Christian religion. Women and children go regularly to church and enjoy themselves singing hymns; as for the men, their only pleasure comes in ringing the church bell, without paying the slightest attention to the words of the catechist. If they were denied these bells, they would never go to mass, as M. du Pratz observed in Louisiana. Thus in the Spanish colonies, the Inquisition is continually occupied with forcing the Indians to attend divine service, and the pickets of the Holy Brotherhood must stand guard at the doors of the churches until the service or the sermon is finished. We can refute with good reason what M. de Montesquieu reports concerning the attachment of American savages to Christianity.

One cannot attach himself sincerely to a religion without knowing its dogmas and its mysteries. The Christian mysteries are too metaphysical to be able to satisfy Americans, who do not understand them, as the missionary Thomas Gage has so well stated.

The Jesuits, who became aware of this distaste, adopted a course of action that helped them attain their ends: they changed the exterior forms of the service into spectacles that pleased the listless Indians. In Paraguay, they put on such comic processions, with such a profusion of statuettes worked by cords, that by now savages come from very far away to see them. All acts of devotion are accompanied by a tragicomedy that can best be compared to the mystery plays performed in Europe, in which God and the angels torture each other in order to make the audience laugh.

No one realized the missions' lack of success among savages better than when the English took Canada. Several were questioned on the articles of faith, which turned out to be entirely unknown to them, although these dogmas had been preached in their lands for already two centuries. Others had a very confused notion of the story of Christ, and when asked who Christ was, they answered that he was a *jongleur,* of French nationality, whom the English hanged in London, that his mother was French, and Pontius Pilate was a lieutenant in the service of Great Britain. M. Douglas, who cites these details, infers from this that Catholic preachers, in order to incite the Iroquois against the English, had intentionally taught them these false things. But I cannot believe that anyone would abuse religion in such a criminal way, and I prefer to impute these childish replies to the Americans' lack of understanding rather than to the sacrilegious intrigues of missionaries.

Inserted in the memoirs of the Baron de la Hontan is a dialogue between him and a Canadian native on some controversial matters. It is superfluous to say that this piece is fictitious, for no Canadian has ever had enough patience or intelligence to argue against the theologians of the Quebec seminary. Yet it is surprising that a modern author, having taken this dialogue literally, should take it upon himself to refute it, and should, in fact, compose a treatise on the philosophy of the Iroquois that he then published in the *Dictionnaire philosophique*. The American languages are so limited, so destitute of words, that it is impossible to express any metaphysical ideas by their means. In none of these languages can one count to more than three;[5] and the savages, no matter how they are taught, never succeed in speaking even only fairly well any European tongue. It would be impossible to translate any book, not only into Algonquin or Brazilian, but not even into Peruvian or Mexican, for the lack of a sufficient quantity of terms proper for setting forth general ideas, as will be more amply demonstrated later. This paucity of words indicates a paucity of ideas; it proves that Americans are not yet out of their childhood. Thus they improve nothing, and stubbornly persist in roaming the woods instead of clearing them to create fertile and pleasant open country. Whereas they observe European colonists enjoying the comforts of life and the fruits of their labors, they take shelter, in the depths of poverty, in horrible huts that they construct as clumsily as their ancestors did in the time of Christopher Columbus; and their architecture has made no more progress than that of the beavers in their land.

If there had been found, in the New World, men inspired by generous sentiments, capable of feeling the incentive of fame, and eager to become learned in the arts and sciences, all the advantage of the discovery of America would have been theirs. By exchanging their gold, their pearls, their emeralds, and their cochineal for our understanding and our secrets; by profiting from our knowledge, our discoveries, our inventions and our instruments, they would have blessed fate for having brought to their shores such clever masters, whom they could repay with some insects, some shining stones, and some yellow dirt. Many nations of ancient Europe recognized that coming under the yoke of the Roman Empire, they ceased being barbarians, for their conquerors had taught them the arts and letters they lacked, and in this they were not mistaken. But the stupidity and laziness of Americans caused them to lose the only advantage they could draw from the arrival of the Europeans.

If they had defended themselves even a little against the invaders, these would not have made bold to slaughter them like animals; if they had shown the slightest inclination for learning,

[5] "*Peottarraro incouroac* signifies, in the language of the Yameos, a people of South America, the number three. Fortunately for those who deal with them, their arithmetic goes no further than that. As unbelievable as that may seem, this is not the only Indian nation where this is true. The Brazilian language, spoken by less crude people, is similarly impoverished, and to count beyond the number three, they are obliged to borrow from the Portuguese tongue." *Voyage de M. de la Condamine,* Paris, 1745, pp. 66, 67.

we would not have come to think of them as the lowest form of the human species. To say that a Spaniard born in America is an "American" is to insult him so cruelly that he can never forgive the offender. Portuguese and English Creoles also consider themselves sorely insulted when they are called "Americans," so superior do they consider themselves to the men of that race; and indeed they are superior in many respects, though not quite so much as they think.

Since it is principally to the climate of the New World that we have attributed the causes vitiating the essential qualities of men and the degeneration of human nature, we are doubtless justified in asking if any derangement has been observed in the faculties of Creoles, that is, of Europeans born in America of parents native to our continent. This interesting question, very important in itself, merits our attention. All animals taken from the Old World to the New have undergone, without any exception, a noticeable deterioration, either in their form or in their instinct. This would lead us immediately to presume that men also have experienced some effects caused by the air, the land, the water, and the food; but since men were better able than animals to preserve themselves against these first influences of the climate, the change in their constitution and the weakening of their mind was not immediately recognized. Yet, in later comparing them with freshly arrived Europeans, some differences seemed to begin to appear; and after repeated observations, it was evident that the degeneracy earlier believed possible was indeed a reality. Finally, we can now affirm with assurance that Creoles of the fourth and fifth generation have less genius, less capacity for knowledge, than Europeans. This belief was universally adopted when Father Benito Feijoo, so well known for the monstrous paradoxes he upheld in his *Theatro Critico,* protested against this opinion and attempted to write a vindication of the American Creoles, who were said to be stupefied.

Though respecting Father Feijoo as a monk superior to Spanish monks, we cannot deny that he has induced an infinity of glaring errors, both by his passion to make himself conspicuous as by his penchant for the miraculous. He has written several formal dissertations to prove that there exists a race of aquatic men endowed with immortal souls. This is enough, in my judgment, to make us challenge his testimony and his authority in every subject he treats; for it is better to believe he is always wrong than to say he is always right, as did Father Sarmiento who in vain rose to the defense of his master.[6] An author who believes in aquatic men cannot be defended.

Studies made of Creoles have shown that in their early youth, just like American children, they give evidence of some acuteness of mind, which then dies out when they outgrow adolescence. They then become listless, wanting in application, stupefied, and are unable to attain perfection in any art or science. Thus, it is proverbially said that they are already blind when other men begin to see, for their understanding diminishes when that of Europeans comes into its full force. Let Father Feijoo wear himself out extolling the sublime genius of Americans and citing what he believes to be favorable facts; it is nonetheless true that American universities have produced no famous men among Creoles. No graduate of the Academy of St. Mark in Lima has ever been able to write even a bad book, yet this school enjoys the best reputation among all American universities. When M. Godin was elected professor of mathematics and astronomy in Peru, he found no student capable of understanding his lessons, and his lectures never were understood in that part of the world. The Jesuits have published some impressive accounts of their college at Santa Fé, where they say they have often counted as many as ten thousand students. It is particularly surprising that of this vast number of students there has come no great teacher, no philosopher, no doctor, no physician, no scientist whose name has crossed the seas and become known in Europe.

It is useless to protest that this total lack of famous men is due to the ignorance and barbarity of the professors, and to the deplorable state to which the sciences are reduced in the West Indies. Those who have received from nature the priceless gift of intellect easily surmount the obstacles of a poor education, and rise by means of their own efforts, just as all great men have risen above their age and above their own masters to whom they almost never owe the least part of their talents and their fame. Thus, the lack of success of Creoles sent by their parents to the different colleges of the New World must be ascribed to

[6] Father M. Sarmiento is the author of *la Demonstration critique et apologétique du Theatro Critico du B. Feijoo,* whose disciple he was. He should have remembered the maxim *nullius addictus jurare in verba magistri.*

a real defect and physical deterioration of constitution, in an unhealthy climate harmful to the human race. Indeed, some of these Creoles have come to study in Europe. Their names have remained as obscure as if they had studied in Mexico or in Lima. They have never produced any study on the animals, the insects, the plants, the minerals, the climate, the peculiarities, or the phenomena of America. We owe all our knowledge of natural history in the Indies to European botanists and naturalists. What would we know without Oviedo, Pison, Margrave, Benzo, Clusius, Merian, Leri, Clayton, Cornut, Barrere, Catesby, Sir Hans Sloane, Feuillée, Plumier, La Condamine, Bouguer, Jussieu, Calm, Browne, and so many others who, to instruct us, have traveled to countries that Creoles could easily have described without ever leaving home, if they'd had the slightest capacity, the slightest interest, the slightest intelligence. We judge them impartially by what they have not done; for, since they have never written anything, we cannot judge them by their works. I believe that is in itself enough to demolish the opinion embraced by Father Feijoo.

Half-breeds, inferior to Creoles, are nevertheless greatly superior to American natives whose blood has not been mixed with that of Europeans. From this we can infer that these last hardly merit the title of rational men. (II, 107–122)

# 3.

## Dom Pernety

*"One simply cannot politely deny facts."*

DE PAUW'S MAIN CRITIC in the polemic over America was DOM ANTOINE-JOSEPH PERNETY, who was born in Roanne on February 13, 1716. As a young man, he became a member of the Benedictine order and was called to the Abbey of Saint-Germain-des-Près in Paris. His early decades offer not much of interest or of variety; it was a life of routinely serving his ecclesiastical functions and of personal study of matters that interested him. In particular, he was attracted by natural history, and even learned to draw so that he could detail the plants he discovered on his walks through Paris.

In 1763, in the capacity of chaplain, he accompanied Bougainville on his expedition to the New World. As one might expect, such a voyage was a crucial experience in his life, and he returned to France either with a new point of view and broader ideas, or else with more conviction and confidence in ideas he might already previously have held. With twenty-eight other Benedictine monks, in June of 1765, he signed a petition requesting dispensation from the rules of the Order. The petition was unfavorably received, and ultimately withdrawn the following year. In 1766 also, he proposed, in general conclave, the liberalizing of the rules of the Order, but recognizing that these efforts too were futile, he quit the Order and went to Berlin to accept the patronage of Frederick the Great.

Frederick's offer was generous indeed; the post of Royal Librarian, membership in the Royal Academy, and the Abbey of Burgel in Thuringen. It would seem, however, that through a confusion in names, this offer was made in error, being really intended originally for Pernety's uncle, Jacques Pernety, author of a work entitled *Lettres sur les physionomies.* But Frederick treated the nephew well nonetheless, especially since he concerned himself with topics of interest to the King. In 1769 he published a *Discours sur la physionomie.* In the same year appeared his *Journal historique du voyage fait aux îles Malouïnes et au détroit de Magellan,* and it was at this moment that the polemic with De Pauw over America was engaged. De Pauw's *Recherches philosophiques* had commanded considerable attention in 1768 and 1769, and Pernety immediately felt called upon to reply. Clearly De Pauw had written without any direct knowledge; clearly his work was biased; clearly he was uncritical of the sources he cited and accepted obvious absurdities because they suited his purpose. It cannot be said, however, that Pernety's answer, the *Dissertation sur l'Amérique et les Américains,* was much more unbiased or unobjective. Pernety, the champion of the New World, was easily carried away by his own enthusiasm, and fell into the same excesses as De Pauw. The two opponents were well worthy of each other.

Pernety's *Dissertation* was published in 1770. De Pauw answered in a *Défense des Recherches philosophiques* (also 1770), and Pernety continued the battle with yet another answer in 1771, the *Examen des Recherches philosophiques sur l'Amérique et les Américains,* which in effect only developed further the same ideas of the *Dissertation* without contributing anything new. Fortunately, De Pauw had the restraint and good sense to drop the matter at this point. An answer to Pernety's answer to his answer to Pernety's critique would hardly have had any interest. In fact, De Pauw seems to have thought little of the *Examen.* The 1772 edition of the *Recherches philosophiques,* now in three volumes, reprints both Pernety's original *Dissertation* and De Pauw's *Défense*, and that is all.

An anonymous work appearing in 1771, *De l'Amérique et les Américains,* is thought to be written by Pernety, and internal evidence would seem to support this belief, for here again the ideas are the same as those expressed in the *Dissertation.* If indeed Pernety was its author, this was the final chapter in his controversy with De Pauw.

Pernety remained happily at his post for many years before finally incurring Frederick's displeasure. He fell from favor when it was brought to the King's attention that he had become interested in the ideas of Swedenborg and was in fact engaged in translating this author into French. Pernety's translations of Swedenborg found publication in France: *Les Merveilles du ciel et de l'enfer* in 1782, and *La Sagesse angélique* in 1786. In 1783, he left Frederick's patronage and returned to Paris, though his stay there was brief for the Archbishop of Paris was hostile to him. He moved south to Valence where lived his brother, then to Avignon, and spent his last years in the south of France.

Pernety had always been interested in the occult. Some early works reflected this interest: *Les Fables égyptiennes et grecques dévoilées* in 1758, in which he treats alchemy and considers the *Iliad* only as an allegorical lesson on this art (it was his belief that Homer had learned alchemy in Egypt); and the *Dictionnaire mytho-hermétique* in the same year. Now in his old age he resumed his occult studies. A good man of pleasant society, he attracted disciples, and in Avignon it appears that he formed a cult of rather vague or unknown principles that at one time had some hundred members. Like De Pauw, he tried to remain apart from the Revolution but was unsuccessful, and he was arrested and detained in prison. In his last years he continued to search for the elixir of longevity, and became convinced that he had found the secret of prolonging life for centuries. He died in Valence in 1801.

## FROM THE DISSERTATION ON AMERICA AND THE NATIVES OF THAT PART OF THE WORLD

### *On The American Soil*

M. DE PAUW had read the accounts of Father Feuillée and of Mr. Frézier, for he cites them; but he did not see the lands they speak of with eyes as objective as theirs. His reflections, which could have been more philosophical, made him forget what he had read in these authors, and unfortunately led him to speak against the truth.

M. de Pauw should take the trouble to go see with his own eyes those lands his authors describe. Enchanted by them, and with enthusiasm, he would change his mind. He would then say with Frézier: "In such good land, it doesn't matter if the soil is not carefully cultivated. It is so fertile, so easy to work, that all one need do is to scratch it with a plow fashioned from a crooked branch drawn by two oxen, and even though the seed be scarcely covered with earth, it yields at least a hundredfold. They need cultivate their vines with no more care than that, in order to get good wine. This fertility and abundance in all things, that are enjoyed in Lima, contribute greatly to the gentle temperament that prevails. The weather is never inclement, for it always maintains a balance between the cold of night and the heat of day. Clouds usually cover the sky, to preserve this fertile climate from the sun's rays which would otherwise be too strong. These clouds never turn to rain that might interrupt delightful walks or other pleasures of life. Sometimes only they descend and form mists that refresh the earth's surface, so that one can always be assured about the next day's weather. If the pleasure of living in a constantly temperate climate were not troubled by frequent earthquakes, I don't believe there is another place in the world more suitable for giving us an idea of earthly paradise, for the land is still fertile in all manner of produce."

And that, sirs, is only one of the regions of this land so abandoned, so ill-favored by nature. How many other such regions could we not similarly praise if they were only known to us! (pp. 27–28)

I could add here what Margrave, Pison, and so many others have said about Mexico, about Brazil, about Louisiana and other regions of North America; but these testimonies, though above suspicion, would only be superfluous. To those people who are knowledgeable about the qualities of the land in these regions, I leave the comparison between reality and what M. de Pauw says about them.

Is he any more justified in describing Americans as a race of degenerate and degraded animals? Is he any more creditable when he speaks of animals? Perhaps he will say that the examples I cite are, at best, exceptions to the rule that he tries to establish as proof of the superiority of the three other parts of the world over America. In that case, we would have to count among the favors Nature granted Europe the fact that here, pigeons lay and hatch only two eggs at a time, while in Peru, these same pigeons lay six or seven times in as many days in a row, hatch them, and that there are as many chicks born as there are eggs. Is it not also by the same favor that in Europe our turnips grow only about as large as a thumb, while in Peru they grow to be the size of the sturdy calf of a man's leg?

Is M. de Pauw any more successful in the conclusions he draws from his philosophical reflections? One can judge by this example. Most plants that are soft and herbaceous in our climate, he tells us, have been found in America, but in the form of woody shrubs. Caterpillars, butterflies, centipedes, scarabs, spiders, frogs and bats exist there, for the most part in gigantic size and in quantities beyond imagining. Dumont tells in his accounts of Louisiana that frogs are seen there weighing as much as thirty-five pounds, and their croaking is like the bellowing of bulls. M. de Pauw concludes from this the ungrateful nature of the soil and a general degeneracy that extends even to the first principles of existence and propagation. Thus I would have been utterly mistaken had I reached an opposite conclusion. I would have thought I was reasoning philosophically in concluding from this prodigious quantity of living things which moreover are of such gigantic size, that the origins of life in that land are far more fecund and far more active than in ours, where all animals—or so it would seem by comparison with those of like species in America—have only a half-life, with only half-perfected bodies, since examples far superior in size and in quality can be found elsewhere.

Yet it seems to me that to reason in this way is to reason logically according to the ideas we have adopted on the improvement of the species: that a plant, instead of continuing to creep and to maintain its soft, weak, and herbaceous nature, should become a bush; that a straight and tall tree should be sturdy and raise its proud head above other small, weak, and stunted trees of the same species; that a giant, or even a tall and well-built European, should have a degree of perfection superior to that of Laplanders or of the people of Greenland or of dwarfs to whom nature seems to have denied matter and form. Fortunately, M. de Pauw is not the authorized spokesman for all Europe to determine our judgment and our ideas on America and its inhabitants, nor to express our sentiments of gratitude toward the New World. If we took him at his word, we would have to consider the New World with the utmost scorn, as being an accursed land that should be abandoned to its dismal fate.

But the daily activities of Europeans gives the lie to all that M. de Pauw writes. We will continue to obtain from America sugar, cocoa, and coffee to gratify our tastes and our senses; woods for veneers and the dyeing of cloth for our luxury and our fancies; balms from Peru and Copahiba, quinine, and sassafras, guaiacum, and a thousand other drugs to cure our maladies; gold and silver—the Christian gods, as they are so wisely named by the savages; gems and furs and cottons to clothe us. And Europe, this land so rich, so fertile, and so abundant in all things, to which nature has given all at the expense of the other hemisphere, still continues to turn to America for all these and many other things that its own soil does not provide.

The location of America in three different zones causes a great diversity of climate; the air is cold or warm according to the region. We can agree with Guedeville that in general the New World is extremely fertile. It has everything we have, and moreover abounds in riches not even found in Europe. The natives of that country lack neither genius, nor strength, nor agility, and among them good prevails over evil. These peoples are fully aware of it. They could say to the Spaniards at the time of the invasion: "Your country must indeed be very sterile or miserable to oblige you to run many risks and dangers to come and invade ours; or you must yourselves be evil men to come with such pleasure to persecute us and chase us from our lands." This reasoning hardly seems to be that of men as stupid as M. de Pauw would wish us to think. I will give him ample reason to recover from his prejudices in this matter after I prove to him that this race of men is not without force and vigor, not a degenerate race, corrupt in the basic physical and moral principles. (pp. 34–37)

### *On The Physical Qualities of Americans*

When I read the work of M. de Pauw, I am reminded of the natives of the Tyrol and the surrounding mountains, who believe their enormous goiters to be a sign of beauty and who mock those who have none. According to this author, the weakest European, the most imbecile, is far superior to all Americans, even to Creoles. Weakened and stupefied, they are veritable automatons that no passion can move, capable only of obeying the impulse of their animal instincts. Clearly they are corrupt and degenerate in their nature and physical constitutions, for we find among them no hunchbacks, no cripples or one-eyed people, except those maimed by accident, while in Europe we encounter many such everywhere.

Undoubtedly M. de Pauw has access to some very special literature concerning America, for I know of no accounts that present Americans as he depicts them. Let us consider what they say. The authors I will cite had no interest in misrepresenting the truth in order to enhance their picture of the natives.

I have read some histories of Canada, reports Baron de la Hontan. The missionaries who wrote them included some descriptions that are rather simple and quite precise of the regions known to them. But they err badly in the picture they give of the manners and customs of the natives. The Recollects and the Jesuits speak of them in an entirely different manner; they had their own reasons for doing so. If I had not understood the language of the natives, I might have believed all that has been written about them. But my own conversations with these people have completely disabused me. Those who have depicted the natives as being as hairy as bears have never in reality seen any natives, for they have neither beards nor any hair on any part of their bodies. In general, they are well-built, of goodly height, and, for Americans, better proportioned than Europeans.

The Iroquois are taller, more courageous and more clever than the others; but less agile and less dexterous in war than in hunting which they never do in large numbers. The Illinois, the Oumanis, the Outagamis and some other tribes are of moderate height. They are as swift as hares, if I may make such a comparison. The Outaouas and most of the northern Indians, with but few exceptions, are cowardly, ugly, and poorly built. The Hurons are brave, enterprising and intelligent; they resemble the Iroquois in their height and facial features. The Indians are all sanguineous, and almost olive in color. In general, they are handsome, and of good height. It is rare to see any who are lame, one-eyed, hunchbacked, blind, or dumb. If there is an occasional one such, his condition is due to an accident. Is it not yet another favor Nature granted to Europe that people afflicted with these infirmities are found here?

But let us continue the portrait of this race of man—these rejects of Nature, according to M. de Pauw, yet far different from this in the eyes of Baron de la Hontan, of M. de Bougainville who lived among them for twenty years, and of many other French officers who fought with them through the last war.

Indians have large black eyes, thick black hair, strong teeth as white as ivory; their breath, according to Baron de la Hontan, is as fresh and clean as the air they breathe even though they almost never eat bread. They are neither as strong nor as vigorous as some Frenchmen as far as carrying heavy loads is concerned, or for lifting a burden and hoisting it up onto their shoulders. On the other hand, they are indefatigable, inured to hardships. They withstand extremes of heat and cold without suffering, for they get constant exercise in hunting, fishing, frequent dancing, and in playing a game similar to handball in which the legs are most important.

The women are of better than average height, as beautiful as one can imagine; but they are so fat, so heavy, and so badly developed that they can appeal only to Indians. Either through exercise, or through their own temperament, they are very healthy, free from paralysis, dropsy, gout, decline, asthma, gravel, and kidney stones—all ailments with which Nature, who already so generously endowed our continent, has chosen to favor us. Nevertheless, she did leave pleurisy to the Canadians, and we also brought them our smallpox. The Americans, in fair exchange, gave us their own malady.

When an Apalachite savage, or any in North America as far north as Labrador, dies a natural death at the age of sixty, they say he has died young, for ordinarily they live eighty or a hundred years. There are many who live even longer. Where, then, is this corruption so prevalent in all the human race in the New World, that causes senses, organs, and all physical faculties to degenerate? Does M. de Pauw then find this degradation, which he stresses on every page of his work, among the other peoples of the continent? No, and a simple glance at accounts of their countries will give evidence to contradict him.

In Cayenne and in Guinea, the natives are physically well-developed, all parts of their bodies being perfectly proportioned. They are of good height, with handsome faces; their hair is long and black and their skin swarthy, yet soft as satin to the touch.

Their women are well-built and some are as beautiful as European women. Bristock says of the Apalachites the same things that Biet reports on the Cayenne natives. The Chevalier de Rochefort pays the same tribute to the inhabitants of Florida, Carolina, and the Caraibes (the islanders as well as those of the mainland), not with respect to the beauty of their faces, but rather to the proportions of their bodies, and their height. They are, he tells us, well-built, with a laughing and pleasant air; their shoulders and hips are broad and all are somewhat given to stoutness. Their mouths are of only average width, and their teeth grow white and close. None are one-eyed, or hunchbacked, or bald, or in any way defective through a natural deformity, only through accident.

If most of these men have some deformity in our eyes—the nose flattened, for instance, or in some cases the forehead, we must not put the blame for this upon Nature, who did not create them so, but rather upon the whims and prejudices of their mothers, who began to flatten their features soon after birth, and continued to do so while nursing them. They believed this would enchance the beauty of their children.

We can reproach the people of our own continent for similar prejudices. I shall speak of this when I discuss the mentality and customs of Americans.

If we travel from the north to the southern extremity of the New World, all the nations we encounter on our way present well-constituted men. These are, if we are to believe Vincent le Blanc and other travelers, the Mexicans, Brazilians, Peruvians, the natives of Paraguay and Chile, and finally the Patagonians. To offer here the testimonies of Margrave, Pison, and other authors above suspicion, would be to fall into repetitions that are already too tiresome. M. de Pauw cites them himself, but he took from them only those details he thought would support his false hypothesis. I will add only that according to Frézier, the Chileans and the other peoples of South America are of good height, have sturdy members, broad stomachs, chests and faces; that in spite of their debaucheries, they live for centuries without infirmities, so robust are they and accustomed to the ravages of the atmosphere; that for long periods of time they endure hunger and thirst, whether in wars or during voyages; and that no one can equal them in resisting fatigue.

Even if M. de Pauw did have access to some reports on particular areas unknown to authors familiar to the public, should he have made them the basis of his work, and reached his conclusions by generalizing from the particular, contrary to all the rules? May I remind him of what he said to the famous M. le Cat of Rouen. In spite of our respect for the extensive erudition of M. de Pauw, we would take the liberty of expressing our surprise at his deciding to revive ancient paradoxes or to establish new ones, at his adopting an opinion and defending an hypothesis so contrary to his own knowledge, and for which in truth he seems to have given his enthusiasm free rein, to the point of protesting that he intended to refute the falsehoods and exaggerations of the Spanish historians.

I cannot conceive how M. de Pauw undertook to deny the existence of Patagonian giants. If we reason strictly according to his own philosophical method, nothing is more convincing than this existence to prove in his eyes the degradation and degeneracy of the human race in America. For in order to prove the sterility of the soil, as well as the degradation of plant life in the New World, does he not tell us that the tender, soft, and herbaceous plants of our continent are to be found in America much taller, much better nourished, much stronger, in the form of woody shrubs—that is, giants of their species in the vegetable kingdom?

But let me give due credit to M. de Pauw, for he does not always substantiate his conclusions with proofs of that sort. He understood perfectly well that the existence of Patagonian giants was likely to demolish his arguments of degeneracy of the human race in the new continent. Therefore he directed all his efforts toward destroying them. But to succeed in destroying giants, one needs the thunderbolts of Jupiter himself, and M. de Pauw did not have these at his disposal. Perhaps these giants have indeed disappeared, but only for those readers dazzled by his specious reasoning. The citations he selects for purposes of contradiction, along with those he leans upon to further his own arguments, create a chaos—but a chaos, fortunately, that only those who have not read the original texts will find difficult to unravel. Examined closely, this disorder is nothing but a cloud easy to dissipate, for truth will always prevail when it is attacked only by negative proofs. Such are M. de Pauw's proofs, and they are the basis of the prejudices shared by all those who, without examination, reject everything that has any aspect of the prodigious. (pp. 37–44)

Among all the accounts of voyages I have cited, there are some that mention not having seen this race of Titans, or even make no mention of them at all. All others confirm having seen them, and having spoken to them. To say with M. de Pauw that these recent authors have related nothing but fables, that they have tried to deceive us, would seem rather hazardous. One simply cannot politely deny facts. As for those accounts that speak of not having seen these Patagonians, these negative proofs are outnumbered by the affirmative proofs of others. It is also very easy to reconcile the two. This race of gigantic men has been seen in the port of St. Julian by some, in the port of Desiré by others, at Cape Gregory and at Boucaut Bay, and elsewhere, by other navigators. Others have gone ashore in the same ports and not seen them.

Should we conclude from this that they do not exist? No, the conclusion would not be logical. You might have one, two, or three houses in town and in the country. I might have called several times to see you, without finding you at home, while others have been more fortunate than I. From this, I would conclude that your existence is not a lie, that the pleasures and fêtes you gave to those who did see you are not mere fables. I would conclude that you do not live continually in only one of these houses, but rather that you move from one to the other according to the season, and that I chose the wrong time to hope to find you. When the wise man, the philosopher, has not ample proofs to acknowledge a certain thing, especially something quite extraordinary, he doubts, but he does not deny. Another type of man denies all that seems extraordinary, to give himself the outward appearance of philosophy. It is fashionable not to be credulous. One doesn't want to be thought one of the ignorant masses, constantly finding new enthusiasms, always ready to accept the most extraordinary things.

The existence of a giant race of humans is just such an extraordinary thing. We have been hearing since the start of the sixteenth century that such a race has been found near the Straits of Magellan. Navigators speak of having seen these giants, spoken to them, eaten and drunk with them. They have described their clothes, their figures, and even their weapons that they have brought back and shown to all who were curious to see them. These testimonies have been successively repeated from 1519 up to the present. Messrs. de la Gyraudais and Guyot brought clothing and weapons of these giants to Paris, made a present of some of them to M. Darboulin in whose home I myself saw and measured them, and where undoubtedly they can still be seen. Yet the existence of these Patagonian giants still remains a problem for many people. How can it be resolved? The solution is not difficult. Let some of our accredited philosophers go to these regions. Let them travel throughout the land and remain there long enough to visit it in different seasons. Let them make inquiries about the inhabitants of Chile and its neighboring regions, about the land occupied by those men called *Chaucahues* with whom they occasionally communicate. If these philosophers then tell us, upon their return, that all their researches have been in vain, the existence of these giants will then become more than doubtful. We might then be justified in regarding it as some sort of fiction, in spite of existing proofs to the contrary that we find in the accounts of the most famous navigators. But while we await the return of these philosophers from this voyage that would be at least as interesting as so many others, we can continue to believe, without being so credulous, it seems to me, that in that part of America there does exist a race of men considerably taller than ours. The details of time and place, the name that Magellan gave them and that we still continue to use for them, all the circumstances surrounding what has been said about them, seem to bear evidence of sufficient truth to overcome the natural bias we might have for the contrary, and to prove to M. de Pauw that the human race is not so degenerate in America as he would wish to persuade us. The infrequent appearance of these colossi has perhaps caused some exaggeration in the reports of their height, but if we were to consider these as estimates rather than as precise measurements, we would see that there is really very little difference among them all. (pp. 60–63)

In demonstrating, in opposition to M. de Pauw, the excellence, the beauty, and the fertility of the American land, we followed him from north to south. Let us now retrace our steps and see if travelers have seen the inhabitants of that hemisphere through the same eyes as that author; if they found the human face fundamentally corrupt in all its physical faculties; if degeneracy had attacked the senses and organs of men; if these men are still today degenerate, cowardly, impotent, without strength or vigor, without any elevation of spirit, without memory, incapable of connecting ideas, superior to animals only in their speech and the use of their hands, inferior to the weakest and least intelligent European.

The Americans in Chile are of a good height, Frézier tells us. They have thick limbs, broad chests and faces, and no beard. Their hair is thick as horsehair, black and flat. Few men can be found elsewhere in the world who can compare with them in agility, in their strength in resisting fatigue, in their skill in going on horseback. In spite of their frequent debauchery, they live centuries without infirmities, so robust are they.

Their natural color is tan, almost copper. This coloration prevails in all America, in the south as in the north. It must be noted, however, that this is not an effect of the qualities of the air they breathe, but rather a particular disposition of the blood, for the descendants of Spaniards who settled there, who married European women and who never consorted with Chilean women, have a clearer white complexion and better blood than Europeans, even though they were born in Chile, nourished in more or less the same way, and suckled by native women.

We cannot attribute this tanned copper color, natural to the inhabitants of Chile, to the Chilean climate, for it is common to all the inhabitants of the two extremities of the New World, and to those who live between the two Tropics. Heat and cold therefore have no effect upon it, and M. de Pauw's conclusions are consequently false.

Are his conclusions any more reliable with respect to the very different degree of heat and cold this side of the Equator and in the same parallel in our continent? He does not know. But I know it is not true that the cold is stronger in the southern hemisphere at the same degree south as on this side of the Equator. Pierre Duclos and Alexandre Guyot twice rounded Cape Horn, in 56° latitude in the southern hemisphere, in the middle of that region's winter; and in fact, in order to avoid the strong currents and contrary winds that are ordinarily encountered near this Cape, they were obliged to voyage south to 60° or so. They have assured me that they did not feel the same severity of cold as in 48° latitude in Europe.

The Frenchmen who settled in the Malviners Islands, in the 52nd parallel, spent three consecutive winters there. Messrs. de la Gyraudais and Guyot put into port in the Straits of Magellan for two winter months. They too have assured me that the cold there was very moderate and even so gentle in the Malviners that the ice that formed over still water was not thick enough to support the weight of a stone of two or three pounds without breaking.

In Chile as in almost all of America, females are so well constituted that they seem to have been excluded from the punishment for the gluttony and disobedience of the first mother of the human race. American women deliver themselves without the help of midwives, and give birth to their children with an ease that our European women would find difficult to believe. Even their confinement lasts only two or three days. If that is a proof of degeneracy in the human race, infirmities and weakness must then be a perfection; and M. de Pauw would be right in saying that we can flatter ourselves for being a thousand times more perfect than Americans.

They rear their children in such manner that they are able to walk without help by the age of six months; and the shortened lifetimes so common among us hardly exist among them. Normally, the length of their lives is greater than the term of ours; their old age is extremely vigorous, and at ninety years of age men still beget children.

Laet even assures us that he has seen savage women still fecund at the age of eighty.

The Caribes live for 150 years and sometimes more. M. de Laudonniere and the seven Frenchmen who escaped from the cruelties of the Spaniards in Florida were received by King Saturiova, who was more than 150 years old and who had about him his descendants unto and including the fifth generation. Vincent le Blanc attributes as long a life to Canadians and to those of the Kashubian kingdom. Picard says the same of Brazilians, others of Peruvians and of the other peoples of America. If such length of life is not proof of a good physical condition, then I confess I do not know what is needed to convince M. de Pauw. (pp. 65–68)

*Of the Qualities of Heart and Mind of Americans*

The opinion on these authors is no less unanimous on the qualities of genius, of mind and of heart of the natives of America than it is on the good constitutions of their bodies. We have seen that in whatever section one may go, one finds well-built men, of good height and of such robust constitution that they are equal to any test. M. de Pauw has nevertheless presented them as a debilitated race, corrupt in its origins. He tells us with the same assurance, but with just as little foundation, that their moral faculties are no less weakened and corrupt. Perhaps he has judged all the people of the new continent by the Peruvians who today live among or near the Spaniards, but if this is so, he has made a serious mistake.

What the natives of Peru have in common with those of Chile and some others, is that they are not lesser drunkards, nor less addicted to women, and that they nevertheless live for centuries. They are also without ambition with respect to the riches they extract from the bowels of the earth to satisfy our greed. But they differ greatly from them in bravery and boldness.

Peruvians today are very timid, weakly, and moreover sly, secretive, and underhanded. These are the attributes of weakness, and of subjugated peoples. The Spaniards have always treated them, and still do, as a stubborn, defeated people against whom they must use their superior force with such tyrannical barbarity that it is equal to the greatest inhumanity. This barbarity, reinforced by the bad treatment Peruvians always receive, has made them fearful. Timidity is always weak and spiritless. But the peoples of the Andes, of Chile, of the regions around Guiana and Mexico have retained their ancient bravery that has preserved them until now from Spanish domination.

Perhaps M. de Pauw was not aware of this, nor of the courage, the bravery, and the liberty all the people of North America and of some regions of South America still enjoy, when he said they had neither the courage to resist slavery, nor the heart to try to escape from it. (pp. 68–70)

M. de Pauw attributes to the natives of the New World a dull-witted indifference toward everything and a stupid insensitivity that form, he tells us, the basis of their character, to the point where no passion has enough intensity to arouse their spirit, and that this is a defect of their nature, a weakness of mind and of body. But should we believe him rather than those who have lived among them for a long time? It is true they are not jealous, and even laugh at Europeans in this regard. One never encounters among them this blind fury we call love. Their friendship, their tenderness, although strong and animated, never lead them into these transports and never carry them to those excesses love inspires in those so possessed by it. Never have women or young girls brought about disorder among them. Women are well-behaved, and their husbands too, not through indifference, but because of their freedom to undo, whenever they wish, the bonds of marriage. Young girls are free, mistresses of their bodies and of their wills; like the young men, they make use of this liberty in whichever way they wish, and their mothers, fathers, sisters or brothers have no right to make any reproaches on this subject.

But Americans are not indifferent toward fame. In fact, they take pride in their merit. When M. de Pauw spoke of them as he did, he did not know of their love of fame, and that their vanity is the sole motive for almost all their actions. (pp. 74–75)

If Americans make no use of geometry, it is because they do not know the meaning of the words *yours* and *mine*. They have no need to set up boundary stones to mark their encroachments. They competently reckon years and months by means of the stars, without knowing the system of astronomy that we use to direct the ships we send to conquer the gold they scorn. Even without astronomy, they take the seasons as they come, just as we do. They sow and reap the fruits of their earth when they are ripe. And thus, content with their land and its produce, they are neither desirous of invading other lands, nor mad enough to imperil their lives and face the dangers of the voyages necessary for such invasions. At night in their huts, as they lie peacefully on their mats and their animal furs, sleep comes to them quickly and easily; whereas Morpheus, the sworn enemy of ambition, of indolence, and of cupidity, flees far from those apartments where the gold stolen from these rustic philosophers glitters and dazzles and sparkles on all sides. Always free—for these children of nature understand the rights of humanity better than we do—they do not know what it is to burden themselves with the heavy chains created by ambition, forged by vanity, and stupidly borne by weakness. These idiotic Americans are capable of defending their lives, without ever having had the idea of taking men away from their families, from the cultivation of their lands, to teach them the cruel and inhuman art of methodically slaughtering each other, and to make of these men, while ambition lies dormant, indolent slaves in some countries, and cruel martinets in others. (pp. 87–88)

What are M. de Pauw's grounds for establishing his paradox that all the peoples of the new continent are inferior in all things to the lowest European? We have seen that in general, Americans, far from being a degenerate race in whom human nature is degraded, possess instead all the characteristics of perfection: good height, well-proportioned bodies, with none among them who are hunchbacked, crippled, blind, dumb, or afflicted with the other infirmities so common in our own continent; strong and vigorous health, a life expectancy well beyond the limit of ours; a healthy mentality, trained, informed, and guided by a truly natural philosophy and, unlike ours, not dependent upon the antiquated notions of our education; a noble and courageous spirit, a generous and kind heart. What more does M. de Pauw require for one to be truly a man? In fact these men, whom with ill-founded vanity we call idiots, say that the name of "savages" we have bestowed upon them would be more appropriate for us; since in truth our actions are contrary to humane principles, or at least to the wisdom that should be the guide for men who take pride in considering themselves more enlightened than they.

This is a fine lesson dictated by the lights of pure reason, healthier in these inhabitants of vast forests or regions left entirely to nature than in the tumultuous enclosures of our cities, where passions becloud reason, where it is more dangerous to live in society than in deserts and forests, where all our knowledge has not yet been able to give us a peaceful existence, where our needs continue to multiply in the midst of plenty, and where all this plenty serves only to render us poorer and more unhappy.

I believe men are made to live together, and that from this mutual dependency come all the advantages of society. But the first design of this union, or social contract, is to oblige all the contracting parties to lend each other mutual assistance and not to allow some to usurp all, or even to authorize such usurpations and to allow others to live in great want.

The American savages understand the nature of man too well to conduct themselves according to principles that offend reason and good sense. At least the majority of them do not live alone; but content with their dealings with men like themselves, they desire no such dealings with those who regard them as very inferior. Prompt to aid each other in all their needs, they refuse to adopt the laws and customs of those who believe they owe nothing to others. The more different their customs are from those of peoples we consider civilized, the more they appear to conform to that primitive law which is engraved by nature in the hearts of all men. We are so accustomed to the yoke under which we succumb without even being aware of it, that we do not stop to think that for this natural law, we have substituted the false ideas of a reason that is enslaved and corrupted by defective education. (pp. 104–106)

Endowed by nature with a noble soul, a generous heart and that calm spirit that views objects without becoming impassioned and attributes to all things their just worth, the peoples of the New World are charitable, obliging and considerate, rendering all the services they can to their European friends as to the people of their own nations, without waiting to be asked. They are not quick to take offense or to be insulted. When a man is not recognized as an enemy, they cannot even suspect that he might wish them harm. But if their good faith is abused, if they are repaid with ingratitude, and if they consider themselves truly offended, then they never forgive and they carry their revenge as far as it will go. It is this furious passion, and not a decided taste for human flesh, that causes some of their tribes to become cannibals. (pp. 107–108)

No, I cannot believe that M. de Pauw attentively read the authors who have written on the new continent, when he traces for us a portrait that is so different from the one I have drawn. How could he not have seen that Louisiana, Virginia, etc., enjoy the best climate in the world; that everything there grows in astonishing abundance, as in Chile, even without the help of laborious cultivation; that the pleasures alone of the natives were sufficient to provide for all their needs, when the sweet tranquillity in which they passed their time was troubled by the arrival of the Spanish and the English, who taught them avarice and greed and made the pass from their age of gold to the age of iron? He would have seen that nature favored no less the men who live in these beautiful lands, for in general they are tall and well-proportioned, with legs and arms of marvelous form, and have not the slightest imperfections on their bodies; that almost all their women are of great beauty, that they are finely shaped, have delicate features, and lack no attractions for our own eyes except that of color; that they are full of spirit, always gay and of good humor, and indeed that their laughter has much charm.

In short, to give a proper idea of the peoples of America, I would objectively believe that in many respects they are more truly men than we in all their manners, worthy of the innocent simplicity of ancient times; that they are savages, in the strict sense of the word, only in our imaginations and in the prejudice of people who are ambitious, miserly, given to luxury and softness, and whom poverty or great anxieties strike in the midst of their alleged wealth. (pp. 118–119)

# 4.

## The Abbé Raynal

*"America hath poured all the sources of corruption on Europe."*

THE ABBÉ GUILLAUME THOMAS FRANÇOIS RAYNAL was one of the most prominent figures of his century. His fame and even his presence were something to be reckoned with throughout Europe during his lifetime, but this glorious reputation did not survive him. He is little known today, and many details of his life remain obscure if not actually unknown. Indeed, such details were obscure even when he was alive, certainly not without reason.

He was born on March 11, 1713 at Saint-Gémiez in the Auvergne, and educated at the Jesuit college at Rodez. He became a member of the Order, was ordained in the priesthood, and had success as both teacher and preacher in Clermont, Toulouse, and Pézenas. But Pézenas was too small a stage for his obvious talents, and in 1747 he left both Pézenas and the Society of Jesus to go to Paris, where he became attached to Saint-Sulpice. Nor was his career at Saint-Sulpice very lengthy; he was dismissed after being found guilty of several acts of simony, and never again permitted to exercise any ecclesiastical function.

There followed a very worldly period in Paris during which Raynal frequented more and more famous people and more and more important salons. In 1747, he had published his *Histoire du Stadhoudérat* and the following year, 1748, his *Histoire du Parlement d'Angleterre*, both of which were poor works and by now long since forgotten. As a schemer and social climber, he succeeded in acquiring the friendship and protection of several prominent personages in the literary world, and through their influence became editor of the *Mercure de France*, a position he held between 1750 and 1754. He became an habitué of the salons of Madame Geoffrin, Helvétius, and Baron Holbach; even Montesquieu honored him with his friendship.

In this milieu, and by his activity in publishing compilations and other such works demanded by popular taste, he rapidly gained a fortune, which was further increased by speculation on colonial products. It seems that Raynal even speculated on the slave trade, and that this in fact was the source of most of his fortune.

His *Histoire philosophique et politique des Établissements et du Commerce des Européens dans les Deux Indes*, after having been announced and much publicized by him for several years before its publication, finally appeared in 1770, in four volumes. Curious indeed that the first edition did not bear the name of the author! This lapse was rectified in the second edition, however, for Raynal then not only published his name but an idealized portrait of himself as well. It quickly became known that Raynal was not the author of the entire work—it was said that he had paid some collaborators; such people as Diderot and Holbach contributed sections; and Book XIX of the work was attributed to Deleyre. Yet none of this diminished Raynal's personal success and fame. Numerous reprints appeared and Raynal even had editions published in other European countries.

In the years following the publication of the *Histoire des Deux Indes*, Raynal traveled to Switzerland and through France, primarily to arrange for foreign publication of his work, and one has almost the sense of a medieval "progress" of a great and munificent lord through those regions. In Geneva, he had statues erected to the heroes of Swiss independence, then insisted his own bust be placed there too. On an island in Lake Lucerne, his own statue was erected in the guise of a statue to Liberty. In Geneva also, he attempted to serve as mediator between two opposing political parties, but did not succeed. In Lausanne, he established three prizes to benefit three needy old men. Passing through Lyons, he was made a member of that city's Academy. In turn, he subsidized there two essay contests, offering a prize of 600 livres for the first contest, on a subject bearing on native industry, and a prize of 1,200 livres for the second, on the vital question: Was America a Mistake?

Meanwhile, the success of the *Histoire des Deux Indes* continued to grow. Its anticlerical sentiment provoked official disapproval, and in 1774 the work was placed on the Index. The continuing notoriety surrounding the work was not of a sort to displease Raynal. It only insured its greater success, and enhanced its author's fame and fortune. In 1779, a judgment was passed prohibiting importation into France of editions published in foreign countries, and in 1781, it was banned by the Parlement of Paris. It was burned by the hand of the public executioner on May 29, 1781, and its author sent into exile.

Raynal first took refuge in Spa, where he met Henry of Prussia who became his protector. He then proceeded to Berlin and expected to be summoned to Potsdam by Frederick II. Frederick, however, had been offended by certain passages in the *Histoire des Deux Indes* and ignored Raynal's presence for several months, until Raynal finally went himself to Potsdam and asked for an audience. He was in fact twice received by the King. During the first audience, Frederick refused to speak of the *Histoire des Deux Indes,* speaking only of the two early *Histoires,* both of which were Raynal's own products and both of which were considered very poor. In the second interview, Frederick allowed Raynal to do most of the talking in order better to judge him, then wrote to D'Alembert in Paris only this comment: "I have seen your Abbé Raynal; he talks a great deal."[1]

After Berlin, Raynal went to Switzerland and, in 1784, he was permitted to return from there to France, though he remained exiled from Paris. He returned to his birthplace where he unostentatiously and very generously aided the improverished farmers of the area. But Saint-Géniez was monotonous and dull for him, and he moved on to Toulouse and then to Marseilles. In 1790 his sentence was annulled and he was permitted to return to Paris. But there he offended the Revolutionaries and his assets were confiscated. He died at Chaillot on March 6, 1796, just a few days before reaching the age of eighty-three.

[1] *"J'ai vu votre abbé Raynal; il parle beaucoup."* See Dieudonné Thiébault, *Mes Souvenirs de vingt ans de séjour á Berlin,* Paris, 1804. Volume III of this work contains a section on Raynal (pp. 155–192) and gives a complete, if anecdotal and not entirely friendly, account of Raynal's exile in Berlin and Potsdam. Thiébault asserts that Raynal received no other audience from Frederick but that when he returned to France he said, *"Je voyais le roi de Prusse tous les jours; il me consultait sur ses affaires les plus secrètes."*

## FROM A PHILOSOPHICAL AND POLITICAL HISTORY [1]

. . . But if they [the Americans] once ceased to have Negroes for slaves, and kings who live at a distance from them for masters, they perhaps would become the most astonishing people that ever appeared on earth. The spirit of liberty which they would imbibe from their earliest infancy; the understanding and abilities which they would inherit from Europe; the activity, which the necessity of repelling numerous enemies would inspire; the large colonies they would have to form; the rich commerce they would have to found on an immense cultivation; the ranks and societies they would have to create; and the maxims, laws, and manners they would have to establish on the principles of reason: all these springs of action would, perhaps, make, of an equivocal and miscellaneous race of people, the most flourishing nation that philosophy and humanity could wish for the happiness of the world.

If ever any fortunate revolution should take place in the world, it will begin in America. After having experienced such devastation, this New World must flourish in its turn and, perhaps, command the Old. It will become the asylum of our people who have been oppressed by political establishments, or driven away by war. The savage inhabitants will be civilized, and oppressed strangers will become free. But it is necessary that this change should be preceded by conspiracies, commotions, and calamities; and that a hard and laborious education should predispose their minds both to act and to suffer.

Young Creoles, come into Europe to exercise and practise what we teach you; there to collect, in the valuable remains of our ancient manners, that vigor which we have lost; there to study our weakness, and draw from our follies themselves those lessons of wisdom which produce great events. Leave in America your Negroes, whose condition distresses us, and whose blood, perhaps, is mingled in all those ferments which alter, corrupt, and destroy our population. Fly from an education of tyranny,

[1] Translated by J. Justamond, London, 1776.

effeminacy, and vice, which you contract from the habit of living with slaves, whose degraded station inspires you with none of those elevated and virtuous sentiments, which can only give rise to a people that will become celebrated. America hath poured all the sources of corruption on Europe. To complete its vengeance, it must draw from it all the instruments of its prosperity. As it hath been destroyed by our crimes, it must be renewed by our vices.

Nature seems to have destined the Americans to a greater share of happiness than the inhabitants of Europe. They have scarce any illness, except inflammations in the lungs, and pleurisies, which are almost as common in the islands as in all other regions, where the transitions from heat to cold are frequent and sudden. The gout, gravel, stone, apoplexies, and a multitude of other scourges of the human race, which are so fatal in other countries, have never made the least ravages there. If the air of the country can be withstood, and the middle age be attained to, this is sufficient to insure a long and happy life. There old age is not weak, languishing, and beset with those infirmities which affect it in our climate. (V, 347–349)

It is surprising that little should have been known of the New World, for so long a time after it was discovered. Barbarous soldiers and rapacious merchants were not proper persons to give us just and clear notions of this hemisphere. It was the province of philosophy alone to avail itself of the information scattered in the accounts of voyages and missionaries, in order to see America such as nature hath made it, and to find out its analogy to the rest of the globe.

It is now pretty certain that the new continent has not half the extent of surface that the old has. At the same time, the form of both is so singularly alike, that we might easily be inclined to draw consequences from this particular, if it were not always necessary to be upon our guard against the spirit of system which often stops us in our researches after truth, and hinders us from attaining it.

The two continents seem to form, as it were, two broad tracks of land that begin from the Arctic pole, and terminate at the tropic of Capricorn, divided on the east and west by the ocean that surrounds them. Whatever may be the structure of these two continents, and the quality or symmetry of their form, it is evident that their equilibrium does not depend upon their position. It is the inconstancy of the sea that constitutes the solid form of the earth. To fix the globe upon its basis, it seemed necessary to have an element which, floating incessantly round our planet, might by its weight counterbalance all other substances, and by its fluidity restore that equilibrium which the conflict of the other elements might have disturbed. Water, by its natural fluctuation and weight, is the most proper element to preserve the connection and balance of the several parts of the globe round its center. If our hemisphere has a very wide extent of continent to the north, a mass of water of equal weight at the opposite part will certainly produce an equilibrium. If under the tropics we have a rich country covered with men and animals; under the same latitude America will have a sea filled with fish. While forests full of trees, bending with the largest fruits, quadrupeds of the greatest size, the most populous nations, elephants and men, are a load upon the surface of the earth, and seem to absorb all its fertility throughout the torrid zone; at both poles are found whales, with innumerable multitudes of cods and herrings, clouds of insects, and all the infinite and prodigious tribes that inhabit the seas, as it were, to support the axis of the earth, and prevent its inclining or deviating to either side: if, indeed, elephants, whales, or men, can be said to have any weight on a globe, where all living creatures are but a transient modification of the earth that composes it. In a word, the ocean rolls over this globe to fashion it, in conformity to the general laws of gravity. Sometimes it covers a hemisphere, a pole, or a zone, which at other times it leaves bare; but in general it seems to affect the equator, more especially as the cold of the poles in some measure contracts that fluidity which is essential to it, and from which it receives all its power of motion. It is chiefly between the tropics that the sea extends itself and is agitated, and that it undergoes the greatest change, both in its regular and periodical motions, as well as in those violent agitations occasionally excited in it by tempestuous winds. The attraction of the sun, and the fermentations occasioned by its continual heat in the Torrid Zone, must have a very remarkable influence upon the ocean. The motion of the moon adds a new force to this influence, and the sea, to conform itself to this double impulse, must, it would seem, flow toward the Equator. Nothing but the flatness of the globe at the poles can possibly account for that immense extent of water that has hitherto concealed from us the lands near the South Pole. The sea cannot easily pass the boundaries of the tropics, if the temperate and frozen zones be not nearer to the center of the earth than the Torrid Zone. It is the sea, therefore, that maintains an equilibrium with the land, and disposes the arrangement of the materials that compose it. One proof that the analogous portions of land, which the two continents of the globe present at first view, are not essentially necessary to its conformation, is that the New Hemisphere has remained covered with the waters of the sea a much longer time than the Old. Besides, if there be an evident similarity between the two hemispheres, there are also differences between them, which will perhaps destroy that harmony we think we observe.

When we consider the map of the world, and see the local correspondence between the isthmus of Suez and that of Panama, between the Cape of Good Hope and Cape Horn, between the Archipelago of the East Indies and that of the Caribbee Islands, and between the mountains of Chile and those of Monomotapa; we are stricken with the similarity of the several forms this picture presents. Land seems on all sides to be opposed to land, water to water, islands and peninsulas scattered by the hand of Nature to serve as a counterpoise, and the sea, by its fluctuation, constantly maintaining the balance of the whole. But if on the other hand we compare the great extent of the Pacific Ocean, which separates the East and West Indies, with the small space which the ocean occupies between the coast of Guinea and that of Brazil; the vast quantity of inhabited land to the north, with the little we know toward the south; the direction of the mountains of Tartary and Europe, which is from east to west, with that of the Cordeleras which run from North to South; the mind is in suspense, and we have the mortification to see the order and symmetry vanish, with which we had embellished our system of the earth. The observer is still more displeased with his conjectures when he considers the immense height of the mountains of Peru. He is then astonished to see a continent so recent, and yet so elevated, the sea so much below the tops of these mountains, and yet so recently come down from the lands that seemed to be effectually defended from its attacks by those tremendous bulwarks. It is, however, an undeniable fact that both continents of the New Hemisphere have been covered with the sea. The air and the land confirm this truth.

The rivers, which in America are wider and of greater extent; the immense forests to the south; the spacious lakes and vast morasses to the north; the almost eternal snows between the tropics; few of those pure sands that seem to be the remains of an exhausted ground; no men entirely black; very fair people under the line; a cool and mild air in the same latitude as the sultry and uninhabitable parts of Africa; a frozen and severe climate under the same parallel as our temperate climates; and lastly, a difference of ten or twelve degrees in the temperature of the Old and New Hemispheres; these are so many tokens of a world that is still in its infancy.

Why should the continent of America be much warmer and much colder in proportion than that of Europe, if it were not for the moisture the ocean has left behind, in quitting it long after our continent was peopled? Nothing but the sea can possibly have prevented Mexico from being inhabited as early as Asia. If the waters that still moisten the bowels of the earth in the New Hemisphere had not covered its surface, the woods would very easily have been cut down, the fens drained, a soft and watery soil would have been made firm, by stirring it up and exposing it to the rays of the sun; a free passage would have been open to the winds, and dikes would have been raised along the rivers; in a word, the climate would have been totally altered by this time. But a rude and unpeopled hemisphere denotes a recent world; when the sea, about its coasts, still flows obscurely in its channels. A less scorching sun, more plentiful rains, and thicker vapors, more disposed to stagnate, are evident marks of the decay or the infancy of nature.

The difference of climate, arising from the waters having lain so long on the ground in America, could not but have a great influence on men and animals. From this diversity of causes must necessarily arise a very great diversity of effects. Accordingly, we see more species of animals, by two-thirds, in the old continent than the new; animals of the same kind considerably larger; monsters that are become more savage and fierce, as the countries have become more inhabited. On the other hand, nature seems to have strangely neglected the New World. The men have less strength and less courage; no beard and no hair; they have less appearances of manhood; and are but little susceptible of the lively and powerful sentiment of love, which is the principle of every attachment, the first instinct, the first band of society, without which all other artificial ties have neither energy nor duration. The women, who are still more weak, are neither favorably treated by nature nor by the men, who have but little love for them, and consider them merely as subservient to their will: they rather sacrifice them to their indolence than consecrate them to their pleasures. This indolence is the great delight and supreme felicity of the Americans, of which the women are the victims, from the continual labors imposed upon them. It must, however, be confessed that in America, as in all other parts, the men, when they have sentenced the women to work, have been so equitable as to take upon themselves the perils of war, together with the toils of hunting and fishing. But their indifference to the sex, which nature has entrusted with the care of multiplying the species, implies an imperfection in their organs, a sort of state of childhood in the people of America, similar to that of the people in our continent who are not yet arrived at the age of puberty. This seems to be a natural defect prevailing in the continent of America, which is an indication of its being a new country. (VII, 142–149)

Whatever may be the case with regard to their origin or their antiquity, which are both uncertain, it is perhaps more interesting to inquire whether those untutored nations are more or less happy than our civilized people. Let us, therefore, examine whether the condition of rude man left to mere animal instinct, who passes every day of his life in hunting, feeding, producing his species, and reposing himself, is better or worse than the condition of that wonderful being who makes his bed of down, spins and weaves the thread of the silkworm to clothe himself, has exchanged the cave, his original abode, for a palace, and has varied his indulgences and his wants in a thousand different ways.

It is the nature of man that we must look for his means of happiness. What does he want, to be as happy as he can be? Present subsistence; and, if he should think of futurity, the hopes and certainty of enjoying that blessing. The savage, who has not been driven into and confined within the frigid zones by civilized societies, is not in want of this first of necessities. If he should lay in no stores, it is because the earth and the sea are reservoirs always open to supply his wants. Fish and game are to be had all the year, and will supply the want of fertility in the dead seasons. The savage has no house, well secured from the access of the external air, or commodious fireplaces; but his furs answer all the purposes of the roof, the garment, and the stove. He works but for his own benefit, sleeps when he is weary, and is a stranger to watchings and restless nights. War is a matter of choice to him. Danger, like labor, is a condition of his nature, not a profession annexed to his birth; a national duty, not a domestic servitude. The savage is serious but not melancholy; and his countenance seldom bears the impression of those passions and disorders that leave such shocking and fatal marks on ours. He cannot feel the want of what he does not desire, nor can he desire what he is ignorant of. Most of the conveniences of life are remedies for evils he does not feel. Pleasure is the mode of satisfying appetites which his senses are unacquainted with. He seldom experiences any of that weariness that arises from unsatisfied desires, or that emptiness and uneasiness of mind that is the offspring of prejudice and vanity. In a word, the savage is subject to none but natural evils.

But what greater happiness than this does the civilized man enjoy? His food is more wholesome and delicate than that of the savage. He has softer clothes, and a habitation better secured against the inclemencies of the weather. But the common people, who are to be the support and basis of civil society, those numbers of men who in all states bear the burden of hard labor, cannot be said to live happy, either in those empires where the consequences of war and the imperfection of the police have reduced them to a state of slavery, or in those governments where the progress of luxury and police has reduced them to a state of servitude. The mixed governments seem to present some prospects of happiness under the protection of liberty; but this happiness is purchased by the most sanguinary exertions, which repel tyranny for a time only, that it may fall the heavier upon the devoted nation, sooner or later doomed to oppression. Observe how Caligula and Nero revenged the expulsion of the Tarquins, and the death of Caesar.

Tyranny, we are told, is the work of the people, and not of kings. But if so, why do they suffer it? Why do they not repel the encroachments of despotism; and while it employs violence and artifice to enslave all the faculties of men, why do they not oppose it with all their powers? But is it lawful to murmur and complain under the rod of the oppressor? Will it not exasperate and provoke him to pursue the victim to death? The complaints of slaves he calls rebellion, and they are to be stifled in a dungeon, and sometimes put an end to on a scaffold. The man who should assert the rights of man would perish in neglect and infamy. Tyranny, therefore, must be endured, under the name of authority.

If so, to what outrages is not the civilized man exposed! If he be possessed of any property, he knows not how far he may call it his own, when he must divide the produce between the courtier who may attack his estate, the lawyer who must be paid for teaching him how to preserve it, the soldier who may lay it waste, and the collector who comes to levy unlimited taxes. If he should have no property, how can he be assured of a permanent subsistence? What species of industry is secured against the vicissitudes of fortune and the incroachments of government?

In the forests of America, if there be a scarcity in the north, the savages bend their course to the south. The wind or the sun will drive a wandering clan to more temperate climates. But if in our civilized states, confined within gates, and restrained within certain limits, famine, war, or pestilence should consume an empire, it is a prison where all must expect to perish in misery, or in the horrors of slaughter. The man who is unfortunately born there is compelled to endure all extortions, all the severities that the inclemency of the seasons and the injustice of government may bring upon him.

In our provinces, the vassal, or free mercenary, digs and plows, the whole year round, lands that are not his own, and the produce of which does not belong to him, and he is even happy if his labor can procure him a share of the crops he has sown and reaped. Observed and harassed by a hard and restless landlord who grudges him even the straw on which he rests his weary limbs, the wretch is daily exposed to diseases, which, joined to his poverty, make him wish for death rather than for an expensive cure, followed by infirmities and toil. Whether tenant or subject, he is doubly a slave; if he should possess a few acres, his lord comes and gathers upon them what he has not sown; if he be worth but a yoke of oxen or a pair of horses, he must employ them in the public service; if he should have nothing but his person, the prince takes him for a soldier. Everywhere he meets with masters, and always with oppression.

In our cities, the workmen and the artist who have no manufacture of their own are at the mercy of greedy and idle masters, who, by the privilege of monoply, have purchased of government a power of making industry work for nothing, and of selling its labors at a very high price. The lower class have no more than the sight of that luxury of which they are doubly the victims, by the watchings and fatigues it occasions them, and by the insolence of the pomp that humiliates and oppresses them.

Even supposing that the dangerous labors of our quarries, mines, and forges, with all the arts that are performed by fire, and that the perils which navigation and commerce expose us to, were less pernicious than the roving life of the savages who live by hunting and fishing; suppose that men who are ever lamenting the sorrows and affronts that arise merely from opinion, are less unhappy than the savages who never shed a tear in the most excruciating tortures; there would still remain a wide difference between the fate of the civilized man and the wild Indian, a difference entirely to the disadvantage of social life. This is the injustice that prevails in the partial distribution of fortunes and stations; an inequality which is at once the effect and the cause of oppression.

In vain does custom, prejudice, ignorance, and hard labor stupefy the lower class of mankind, so as to render them insensible of their degradation; neither religion nor morality can hinder them from seeing and feeling the injustice of the arrangements of policy in the distribution of good and evil. How often have we heard the poor man expostulating with heaven, and asking what he had done that he should deserve to be born in an indigent and dependent station? Even if great conflicts were inseparable from the more exalted stations, which might be sufficient to balance all the advantages and all the superiority that the social state claims over the state of nature, still the obscure man, who is unacquainted with those conflicts, sees nothing in a high rank but that affluence which is the cause of his own poverty. He envies the rich man those pleasures to which he is so accustomed that he has lost all relish for them. What domestic can have a real affection for his master, or what is the attachment of a servant? Was ever prince truly beloved by his courtiers, even when he was hated by his subjects? If we prefer our condition to that of the savages, it is because civil life has made us incapable of bearing some natural hardships which the savage is more exposed to than we are, and because we are attached to some indulgences that custom has made necessary to us. Even in the vigor of life, a civilized man may accustom himself to live among savages, and return to the state of nature. We have an instance of this in that Scotchman who was cast away on the island of Fernandez, where he lived alone, and was happy as soon as he was so taken up with supplying his wants as to forget his own country, his language, his name, and even the articulation of words. After four years, he felt himself eased of the burden of social life, when he had lost all reflection or thought of the past and all anxiety for the future.

Lastly, the consciousness of independence being one of the first instincts in man, he who enjoys this primitive right, with a moral certainty of a competent subsistence, is incomparably happier than the rich man, restrained by laws, masters, prejudices and fashions, which incessantly remind him of the loss of his liberty. To compare the state of the savages to that of children, is to decide at once the question that has been so warmly debated by philosophers, concerning the advantages of the state of nature above those of social life. Children, notwithstanding the restraints of education, are in the happiest age of human life. Their habitual cheerfulness, when they are not under the schoolmaster's rod, is the surest indication of the happiness they feel. After all, a single word may determine this great question. Let us ask the civilized man whether he be happy: and the savage whether he be unhappy. If they both answer in the negative, the dispute is at an end.

You civilized nations, this parallel must certainly be mortifying to you! But you cannot too strongly feel the weight of the calamities under which you are oppressed. The more painful this sensation is, the more will it awaken your attention to the true causes of your sufferings. You may at least be convinced that they proceed from the confusion of your opinions, from the defects of your political constitutions, and from capricious laws, which are in continual opposition to the laws of nature. (VII, 153–160)

. . . Let us conclude. But let us first give a rapid sketch of the good and of the evil produced by the discovery of the East and West Indies.

This great event hath improved the construction of ships, navigation, geography, astronomy, medicine, natural history, and some other branches of knowlege; and these advantages have not been attended with any known inconvenience.

It has procured to some empires vast domains, which have given splendor, power, and wealth, to the states which have founded them. But what expenses have not been lavished to clear, to govern, or to defend these distant possessions. When these colonies shall have acquired that degree of culture, knowledge, and population which is suitable for them, will they not detach themselves from a country which has founded its splendor upon their prosperity? We know not at what period this revolution will happen; but it must certainly take place.

Europe is indebted to the New World for a few conveniences, and a few luxuries. But before these enjoyments were obtained, were we less healthy, less robust, less intelligent, or less happy? Are these frivolous advantages, so cruelly obtained, so unequally distributed, and so obstinately disputed, worth one drop of that blood which has been spilt, and which will still be spilt for them? Are they to be compared to the life of a single man? And yet, how many lives have hitherto been destroyed; how many are at present devoted; and how many will not hereafter be sacrificed to supply chimerical wants, which we shall never be persuaded to get rid of, either by authority or reason.

The voyages undertaken upon all the seas have weakened the principle of national pride; they have inspired civil and religious toleration; they have revived the ties of original fraternity; have inspired the true principles of a universal system of morality, founded upon the identity of wants, of calamities, of pleasures, and of the analogies common to mankind under every latitude; they have induced the practice of benevolence toward every individual who appeals to it, whatever his manners, his country, his laws, and his religion may be. But at the same time, the minds of men have been turned to lucrative speculation. The sentiment of glory has been weakened. Riches have been preferred to fame; and everything which tended to the elevation of mankind has visibly inclined to decay.

The New World has multiplied specie amongst us. An earnest desire of obtaining it has occasioned much exertion upon the face of the globe; but exertion is not happiness. Whose destiny has been ameliorated by gold and silver? Do not the nations who dig them from the bowels of the earth, languish in ignorance, superstition, ignorance and pride, and all those vices which it is most difficult to eradicate, when they have taken deep root. Have they not lost their agriculture and their manufactures? Their existence, is it not precarious? If an industrious people, proprietors of a fertile soil, should one day represent to the other people that they have too long carried on a losing trade with them, and that they will no longer give the thing for the representation, would not this sumptuary law be a sentence of death against that region which has none but riches of convention, unless the latter, driven by despair, should shut up its mines, in order to open furrows in the ground?

The other powers of Europe may perhaps have acquired no greater advantage from the treasures of America. If the repartition of them has been equal, or proportionate between them, neither of them have decreased in opulence, or increased in strength. The analogies which existed in ancient times still exist. Let us suppose that some nations should have acquired a greater quantity of metals than the rival nations, they will either bury them, or throw them into circulation. In the first instance, this is nothing more than the barren property of a superfluous mass of gold. In the second, they will acquire only a temporary superiority, because in a short space of time all vendible commodities will bear a price proportionate to the abundance of the signs which represent them.

Such are then the evils attached even to the advantages which we owe to the discovery of the East and West Indies. But how many calamities, which cannot be compensated, have not attended the conquest of these regions?

Have the devastators of them lost nothing by depopulating them for a long species of ages? If all the blood that has been spilt in those countries had been collected into one common reservoir, if the dead bodies had been heaped up in the same plain, would not the blood and the carcasses of the Europeans have occupied a great space in it? Has it been possible speedily to fill up the void which these emigrants had left in their native land, infected with a shameful and cruel poison from the New World, which attacks even the sources of reproduction?

Since the bold attempts of Columbus and of Gama, a spirit of fanaticism, till then unknown, has been established in our countries, which is that of making discoveries. We have traversed, and still continue to traverse, all the climates from one pole to another, in order to discover some continents to invade, some islands to ravage, and some people to spoil, to subdue, and to massacre. Would not the person who should put an end to this frenzy deserve to be reckoned among the benefactors of mankind?

The sedentary life is the only favorable one to population. The man who travels leaves no posterity behind him. The land forces have created a multitude of persons devoted to celibacy. The naval forces have almost doubled them; with this difference, that the latter are destroyed by illnesses on board ship, by shipwrecks, by fatigue, by bad food, and by the change of climate. A soldier may return to some of the professions useful to society. A sailor is a sailor forever. When he is discharged from the service, he is of no further use to his country, which is under the necessity of providing a hospital for him.

Long voyages have introduced a new species of anomalous savages. I mean those men who traverse so many countries and who in the end belong to none; who take wives wherever they find them, and that only from motives of animal necessity; those amphibious creatures who live upon the surface of the waters; who come ashore only for a moment; to whom every habitable latitude is equal; who have, in reality, neither fathers, mothers, children, brothers, relations, friends, nor fellow citizens, in whom the most pleasing and the most sacred ties are extinct; who quit their country without regret; who never return to it without being impatient of going out again; and to whom the habit of living upon a dreadful element gives a character of ferociousness. Their probity is not proof against the crossing of the line; and they acquire riches in exchange for their virtue and their health.

This insatiable thirst of gold, has given birth to the most infamous and the most atrocious of all traffics, that of slaves. Crimes against nature are spoken of, and yet this is not instanced as the most execrable of them. Most of the European nations have been stained with it, and a base motive of interest has extinguished in their hearts all the sentiments due to our fellow creatures. But without these assistances, these countries, the acquisition of which has cost so dear, would still be uncultivated. Let them then remain fallow; if, in order to cultivate them, it be necessary that man should be reduced to the condition of the brute, in the person of the buyer, of the seller, and of him who is sold.

Shall we not take into our account the complication which the settlements in the East and West Indies have introduced in the machine of government? Before that period, the persons proper to hold the reins of government were infinitely scarce. An administration more embarrassed has required a more extensive genius, and greater depth of knowledge. The cares of sovereignty, divided between the citizens placed at the foot of the throne, and the subjects settled under the equator, or near the pole, have been insufficient for both the one and the other. Everything has fallen into confusion. The several states have languished under the yoke of oppression, and endless wars, or such as were incessantly renewed, have harassed the globe and stained it with blood.

Let us stop here, and consider ourselves as existing at the time when America and India were unknown. Let me suppose that I address myself to the most cruel of the Europeans in the following terms. There exist regions which will furnish you with rich metals, agreeable clothing, and delicious food. But read this history, and behold at what price the discovery is promised to you. Do you wish or not that it should be made? Is it to be imagined that there exists a being infernal enough to answer this question in the affirmative! Let it be remembered that there will not be a single instant in futurity when my question will not have the same force. (VIII, 366–372)

# 5.

## Dr. William Robertson

*"A proof of some feebleness in their frame, still more striking, is the insensibility of Americans to the charms of beauty, and the power of love."*

THE SCOTTISH HISTORIAN, PRESBYTERIAN minister, and politician, WILLIAM ROBERTSON, was born in Borthwick, Midlothian, on August 19, 1721. Trained at the University of Edinburgh, he took up ministerial duties in nearby Gladsmuir in 1743 and was active also in politics during most of his life as a member of the General Assembly, later elected moderator of this body, and as a leader of the moderate party.

His first great work, *History of Scotland during the Reigns of Queen Mary and King James VI*, published in 1759, made him famous almost immediately and was directly responsible for Robertson's being appointed Principal of Edinburgh University in 1762 and Historiographer Royal in 1763. By this time he was engaged in writing his second work, *History of the Reign of the Emperor Charles V*, published in 1769. This work in turn led him to his studies on America, for in *Charles V* he had intentionally omitted all discussion of the Spanish colonies in America. The subject appeared to him so fascinating and important as to deserve a separate study; it could only suffer by limited and superficial consideration in *Charles V*.

*The History of America* (1777) is in reality a history of Spanish America, for although Robertson indeed wished to discuss the English colonies, their revolt against the Crown made him withhold his texts until the course of contemporary events became settled. He never completed these sections himself, though his histories of Virginia and of New England were added to the work after his death.

If the *History of America* seems defective in some respects today, it must be remembered that research for the work was severely hampered. This indefatigable correspondent and researcher was denied access to the Spanish *Archivo* at Simancas. His preparation and documentation was in large part based on literary sources rather than historical, and it can perhaps be understood why the ideas of Buffon and Raynal, both so widely read for so long, should have entered his texts.

The success of *America* was enormous and immediate, just as his previous successes had been, and translations into other European languages followed. In 1777, Robertson was elected Corresponding Member of the Royal Academy in Madrid, but Spain remained hostile to the work. Indeed, it was prohibited first in Spain itself and subsequently in Spanish America and in the Philippine Islands, though as always happens in these cases, the ban did not keep it from being widely read.

This was the last of Robertson's great works, although in 1791, he yet published *Historical Disquisitions concerning the Knowledge Which the Ancients Had of India.* He died on June 11, 1793.

## FROM THE HISTORY OF AMERICA

WHEN we survey the face of the habitable globe, no small part of that fertility and beauty which we ascribe to the hand of nature, is the work of man. His efforts, when continued through a succession of ages, change the appearance and improve the qualities of the earth. As a great part of the ancient continent has long been occupied by nations far advanced in arts and industry, our eye is accustomed to view the earth in that form which it assumes when rendered fit to be the residence of a numerous race of men, and to supply them with nourishment.

But in the New World, the state of mankind was ruder, and

the aspect of nature extremely different. Throughout all its vast regions, there were only two monarchies remarkable for extent of territory, or distinguished by any progress in improvement. The rest of this continent was possessed by small independent tribes, destitute of arts and industry, and neither capable of correcting the defects nor desirous of ameliorating the condition of that part of the earth allotted to them for their habitation. Countries occupied by such people were almost in the same state as if they had been without inhabitants. Immense forests covered a great part of the uncultivated earth; and as the hand of industry had not taught the rivers to run in a proper channel, or drained off the stagnating water, many of the most fertile plains were overflowed with inundations, or converted into marshes. In the southern provinces, where the warmth of the sun, the moisture of the climate, and the fertility of the soil combine in calling forth the most vigorous powers of vegetation, the woods are so choked with its rank luxuriance as to be almost impervious, and the surface of the grround is hid from the eye under a thick covering of shrubs and herbs and weeds. In this state of wild unassisted nature, a great part of the large provinces in South America, which extend from the bottom of the Andes to the sea, still remain. The European colonies have cleared and cultivated a few spots along the coast, but the original race of inhabitants, as rude and indolent as ever, have done nothing to open or improve a country possessing almost every advantage of situation and climate. As we advance toward the northern provinces of America, nature continues to wear the same uncultivated aspect, and in proportion as the rigor of the climate increases, appears more desolate and horrid. There the forests, though not encumbered with the same exuberance of vegetation, are of immense extent; prodigious marshes overspread the plains, and few marks appear of human activity in any attempt to cultivate or embellish the earth. No wonder that the colonies sent from Europe were astonished at their first entrance into the New World. It appeared to them waste, solitary, and uninviting. When the English began to settle in America, they termed the countries of which they took possession the wilderness. Nothing but their eager expectation of finding mines of gold could have induced the Spaniards to penetrate through the woods and marshes of America, where, at every step, they observed the extreme difference between the uncultivated face of nature and that which it acquires under the forming hand of industry and art.

The labor and operations of man not only improve and embellish the earth but render it more wholesome and friendly to life. When any region lies neglected and destitute of cultivation, the air stagnates in the woods; putrid exhalations arise from the waters; the surface of the earth, loaded with rank vegetation, feels not the purifying influence of the sun or of the wind; the malignity of the distempers natural to the climate increases, and new maladies, no less noxious, are engendered. Accordingly, all the provinces of America, when first discovered, were found to be remarkably unhealthy. This the Spaniards experienced in every expedition into the New World, whether destined for conquest or settlement. Though by the natural constitution of their bodies, their habitual temperance, and the persevering vigor of their minds they were as much formed as any people in Europe for active service in a sultry climate, they felt severely the fatal and pernicious qualities of those uncultivated regions through which they marched, or where they endeavored to plant colonies. Great numbers were cut off by the unknown and violent diseases with which they were infected. Such as survived the destructive rage of those maladies were not exempted from the noxious influence of the climate. They returned to Europe, according to the description of the early Spanish historians, feeble, emaciated, with languid looks, and complexions of such a sickly yellow color, as indicated the unwholesome temperature of the countries where they had resided.

The uncultivated state of the New World affected not only the temperature of the air but the qualities of its productions. The principle of life seems to have been less active and vigorous there than in the ancient continent. Notwithstanding the vast extent of America and the variety of its climates, the different species of animals peculiar to it are much fewer in proportion than those of the other hemisphere. In the islands, there were only four kinds of quadrupeds known, the largest of which did not exceed the size of a rabbit. On the continent, the variety was greater; and though the individuals of each kind could not fail of multiplying exceedingly when almost unmolested by men, who were neither so numerous nor so united in society as to be formidable enemies to the animal creation, the number of distinct species must still be considered as extremely small. Of two hundred different kinds of animals spread over the face of the earth, only about one-third existed in America at the time of its discovery. Nature was not only less prolific in the New World, but she appears likewise to have been less vigorous in her productions. The animals originally belonging to this quarter of the globe appear to be of an inferior race, neither so robust nor so fierce as those of the other continent. America gives birth to no creature of such bulk as to be compared with the elephant or rhinoceros, or that equals the lion and tiger in strength and ferocity. The tapir of Brazil, the largest quadruped of the ravenous tribe in the New World, is not larger than a calf six months old. The puma and jaguar, its fiercest beasts of prey, which Europeans have inaccurately denominated lions and tigers, possess neither the undaunted courage of the former nor the ravenous cruelty of the latter. They are inactive and timid, hardly formidable to man, and often turn their backs upon the least appearance of resistance. The same qualities in the climate of America which stinted the growth and enfeebled the spirit of its native animals have proved pernicious to such as have migrated into it voluntarily from the other continent, or have been transported thither by the Europeans. The bears, the wolves, the deer of America are not equal in size to those of the Old World. Most of the domestic animals with which the Europeans have stored the provinces wherein they settled have degenerated with respect either to bulk or quality, in a country whose temperature and soil seem to be less favorable to the strength and perfection of the animal creation.

The same causes which checked the growth and the vigor of the more noble animals were friendly to the propagation and increase of reptiles and insects. Though this is not peculiar to the New World, and those odious tribes, nourished by heat, moisture, and corruption, infest every part of the torrid zone, they multiply faster, perhaps, in America, and grow to a more monstrous bulk. As this country is on the whole less cultivated and less peopled than the other quarters of the earth, the active principle of life wastes its force in productions of this inferior form. The air is often darkened with clouds of insects, and the ground covered with shocking and noxious reptiles. The country around Portobelo swarms with toads in such multitudes as hide the surface of the earth. At Guayaquil, snakes and vipers are hardly less numerous. Cartagena is infested with numerous flocks of bats, which annoy not only the cattle but the inhabitants. In the islands, legions of ants have, at different times, consumed every vegetable production and left the earth entirely bare as if it had been burnt with fire. The damp forests and rank soil of the countries on the banks of the Orinoco and Marañon teem with almost every offensive and poisonous creature which the power of a sultry sun can quicken into life.

The birds of the New World are not distinguished by qualities so conspicuous and characteristic as those which we have observed in its quadrupeds. Birds are more independent of man, and less affected by the changes which his industry and labor make upon the state of the earth. They have a greater propensity to migrate from one country to another, and can gratify this instinct of their nature without difficulty or danger. Hence the number of birds common to both continents is much greater than that of quadrupeds; and even such as are peculiar to America nearly resemble those with which mankind were acquainted in similar regions of the ancient hemisphere. The American birds of the Torrid Zone, like those of the same climate in Asia and Africa, are decked in plumage which dazzles the eye with the beauty of its colors; but nature, satisfied with clothing them in this gay dress, has denied most of them that melody of sound and variety of notes which catch and delight the ear. The birds of the temperate climates there, in the same manner as in our continent, are less splendid in their appearance, but, in compensation for that defect, they have voices of greater compass, and more melodious. In some districts of America, the unwholesome temperature of the air seems to be unfavorable even to this part of the creation. The number of birds is less than in other countries, and the traveler is struck with the amazing solitude and silence of its forests. It is remarkable, however, that America, where the quadrupeds are so dwarfish and dastardly, should produce the condor, which is entitled to pre-eminence over all the flying tribe in bulk, in strength, and in courage. (I, 221–226)

Almost two centuries elapsed after the discovery of America before the manners of its inhabitants attracted, in any considerable degree, the attention of philosophers. At length they discovered that the contemplation of the condition and character of the Americans, in their original state, tended to complete our knowledge of the human species, might enable us to fill up a considerable chasm in the history of its progress, and lead to speculations no less curious than important. They entered upon this new field of study with great ardor; but, instead of throwing light upon the subject, they have contributed, in some degree, to involve it in additional obscurity. Too impatient to inquire, they hastened to decide, and began to erect systems when they should have been searching for facts on which to establish their foundations. Struck with the appearance of degeneracy in the human species throughout the New World, and astonished at beholding a vast continent occupied by a naked, feeble, and ignorant race of men, some authors of great name have maintained that this part of the globe had but lately emerged from the sea and become fit for the residence of man; that everything in it bore marks of a recent origin; and that its inhabitants, lately called into existence, and still at the beginning of their career, were unworthy to be compared with the people of a more ancient and improved continent. Others have imagined that, under the influence of an unkindly climate, which checks and enervates the principle of life, man never attained in America the perfection which belongs to his nature, but remained an animal of an inferior order, defective in the vigor of his bodily frame and destitute of sensibility, as well as of force, in the operations of his mind. In opposition to both these, other philosophers have supposed that man arrives at his highest dignity and excellence long before he reaches a state of refinement; and, in the rude simplicity of savage life, displays an elevation of sentiment, an independence of mind, and a warmth of attachment for which it is vain to search among the members of polished societies. They seem to consider that as the most perfect state of man which is the least civilized. They describe the manners of the rude Americans with such rapture, as if they proposed them for models to the rest of the species. These contradictory theories have been proposed with equal confidence, and uncommon powers of genius and eloquence have been exerted, in order to clothe them with an appearance of truth. (I, 247–248)

. . . The human body is less affected by climate than that of any other animal. Some animals are confined to a particular region of the globe, and cannot exist beyond it; others, though they may be brought to bear the injuries of a climate foreign to them, cease to multiply when carried out of that district which nature destined to be their mansion. Even such as seem capable of being naturalized in various climates, feel the effect of every remove from their proper station, and gradually dwindle and degenerate from the vigor and perfection peculiar to their species. Man is the only living creature whose frame is at once so hardy and so flexible that he can spread over the whole earth, become the inhabitant of every region, and thrive and multiply under every climate. Subject, however, to the general law of nature, the human body is not entirely exempt from the operation of climate; and, when exposed to the extremes either of heat or cold, its size or vigor diminishes.

The first appearance of the inhabitants of the New World filled the discoverers with such astonishment that they were apt to imagine them a race of men different from those of the other hemisphere. Their complexion is of a reddish brown, nearly resembling the color of copper. The hair of their head is always black, long, coarse, and uncurled. They have no beard, and every part of their body is perfectly smooth. Their persons are of a full size, extremely straight, and well proportioned. Their features are regular, though often distorted by absurd endeavors to improve the beauty of their natural form, or to render their aspect more dreadful to their enemies. In the islands where four-footed animals were both few and small, and the earth yielded her productions almost spontaneously, the constitution of the natives, neither braced by the active exercises of the chase, nor invigorated by the labor of cultivation, was extremely feeble and languid. On the continent, where the forests abound with game of various kinds, and the chief occupation of many tribes was to pursue it, the human frame acquired greater firmness. Still, however, the Americans were more remarkable for agility than strength. They resembled beasts of prey, rather than animals formed for labor. They were not only averse to toil, but incapable of it; and when roused by force from their native indolence and compelled to work, they sank under tasks which the people of the other continent would have performed with ease. This feebleness of constitution was universal among the inhabitants of those regions in America which we are surveying, and may be considered as characteristic of the species there.

The beardless countenance and smooth skin of the American seems to indicate a defect of vigor, occasioned by some debility in his frame. He is destitute of one sign of manhood and of strength. This peculiarity, by which the inhabitants of the New World are distinguished from the people of all other nations, cannot be attributed, as some travelers have supposed, to their mode of subsistence. For though the food of many Americans be extremely insipid, as they are altogether unacquainted with the use of salt, rude tribes in other parts of the earth have subsisted on aliments equally simple, without this mark of degradation, or any apparent symptom of a diminution in their vigor.

As the external form of the Americans leads us to suspect that there is some natural debility in their frame, the smallness of their appetite for food has been mentioned by many authors as a confirmation of this suspicion. The quantity of food which men consume varies according to the temperature of the climate in which they live, the degree of activity which they exert, and the natural vigor of their constitutions. Under the enervating heat of the Torrid Zone, and when men pass their days in indolence and ease, they require less nourishment than the active inhabitants of temperate or cold countries. But neither the warmth of their climate nor their extreme laziness will account for the uncommon defect of appetite among the Americans. The Spaniards were astonished with observing this, not only in the islands, but in several parts of the continent. The constitutional temperance of the natives far exceeded, in their opinion, the abstinence of the most mortified hermits; while, on the other hand, the appetite of the Spaniards appeared to the Americans insatiably voracious; and they affirmed that one Spaniard devoured more food in a day than was sufficient for ten Americans.

A proof of some feebleness in their frame, still more striking, is the insensibility of the Americans to the charms of beauty and the power of love. That passion, which was destined to perpetuate life, to be the bond of social union, and the source of tenderness and joy, is the most ardent in the human breast. Though the perils and hardships of the savage state, though excessive fatigue on some occasions, and the difficulty at all times of procuring subsistence may seem to be adverse to this passion, and to have a tendency to abate its vigor, yet the rudest nations in every other part of the globe seem to feel its influence more powerfully than the inhabitants of the New World. The Negro glows with all the warmth of desire natural to his climate; and the most uncultivated Asiatics discover that sensibility, which, from their situation on the globe, we should expect them to have felt. But the Americans are in an amazing degree strangers to the force of this first instinct of nature. In every part of the New World the natives treat their women with coldness and indifference. They are neither the objects of that tender attachment which takes place in civilized society, nor of that ardent desire conspicuous among rude nations. Even in climates where this passion usually acquires its greatest vigor, the savage of America views his female with disdain, as an animal of a less noble species. He is at no pains to win her favor by the assiduity of courtship, and still less solicitous to preserve it by indulgence and gentleness. Missionaries themselves, notwithstanding the austerity of monastic ideas, cannot refrain from expressing their astonishment at the dispassionate coldness of the American young men in their intercourse with the other sex. Nor is this reserve to be ascribed to any opinion which they entertain with respect to the merit of female chastity. That is an idea too refined for a savage, and suggested by a delicacy of sentiment and affection to which he is a stranger. (I. 250–253)

The operation of political and moral causes is still more conspicuous in modifying the degree of attachment between the sexes. In a state of high civilization, this passion, inflamed by restraint, refined by delicacy, and cherished by fashion, occupies and engrosses the heart. It is no longer a simple instinct of nature; sentiment heightens the ardor of desire, and the most tender emotions of which our frame is susceptible, soothe and agitate the soul. This description, however, applies only to those who by their situation are exempted from the cares and labors of life. Among persons of inferior order, who are doomed by their condition to incessant toil, the dominion of this passion is less violent; their solicitude to procure subsistence, and to provide for the first demand of nature, leaves little leisure for attending to its second call. But if the nature of the intercourse between the sexes varies so much in persons of different rank in polished societies, the condition of man, while he remains uncivilized, must occasion a variation still more apparent. We may well suppose, that amidst the hardships, the dangers, and the simplicity of savage life, where subsistence is always precarious and often scanty, where men are almost continually engaged in the pursuit of their enemies or in guarding against their attacks, and where neither dress nor reserve are employed as arts of female allurement, that the attention of the Americans to their women would be extremely feeble, without imputing this solely to any physical defect or degradation in their frame.

It is accordingly observed that in those countries of America, where, from the fertility of the soil, the mildness of the climate, or some farther advances which the natives have made in improvement, the means of subsistence are more abundant, and the hardships of savage life are less severely felt, the animal passion of the sexes becomes more ardent. Striking examples of this occur among some tribes seated on the banks of great rivers well stored with food, among others who are masters of hunting grounds abounding so much with game that they have a regular and plentiful supply of nourishment with little labor. The superior degree of security and affluence which these tribes enjoy is followed by their natural effects. The passions implanted in the human frame by the hand of nature acquire additional force; new tastes and desires are formed; the women, as they are more valued and admired, become more attentive to dress and ornament; the men, beginning to feel how much of their own happiness depends upon them, no longer disdain the arts of winning their favor and affection. The intercourse of the sexes becomes very different from that which takes place among their ruder countrymen; and as hardly any restraint is imposed on the gratification of desire, either by religion, or laws, or decency, the dissolution of their manners is excessive. (I, 255–256)

But though the hand of nature has deviated so little from one standard in fashioning the human form in America, the creation of fancy hath been various and extravagant. The same fables that were current in the ancient continent have been revived with respect to the New World, and America too has been peopled with human beings of monstrous and fantastic appearance. The inhabitants of certain provinces were described to be pygmies of three feet high; those of others to be giants of an enormous size. Some travelers published accounts of people with only one eye; others pretended to have discovered men without heads, whose eyes and mouths were planted in their breasts. The variety of nature in her productions is indeed so great that it is presumptuous to set bounds to her fertility, and to reject indiscriminately every relation that does not perfectly accord with our own limited observation and experience. But the other extreme, of yielding a hasty assent, on the slightest evidence, to whatever has the appearance of being strange and marvelous, is still more unbecoming a philosophical inquirer, as, in every period, men are more apt to be betrayed into error by their weakness in believing too much, than by their arrogance in believing too little. In proportion as science extends, and nature is examined with a discerning eye, the wonders which amused ages of ignorance disappear; the tales of credulous travelers concerning America are forgotten; the monsters which they describe have been searched for in vain; and those provinces where they pretend to have found inhabitants of singular forms are now known to be possessed by people nowise different from the other Americans.

Though those relations may, without discussion, be rejected as fabulous, there are other accounts of varieties in the human species in some parts of the New World which rest upon better evidence, and merit more attentive examination. This variety has been particularly observed in three different districts. The first of these is situated in the isthmus of Darien, near the center of America. Lionel Wafer, a traveler possessed of more curiosity and intelligence than we should have expected to find in an associate of buccaneers, discovered there a race of men few in number but of a singular make. They are of low stature, according to his description, of a feeble frame, incapable of enduring fatigue. Their color is a dead milk white; not resembling that of fair people among Europeans, but without any tincture of a blush or sanguine complexion. Their skin is covered with a fine hairy down of a chalky white; the hair of their heads, their eyebrows, and eyelashes are of the same hue. Their eyes are of a singular form, and so weak that they can hardly bear the light of the sun; but they see clearly by moonlight, and are most active and gay in the night. No race similar to this has been discovered in any other part of America. Cortés, indeed, found some persons exactly resembling the white people of Darien among the rare and monstrous animals which Montezuma had collected. But as the power of the Mexican empire extended to the provinces bordering on the isthmus of Darien, they were probably brought thence. Singular as the appearance of those people may be, they cannot be considered as constituting a distinct species. Among the Negroes of Africa, as well as the natives of the Indian islands, nature sometimes produces a small number of individuals with all the characteristic features and qualities of the white people of Darien. The former are called Albinos by the Portuguese, the latter Kackerlakes by the Dutch. In Darien, the parents of those *whites* are of the same color as the other natives of the country; and this observation applies equally to the anomalous progeny of the Negroes and Indians. The same mother who produces some children of a color that does not belong to the race brings forth the rest with the complexion peculiar to her country. One conclusion may then be formed with respect to the people described by Wafer, the Albinos and the Kackerlakes: they are a degenerated breed, not a separate class of men; and from some disease or defect of their parents, the peculiar color and debility which mark their degradation are transmitted to them. As a decisive proof of this, it has been observed that neither the white people of Darien nor the Albinos of Africa propagate their race; their children are of the color and temperament peculiar to the natives of their respective countries.

The second district that is occupied by inhabitants differing in appearance from the other people of America is situated in a high northern latitude, extending from the coast of Labrador toward the pole, as far as the country is habitable. The people scattered over those dreary regions are known to the Europeans by the name of Esquimaux. They themselves, with that idea of their own superiority which consoles the rudest and most wretched nations, assume the name of *keralit*, or *men*. They are of a middle size and robust, with heads of a disproportioned bulk and feet as remarkably small. Their complexion, though swarthy, by being continually exposed to the rigor of a cold climate, inclines to the European white rather than to the copper color of America; and the men have beards which are sometimes bushy and long. From these marks of distinction, as well as from one still less equivocal, the affinity of their language to that of the Greenlanders, which I have already mentioned, we may conclude with some degree of confidence that the Esquimaux are a race different from the rest of the Americans.

We cannot decide with equal certainty concerning the inhabitants of the third district, situated at the southern extremity of America. These are the famous Patagonians, who, during two centuries and a half, have afforded a subject of controversy to the learned, and an object of wonder to the vulgar. They are supposed to be one of the wandering tribes which occupy that vast but least-known region of America, which extends from the River De la Plata to the Straits of Magellan. Their proper station is in that part of the interior country which lies on the banks of the River Negro; but in the hunting season they often roam as far as the straits which separate Tierra del Fuego from the main land. The first accounts of this people were brought to Europe by the companions of Magellan, who described them as a gigantic race, above eight feet high, and of strength in proportion to their enormous size. Among several tribes of animals, a disparity in bulk as considerable may be observed. Some large breeds of horses and dogs exceed the more diminutive races in stature and strength, as far as the Patagonian is supposed to rise above the usual standard of the human body. But animals attain the highest perfection of their species only in mild climates, or where they find the most nutritive food in greatest abundance. It is not then in the uncultivated waste of the Magellanic regions and among a tribe of improvident savages that we should expect to find man possessing the highest honors of his race, and distinguished by a superiority of size and vigor far beyond what he has reached in any other part of the earth. The most explicit and unexceptionable evidence is requisite in order to establish a fact repugnant to those general principles and laws which seem to affect the human frame in every other instance, and to decide with respect to its nature and qualities. Such evidence has not hitherto been produced. (I, 259–263)

# 6.

## The Abbé Roubaud

*"The degeneration of nature in these regions is as chimerical as the state of barbarity of the inhabitants was true."*

THE ABBÉ PIERRE JOSEPH ANDRÉ ROUBAUD, born in Avignon in June 1730 into a poor family, was directed by his parents toward an ecclesiastical career. As a young man, he left his home region for Paris, determined to earn his existence by his pen. He contributed his first articles to the *Journal de Commerce* and soon became that journal's most important contributor. Strongly independent in every way, he wrote on history and politics, and in many of his articles he attacked current administrative abuses. In addition to the *Journal de Commerce,* his articles appeared in the *Gazette d'Agriculture,* the *Journal de l'Agriculture,* and the *Nouvelles Ephémérides du Citoyen.* In 1774, some articles he had contributed to the *Journal de l'Agriculture* provoked an argument with Linguet, who refuted him in his own *Journal* of that year. Because of his independence and outspokenness, Roubaud was exiled from Paris in 1775 and took up residence in Normandy.

Up to this time, he had already published a few political and historical works; *La politique indienne* had appeared in Paris in 1768, and in 1775 he published *Récréations économiques* (also Paris). His most important work, however, was the *Histoire générale de l'Asie, de l'Afrique, et de l'Amérique* (Paris, 5 vols., 1770–1775). In this work, he gives a well-documented history of America since the time of its discovery, and takes strong issue with De Pauw and his remarks on degeneracy in the New World. His point of view is clear: the discovery was itself a magnificent achievement of man, but the conquest of America, the exploitation of its resources and its peoples brought only catastrophe to both the Old World and the New. He brings his history of the North American colonies up to the present year (1775) and ends with predicting the successful revolution of these colonies and the eventual liberation of all America from European control.

Roubaud's exile lasted only one year. In 1776 he was permitted to return to Paris where presumably he lived for the rest of his life. His studies after his return were directed rather toward language than toward history and politics, although it is difficult to say whether this was the result of official pressures or simply of a change of emphasis in his own interests. In 1784 appeared his *Nouveaux Synonymes français* (Paris, 4 vols.). After this, he lived in such obscurity that even his death was unnoticed and it has been impossible to date it. It has been placed in various years between 1791 and the end of the century. His pension of 3,000 francs had been stopped at the time of the Revolution, but in 1795, along with other men of letters awarded pensions by the convention, he was granted a pension of 2,000 francs. It seems, however, that Roubaud was already dead at this time, his obscurity such that the authorities were not even aware of his death.

## FROM THE GENERAL HISTORY OF ASIA, AFRICA, AND AMERICA

. . . UP TO this point we have limited ourselves to resuming the work of M. de Pauw and to bringing together his proofs for his opinions. We are confident that our analysis of the *Recherches philosophiques sur les Américains* presents the substance of the work, without dissimulation or alteration. Does not this picture of America, as offered by De Pauw, seen drawn as a caricature? Can history present this hemisphere in its reality by accumulating error upon error? Was nature in reality so crushed under some mysterious burden that it could offer only the terrifying spectacle of the world's decreptitude?

After the discovery of the new continent, an American philosopher, drawing judicious conclusions from uncontestable truths, could easily have given a totally different and horrible idea of Europe. He could have said:

"What is this land that spews up so many plagues upon us, this land we have neither harmed nor coveted? It engenders monsters, and these monsters flee across broad seas and through the most frightful perils to escape from its even greater evils. Hunger and despair create brigands; only the most extreme hunger could have thrown these brigands into such excessive despair. What do they seek in our lands? Gold? Do these madmen believe that gold nourishes and clothes men? What are they seeking in the heart of our green stones that they break them with picks and hammers?

"They bring grains and plants, doubtless poisoned, for these barbarians bring only desolation; or if they are strong and healthy plants, they must have been stolen from fertile lands. Their own land must reject them, since they come to plant them in ours. If our earth nourishes them though they be alien to it, our own products must wither in their soil. Perhaps nature has a horror of their domestic animals, just as we ourselves hold them in execration. And what of these monsters with which they fight and by which they triumph? What of these horses without which they can hardly get about, for they are so feeble and so weak? these dogs who seem no more ferocious than their masters, for they are less treacherous? These are the worthy companions of their exploits, and they owe their triumphs to them, and to their terrifying arms forged in hell. The cowards would not have dared to fight on equal terms. They pierce our hearts when we receive them with open arms. Cowardly subowners of our women, they have the courage to be cruel only after having assured their success through the blackest of treacheries. Let them boast of their arts: they practice only those of corruption and destruction, the arts of treachery and ferocity. The arts fit for men would have made their nature more gentle.

"They tell about the marvels of their lands, these unfortunates who come to make their lives among ours, and what do they teach us of the customs of their country? Mothers thrust aside their children from the very moment they are born. The poor unfortunate babes fall into the murderous hands of mercenary nurses who condemn them to the torture of being bound and suffocated. Babies, young girls, even pregnant women, submit their bodies to the torture of being pressed tight by fish bones from the northern seas, for it is recognized that a weak and misguided Nature would create only deformed creatures if she were not resisted by infallible corrective measures. They build houses upon houses wherein people live one upon the other and breathe an air poisoned by their breath, their filth, by the effluvia of cemeteries, of hospitals, and of disgusting trades. They esteem arts and men only in inverse proportion to their usefulness, and their most precious citizens, those who nourish all the others, are vilified, so suppressed and so crushed that they are left with not even enough food for themselves.

"Should we think their climate so kind when they believe nature can create only monsters there, when it does not respond to their needs, when they abandon it with such eagerness and satisfaction? when they admit that in general their lives are shorter than ours, and consequently their constitutions less strong? How impure their blood must be! They have brought us their fearful malady, the smallpox, and it has caused, if that be possible, even more devastation than their violence. Their malady so aggravates our endemic disease, to which they've given our name, that they become quickly covered with horrible ulcers, and their lives are soon ended, while it hardly affects us at all and we reach a very old age. Don't their beards and all the hair that covers their bodies indicate the class of animals they belong to? What should we think of the fine laws of a country where even the basic elements of justice are unknown? Should we credit a large population to such a country when the land seems so hostile, barely able to produce a few handfuls of men for such astonishing undertakings? These men are reduced to demanding help from their animals, to turning their dogs and their horses into conquerors. As for the religion they want to impose upon us, they do not believe in it themselves if it prohibits injustice and crime, while we could not accept it if it orders or permits them."

Our philosopher, by wise and ingenious reflection upon authenticated and uncontrovertible facts, could carry the development of this text just as far as De Pauw carried his *Recherches sur les Américains,* and in treating the truth in the same manner, he could give the most horrendous and unfaithful picture imaginable of Europe.

De Pauw has tried to explain the chaos of ancient America. He has drawn much enlightenment from the darkness that surrounds it. But was this country indeed as grotesque as he shows it to be with such knowledge and philosophy? If his only purpose was to establish the prodigious superiority of our hemisphere over the other, he would not have promised, in his *Discours préliminaire*, a *"portrait surprennant par sa nouveauté."* Futilely and laboriously, he would have demonstrated a truth already amply demonstrated to all the universe; he would not have been forced to deny America all the advantages historians attribute to it. In conceding to America all it could rightfully ask, it would still have remained infinitely inferior to our own continent.

His particular design was to prove the decadence, the degeneracy, and the failings of nature in the Western regions. He repeats it on every page: it is not a new view that he is publishing. But did he succeed? There is room for doubt. For the most part, his assertions are false, and even if they were strictly true, he would still have deduced false consequences from them.

*Degeneracy* is the passage from a more perfect state to a less perfect state; the proof of degeneracy is established by means of a comparison between the two states. To attribute degeneracy to nature in America, M. de Pauw would have had to ascertain either (1) by authenticated sources that it was less vigorous at the time of the discovery than it had been earlier, or (2) by philosophical reasoning that the natural state itself is much less crude than that of America. It is impossible to prove the first of these points: it would be extremely difficult to prove the second. De Pauw did not, and probably never will, undertake to do one or the other.

A land reduced to sterility through being exhausted would be a degenerate land. A race of men condemned to a state of old age at the moment of maturity would be a degenerate race. In America, the land was naturally very fertile, and the human race naturally long-lived.

This is not a vain dispute over mere words. When words express the particular opinion of the author and the specific nature of his thought, the dispute becomes one concerning fundamentals. We cannot accuse De Pauw of not knowing the meanings of such words as degeneration, decay, degradation, decreptitude, etc. His system bears upon their natural meaning.

If he had wanted to say merely that America was uncultivated, and that mankind there was primitive or uncivilized, he would have said it. He would have said nothing more, and he would have said nothing new.

The author recognizes that "nature, lacking direction at the hand of man, succumbed under its own efforts in America, and if man directed the efforts of nature, fertility would not be totally lost." Therefore the land itself was fertile, although man did not know how to turn this fertility to his advantage, which *does not equal sterility,* physically speaking, as the author adds. I say *physically speaking* because it is a question of the physical qualities of the American soil.

The degeneration of nature in these regions is therefore as chimerical as the state of barbarity of the inhabitants was true. America was uncultivated because its men were still in a state of infancy. But how was this infancy perpetuated to such a point that barely two nations had begun to become civilized, whereas our own continent was entirely covered with nations that had been more or less civilized for so many centuries?

America was, so to speak, a new land. At the time of its discovery, its surface still offered the appearance of a sea strewn with islands and peninsulas, almost like a land intersected in all directions by water that was either free-flowing or stagnant.

High mountains, great rivers, vast forests, all opposed invincible obstacles to communication between its sparse tribes. The torrents could be contained, the rivers directed, the marshes reclaimed, and forests cut down only by means of the strong arms of numerous groups. The American tribes were scattered and isolated. For Americans to become civilized, it would have been necessary for all its inhabitants, all by their individual means, to raise themselves to the point of civilization, whereas in our own hemisphere, a single civilized nation could have transmitted its culture from nation to nation over the entire extent of our continent.

Americans, maintained by circumstances in a state bordering upon savageness, had the longest and most difficult course to run before attaining the fundamentals of civilized society. For the most part, they were hunters, and the wild hunter seeks solitude, shies away from human habitation, and at each step withdraws from social existence, as De Pauw has so well noted. They were hunters because they had more forests about them than pasture lands, more game than fruit in their forests, more faith in the consumption of game than in that of roots that could be poisonous. They were more in need of defending their provisions and their persons against bears, wolves, tigers, foxes, and other prevalent carnivorous animals, than they were of letting them multiply by abandoning too soon this natural state of warfare in order to raise troops and crops. Like hunting, fishing —the resources of some of the peoples—offered a more or less solitary life.

We can say that their ingenuity, if we can speak in such terms, had attained perfection in the hunting life, in their alimentary discoveries, and especially in the composition and preparation of nutritious powders and pastes which, condensed and considerably reduced in volume, assured them of adequate and convenient sustenance during their long treks across barren regions and after unsuccessful hunts. With all our arts, our knowledge, and our research we are only now barely learning to insure ourselves, through similar discoveries, against famine aggravated by drought; and if we have indeed developed some nutritious powders, we have had to copy the processes of these peoples. (V. 56–62)

Do we dare compare the physical American man with the European? Which of the two has been endowed with the stronger constitution? One soon collapses under the effects of the elements; the other bears them lightly. One can withstand neither hunger nor thirst, nor intemperance; the other supports opposing extremes equally well. One betrays, under torture, the delicacy of a child; the other displays, in the most fearful torments, a superhuman strength. One can sustain neither indolence nor excessive labor; the other is tired neither by action nor by repose. One, in an air so pure, eating succulent food, under the care of science and industry, early reaches the term of his existence; the other, in an atmosphere heavy with impurities, with dubious and precarious sustenance, with no resources save those of his own strength, prolongs his life beyond limits known to us.

Do we dare ask which of these two men is superior to the other? The first is European; the second, American.

What a powerful conclusion De Pauw would have drawn from this comparison, if the American had occupied the place of the European! And yet, it is from these accumulated proofs of strength of the Indian that he deduces his weakness. Without burdening ourselves with ingenious subtleties, we will only ask him which physical constitution he would adopt for himself, if he had the choice.

Fairness does not permit us to hide the fact that the American's physical superiority is due to his training and his savage existence, rather than to an inherited strength and the generosity of nature. But even among the savages of both hemispheres, are there any to whom the American would cede, at least without contest, his superiority? And if it were true that the American is a sort of miscarriage of nature, that his blood is so cold, his nerves so slack, his arm so weak, his morals so corrupt, and his very existence so sickly in itself, that he breathes only foul air, eats only fish, lives only in an atmosphere of death, how could he then survive so many dangers and his own organic debility to reach so effortlessly such an advanced age? (V. 80–81)

The discovery of America remains the most memorable revolution this globe has witnessed by the hand of man; the conquest of America remains the most shocking calamity humanity has suffered by the hand of man.

These events have changed the face of the universe. Is the earth, because of them, more prosperous? Where is wealth? Where is peace? Where is happiness?

And what remains of the former America? The sky, the earth, and the memory of nations destroyed.

No, I am mistaken. There still remain slaves and savages. These slaves are the most brutalized of mortals, and their state of lethargic stupidity is the lowest degree of human misery. These savages are constantly attacked, pursued, perverted, and destroyed by our arms, our intrigues, our vices, our maladies, our liquors, etc. They are like children become enervated and corrupt.

There has been a fearful exchange of evils between Europe and America, and there has not been a reciprocal exchange of good.

Smallpox, transplanted into America, has not been less destructive there than the American malady, known by that name, has been in Europe.

Americans possessed some secrets; we did not learn them.

Europe possessed many arts; we did not teach them to the Americans.

Some corners of the New World have been cultivated. By whom? By Africans and by Americans. For whom? For Europeans.

I would hope these natives might be converted into true Christians, so that religion itself might be comforted by their virtues and by their blessedness for having been sacrificed to the sacrilegious excesses of the most impious barbarity.

A beacon of light was raised, dissipating the darkness that enveloped Physics, Astronomy, and Geography. A ball of fire descended, igniting cupidity, jealousies, and hatreds whose explosions cover all the surface of the earth.

May day never break again, if it must only throw light on a world full of such crimes!

The Old World caught up the New in its vortex; but in the collision of these two bodies, the stronger could not crush the weaker without being itself rent and broken.

Perhaps more than twenty million Indians perished in America; many more men were lost to our own continent. It is estimated that Spain spewed eight million men over the New World. Have Portugal, England, France, Germany, Holland, and other countries lost any less than that, especially if we count the many victims of wars and of navigation? Even now, Great Britain is losing men day after day in order to populate this vast desert. Africa has already lost nearly twelve million of its own to it, and continues to sacrifice, each year, more than sixty thousand.

Africa! What connection was there between Africa and the crimes of Europeans in America? The same connection Barbary discovered between a barren land and men suited to that climate, between an unproductive desert and beasts of burden, between thirst for blood quenched and the thirst for riches aroused, between crime and crime.

Fallow lands, sores on the earth, have become more extensive in Europe. Look especially at Spain. Does the cultivation of a few regions in America compensate for these vast and deep wounds?

What does it matter that Europe might have opened up new outlets for its products, when it has curtailed its own abundance and brought about famines! Will you harvest on your own land without having sown, and will you sow on foreign soil without reaping?

And what were these new outlets? Europeans who went to America to enjoy the natural products of their own homeland. Does the relocation of consumers constitute a new market?

Gold, either stolen or purchased at the cost of American blood, flowed over Europe in waves; and it scorched a good part of the land. Foolishly it was thought to be the wealth of nations, even to the point of financing them completely; and it rendered fiscal greed unrestrained. Vices and errors converted it into a universal instrument for all manner of disorder, and all became politically, socially, and morally venal.

The conquest was still recent when Garcilaso de la Vega noted the depreciation of currency brought about by the abundance of gold, and the increase in cost of commodities proportionate to the multiplying of specie. A specific amount of commodities, in the balance of exchanges, is worth eight times its weight in metal since Europe struck eight times the coins it had before. What did Europe gain from this? It converted its strong currency into small change.

The treasures of the New World brought Philip II to bankruptcy. Portugal, draining more than forty million livres from Brazil each year, found itself barely provided with five million depreciated coins. Spain fell into a most weakened state by drawing these mountains of gold from the mines of Chile, of Mexico, and of Peru. I say mountains of gold because the production of these mines is inestimable. All of Europe, that an American might well believe to be covered with precious metals over its entire surface, all of Europe is crushed under debts and flooded with paper currency of no value.

These nations demanded gold from all of America. They lavished it on more fertile lands in order to buy the products these lands offered. Gold continues to flow; the mines will become exhausted, and the habit of these outrageous expenditures will remain. What will happen then?

This tribute, it is said, has fostered our trade with the Indies. Not only has it fostered it, it has expanded this ravenous trade excessively. Gold, in flowing rapidly from its sources in America across Europe, carried off our population, our manufactures, our fertile earth, into the abyss that is the Indies.

We have sacrificed, we do now sacrifice, and we will continue to sacrifice the capital derived from our cultivation and our industry to our passion for consuming limitless quantities of spices that burn our throats, tea that parches our mouths, drugs that poison us, and fabrics that mock the loss of our agriculture and our arts.

America gave us some food plants. The potato, for instance, is one of the most precious gifts we have from the New World. But do we dare boast about such resources against famine? Would we hunger after potatoes if we had not blighted our own grain?

We take furs from America. Degenerate race! Must we protect ourselves from a temperate climate with armor produced by the north against the cold of the north?

America introduced us to tobacco. Yes, the great need for a powder, useless and even dangerous, has made nations prey to the fiscal system which encouraged this need and now greedily exploits it.

It increased our supply of coffee, and Europe quenched its thirst with a harmful beverage. In many provinces of France and Germany and other countries, we find its addicts doing without bread in order to drink coffee.

It gave us cochineal, pearls, emeralds, and diamonds. Children! How long will you continue to buy dyes at the price of your sustenance? Will you still ask for baubles on your deathbeds?

We get our sugar from the same country. The Provence Islands have produced sugar, Sicily has produced it, European Turkey and part of southern Europe will produce it. Africa will produce it, and it would flourish under our own care if we were not still half barbarians.

To enjoy these products freely, these products nourished by blood and still dripping with blood, we have established in those regions two sorts of domination, one over the natives and the other over our transplanted subjects. The first is tyranny, the second monopoly. The difference is in name only. . . .

Europe based its glory, its power, its very salvation on possessions that were distant, precarious, useless, acquired at great cost, cultivated at great cost, defended at great cost, and maintained at great cost. Empires forsook their own solid foundations, and debased themselves in order to expand and to lean on broken reeds.

The opinion was formed that trade—especially distant maritime trade, the most casual, the most perilous, the most costly of all, that ruinous trade that absorbs what is necessary in return for what is superfluous—would produce wealth, simply because it carried from one climate to another the riches produced everywhere by agriculture; and plows were thrown into the sea.

It is an error to believe, with Montesquieu, that nations considering America as an object for trade were wiser than those considering it as an object for conquest. Their law was created by necessity. The conquerors left no mines to invade, nor thrones to usurp, nor nations to enslave, nor tribute to impose. What then was left for the others? Only deserts to populate and to cultivate in order to obtain new products in exchange for their own. (V, 186–191)

# 7.

## Joseph Mandrillon

*"I dare to state it: the discovery of America was an evil."*

JOSEPH MANDRILLON, born in 1743 in Bourg-en-Bresse, was trained for a business career and spent several years in banking before going to America to make business contacts. Upon his return, he went to Amsterdam where he established himself in business. He was actively involved in political questions in Holland at the time, and wrote several articles opposing the ideas of those in power. When the French Revolution broke out, he returned to Paris and joined the Constitutional Republican party; he strongly opposed the more vindictive faction of the party during the Reign of Terror, but with not much success. In 1793 he was arrested, charged with corresponding with the Duke of Brunswick. The death sentence was passed by a Revolutionary court, and he was guillotined on January 7, 1794.

In Amsterdam in 1784, he published his *Recherches philosophiques sur la Découverte de l'Amérique,* which was in answer to the question Raynal had proposed to the Academy of Lyons. According to this work, the discovery of America had indeed been a mistake. It had brought untold misery to the Americans, and great misfortunes to Europe. There had been some advantages, certainly, both to America and to Europe, but these advantages were slight compared to the harm that had already been done over centuries.

There is no mistaking Mandrillon's strongly negative point of view in this work. Nevertheless, the conclusion seems to suggest some mitigation. Up to now, the discovery had been a mistake. But now, the English colonies had revolted and the new United States had been formed. Perhaps this new nation could succeed in civilizing the rest of America. Perhaps it might be possible one day, if America is judiciously governed by laws based on nature and morality, to review the question and discover that, in the long run, the good has after all outweighed the evil.

## FROM THE PHILOSOPHICAL INVESTIGATIONS ON THE DISCOVERY OF AMERICA

(*America has known only unhappiness at the hands of Europeans. The conquerors' greed for gold and precious stones brought persecutions, tortures, and death to millions of Americans, and destruction of the American cities and civilizations. Incompetent European administrators, concentrating upon the mines, allowed the land to lie fallow and to deteriorate. The great losses of the native population brought about the importation of slaves, the worst crime of all. Missionaries and the Inquisition tried to impose their religion, and* "the immoderate zeal of religion cost the Indians almost as much blood and tears as had the chains of despotism and the tyranny of laws." (p. 31) *Those Indians who accepted Christianity did so through fear, and thus was hyprocrisy born in their simple hearts.*)

TO COUNTERBALANCE these evils, I need only present the blessings the discovery of America brought to its natives. But in spite of all my research, and the great desire I might have to enumerate these blessings, I have found none of any kind in ethics or in politics. Before the arrival of the Europeans, the peoples of the New World lived in peace and happiness. Their desires did not exceed the limits of their possibilities. Much of their land, it is true, bristled with thorns and was covered with forests; cultivation was unknown or neglected. These same lands, improved by the art of agriculture, are now very productive; their air is more pure and more healthy, life there more agreeable and less injurious. These natives did not know the art of forging iron, so that they were deprived of many commodities and unable to exploit their forests, to improve the cultivation of their land. Certainly America is indebted to Europe for this amelioration. Yet is it not likely that the Mexicans and the Peruvians, whose empires were so brilliant and who had already made such progress in the arts of civilization, would have perfected their own knowledge and transmitted it to the rest of America? Certainly these nations would not have sold their services at the terrible cost exacted by the Europeans! Reciprocal advantages would have been better established and far more extensive. It is therefore evident that all of America would sooner or later have become civilized without the help of Europe.

Furthermore, one cannot desire what one does not know. The Indian, even if less well educated, would not have been any less content, since his knowledge was sufficient for his happiness. If we examine the condition of the savages and other natives of America, we will see that they are now no better educated nor more civilized, even though Europeans have been governing them for nearly three centuries. On the contrary: they feel toward us a natural distrust and a relentless hatred that is passed on from one generation to the next. They believe, as did their ancestors, that we came only to chase them from their lands and to destroy the happiness they enjoyed. Indeed, is it not natural that they should consider themselves the sole true proprietors of this immense region, and that they consequently should see us only as unjust usurpers? (pp. 33–35)

We have shown the evils this discovery brought to America, and the very small advantage it derived from it. Let us consider now the evils caused in Europe:

1. Because of this discovery, depopulation was extensive in Europe, and especially in Spain.

2. Europeans brought back from America that shameful malady that causes such great ravages among them.

3. The quantities of gold and silver obtained from America has increased the cost of basic commodities, while the wages of workers has not increased proportionately. (p. 38)

To put some order into the fearful chaos of evils caused by the discovery of America, we have had to divide the subject, unfortunately so vast, into several different headings. But alas! the sum of the blessings is so small that it can be presented from a single point of view. We would be fortunate indeed if these advantages were sufficient to mitigate, by their utility, the painful effect of all the evils.

What advantages could the discovery of the New World have obtained for Europe?

All these advantages consist in the acquisition of American natural products, such as beaver fur, indigo, woods used in dyeing, cochineal, cotton, cocoa, sugar, medicinal plants, gold, silver, pearls and precious stones, articles which have given the greatest expansion to commerce. Above all, we owe to America our progress in geography, shipbuilding, navigation, astronomy, and natural history. (pp. 50–51)

What conclusions can we draw from a just comparison of these evils and these blessings?

After the account I have just given of the harm and the good the discovery of America brought to both hemispheres, I must still state the case for humanity and for the arts and sciences. At first glance, it is painfully obvious that men owe their increased knowledge only to causes that offend humanity. Though he may be more enlightened, is man happier because of it? This test alone should resolve the question, or at least help us to resolve it.

If the arts and sciences can develop and grow only by increasing the totality of evil, man would no doubt be better off happy rather than wise. Can the most valuable acquisition of knowledge compensate for the loss of a single drop of blood? Of what importance is it to the universe that Rome might possess one more masterpiece among its many, if its acquisition is the result of a crime? Could we excuse the inhuman artist who, in order to paint more realistically the paleness of death, stabs a fellow creature with one hand, and with barbaric enthusiasm traces on his canvas the expression of pain and of death with the other? Such is the vanity of men that, to gain celebrity, they scorn all that is decent and virtuous.

I dare to state it: the discovery of America was an evil. Never can the advantages it brought about (no matter how one considers or depicts them) compensate for the harm it has caused.

For a long time to come, America will continue to suffer the consequences of the shocking despotism of Europeans. The little attention we give to improving the lot of its population, its agriculture, and especially its civilization, does not give room to hope that Europeans will ever have the good fortune and the honor of overcoming obstacles and of restoring to the savages lost in the interior that natural confidence that was originally the basis of their character. It is not the Europeans who will make flourish those lands they have devastated. In the depths of silence, destiny prepared a revolution that was to astonish both hemispheres. A people shackled by a tyrannic monopoly proclaimed this revolution in the precious name of liberty. To the independent colonies will go the honor of civilizing the rest of America. Their strength will grow by degrees; other colonies will follow their example, and we will eventually see as many different civilized states in that part of the world as there are in Europe.

The memory of the evil of Europeans will probably serve as an example one day to future navigators and future conquerors in their discoveries and conquests. They will have learned from us that unknown or subjugated nations are especially deserving of consideration since such discoveries and conquests always damage their happiness, however feeble or strange this happiness might seem to be.

Depending upon the character and training of the Americans before their country became known to us, they surely enjoyed, like us, a happiness that was natural to them and unknown to us; for nature is universally the mother and the teacher of mankind. There are as many kinds of happiness as there are different conditions among men. Each individual, each race, each nation on the surface of the globe, has its joys and its griefs that are characteristic of it and in harmony with its existence. That which creates happiness for one often causes torment for the other. The philosopher is happy in his solitude, while the man of the world is unhappy when he is alone. It follows from these truths that Europeans, in trying to bring their own happiness to the Indians, brought them only grief.

If, in this state of things, Europeans could right the wrongs they have endured and those they have caused the Americans to suffer, this would at least be an improvement for both. They could, by means of sincere reconciliation, be pleased with the knowledge they would never have gained without the discovery of America, and console themselves for having gained it at such great cost by the hope of seeing it serve the cause of common happiness.

But far from being able to rectify these wrongs, Europeans are barely capable of diminishing these sorrowful effects. Those very advantages they have gained are hardly sufficient to compensate for those they continue anxiously and ambitiously to covet. Such are the unfortunate consequences of possession: the greater the desire for them has been, the less their enjoyment once attained.

According to an opinion generally held, nature keeps good and evil in perfect balance, and if this balance is not recognized by some individuals, it is because these goods and these evils are impartially distributed over the earth. Accustomed to desiring an ideal happiness, men always believe themselves more unfortunate than they really are. They become so familiar with their possessions that surfeit soon replaces their enjoyment of them. Such is the cause of most of the ills constantly tormenting man.

As soon as we accept these truths, it becomes easy to realize how much the Indians, subjugated by force, must have suffered at our hands. We so greatly increased their sufferings that we forced them to recognize as advantages those things they unthinkingly enjoyed before and of which they are now deprived. They learned to love their country, to value their liberty, only when they were deprived of both. In short, Europeans appropriated everything, men and animals, unto themselves.

In enumerating the blessings this region gave to us, if we except the progress made in geography, navigation, and astronomy, I find none Europe could not have done without. Perhaps this idea will seem astonishing at first, but let us examine it.

Is Europe any happier with the products America gave it, and could Europe not have existed just as easily without them? It does not follow from the fact that commerce has been greatly expanded, that the resources of a state are increased in proportion to this expansion. In fact, it is through a too great expansion that we lose the fruits of its initial advantages. When trade has reached its last phase, it begins to make us slaves of superfluities, of opulence, of avarice; and men, crushed under the weight of luxury, weakened by delicacies and refinements of all sorts, lose their taste for morality. Quickly become corrupt and corrupters, they scorn virtue and thus overthrow the foundations of just principles. Without these refinements of taste, what need did we have for the fur of the beaver or of other such animals? Are we the better protected? and would not the fleece from our own sheep, the fur of our own European animals, have served just as well?

Could not our artists, with their ingenuity and the mixture of our own dyes, have compensated for cochineal and indigo? And of what use is it to humanity that our painters and our dyers have one or two more colors, a livelier red or a lovelier blue, than those they had before? Would our women be less gracious, our love less tender, our passion for them less vivid, if they had no rouge? Perhaps if they did not have these deceptive aids so readily at hand, they would more carefully guard against the destructive effects of the late hours and refined foods that so quickly damage their charms, that cause wrinkles at an age when roses should only start to appear. Charming village maidens! I appeal to the freshness of your complexion! It is an eloquent proof for us that nothing is more beautiful than simple nature.

Could cotton be such a rich acquisition? Who knows if its discovery and its use have not caused us to neglect possible experiments with hemp and flax. Without this new product, we might already have discovered—as we perhaps shall someday—the means of treating their thread in such a way as to give it as much warmth, suppleness, and whiteness. It is these three properties alone which have given cotton its reputation.

With respect to the woods used in dyeing, we cannot deny how useful they are; but we cannot consider their possession as necessary to man since they are used only in superfluous things. And further, it is to our excessive sensuality that sugar owes its great consumption here. Our fathers were unfamiliar with it and existed very well without it. The product of our industrious bees was enough for them, and probably we would ourselves prefer honey to sugar if we were wise enough not to multiply our needs by ever-new desires and to resist the pernicious inclination to drink liqueurs. We might also add that the use of sugar has greatly harmed the products of our earth through the loss of our beehives. This commodity and coffee, whose consumption has been favored by the American production, have brought inestimable damage to our native beverages and consequently to that industry, without counting the damage to health.

As for medicinal plants, could not our clever and industrious doctors do without those that come to us from America? Are not our bodies shaped today as they were three centuries ago? Even though they lacked remedies, did our ancient and famous doctors complain that they lacked means for relieving illness? Far from supposing that deaths occurred more easily at that time, we can note that man was more vigorous and lived longer. Was this because there were fewer remedies and less superfluity in the art of medicine? You might well answer that if men today are less robust and their lives shorter, only the disorders of their habits and morals are responsible. I agree. But which medicinal plant from America can overcome their debility or lengthen their days? Can you name one?

As for quinine, we might well wonder if Providence placed fevers in our climate and their remedy in Africa!

If it were true that the happiness of man consists in riches, the simple extraction of precious stones and metals would suffice to make us consider the discovery of America as the greatest of blessings. But alas, it is from the heart of wealth and luxury that arise most of the evils which distress society. One would think that the mines of America, in enriching Europe, would have lavished more ease upon it, more prosperity. Far from it! We have demonstrated all its dismal consequences, especially for the poorest and the hardest-working class of citizens.

As far as geography, navigation, and astronomy are concerned, we cannot deny that these are blessings so useful to the development of the human spirit that they alone would balance the sum of harm caused by the discovery of America if we could only accept the idea that men are better off wise than happy. But who would dare say such a thing? Who is that serious-minded man who cannot see that the course of evil is prompt and rapid, while that of good is slow and belated?

I have yet only to speak of natural history. Europe has been enriched by a prodigious number of birds, animals, and plants of all sorts, whose existence we did not even suspect and which have served to broaden our knowledge of nature itself. Up to now, only curiosity has gained by this, for it really affects our happiness very little if our herbaria be more complete and our collections richer in cold and sterile exhibits. God forbid that I should consider the work of our naturalists as useless or indifferent! Quite to the contrary, I agree that it is always well, always interesting, to acquire new specimens: the better we know nature, the better we can follow her course. Besides, even if the only result of the sight of these admirable varieties of animals, vegetables, and minerals distributed over the earth by the beneficent hand of the Creator is to inspire in us a deeper respect and a greater gratitude, the work of these famous naturalists would console us in part for the evils of the New World.

"To preserve and to enhance the blessings caused by the discovery of America," we must appreciate and not abuse them.

Appreciating them, we must encourage agriculture throughout all the lands we possess in the New World. We must keep men honest and gentle to direct this work, and generously recompense their efforts so that they will have no other concern, no other desire, than the common good. We must appoint upright and intelligent inspectors to supervise the harvests and their shipment to Europe. The qualifications of these employees should be established by public examination, to avoid all dangers of complicity or dishonesty. And to reward the zeal and the disinterested service of these inspectors, the government should offer them the choice of remaining where they are or returning at the end of a fixed period of time to their homeland, with appropriate pensions.

Another object the European powers should not lose sight of is that as long as they possess land in those regions of the world, they must above all apply themselves to the task of civilizing the savages, and that by means of gentleness, patience, and kindness, they should merit in turn their entire confidence. It is essentially important to the good of all that reforms be made in the laws and regulations concerning America, that the rights of man be more firmly established there, and more assured, that the relation between the two hemispheres be more serviceable. When these improvements have been accomplished, we must try to find the means for preserving all the advantages nature bestowed upon the European earth. Neither fashion, nor greed, nor the too great abundance of American products should in any way injure European cultivation, and the excess of such production should not affect the hopes and the advantages of the European cultivator. Commerce and industry will be able to expand only on the basis of the surplus of these products, a surplus the cultivator and citizens can do without.

Once the advantages of America are appreciated, it will be difficult to misuse them. On the contrary, they will rapidly increase and perhaps one day our children will be able to say: "In spite of all the evils caused by the New World, its discovery was nevertheless a blessing."

These blessings will then exist, and will no longer be chimerical. In short, to preserve and to enhance the advantages we have acquired, we need only know how properly to profit by our knowledge. Let this knowledge no longer be an endless source of disagreement among those who share it. It is especially important to learn to recognize in others the degree of intelligence with which they are endowed, and to cooperate unanimously in the progress of the arts and sciences in general. This unanimity is all the more essential since it is inestimably valuable to society. Just as beneficial rays that feed nature and endow life reach us endlessly from the sun, so from the successful cooperation of learned men will endlessly emanate rays of light that will dissipate all shadows of ignorance and error in the rest of humanity.

It is most important for humanity to find the means to correct the evils that afflict it. The task is difficult. The remedy requires a reformation of our habits and morals and of our very laws. Even if our legislators were all persuaded of the necessity of this reform, if sovereigns themselves encouraged this work, it still remains doubtful that it could be carried, I don't say to perfection itself, but to its complete execution. A universal code to which one could apply rules to be observed by all nations having relations with America seems to me as improbable as the reality of universal peace. And yet it is only with such unanimity, with such a code, that we could try the means to obviate the ills of humanity, especially those caused by the discovery of America. The means of preserving the blessings it produced depend upon the same reform.

As soon as we try to weigh the advantages and the inconveniences of diverse governments in order to form a whole suitable for diverse peoples, to reveal all the different aspects in which the good and evil of America have appeared, this immense labor is no longer within the capabilities of a single individual. To attempt it would be reckless. The corruption of our morals, in making us familiar with vice, inclines us more to evil. We come to think that for the sake of our own pleasure, the fact that the peace of some obscure individuals should be troubled is unimportant. The ease with which most men exercise their unjust rights makes them count for nothing the joy of being honorable.

If most of our laws were not in conflict with those of nature, men would early learn to respect them. Great advantages would follow: a charitable affection for the unfortunate, and more wisdom in the distribution of benefits. We would see ruling society those affectionate bonds which, drawing men closer together, seem to form of mankind one single family.

Let laws be based upon the principles prescribed by morality and by nature. Then dignity and honors will be no more than the rewards of the zeal, the capabilities, and the virtue of each citizen. It is upon intelligent choice that depends the science of ruling hearts and minds, of causing truth to be loved, of maintaining and encouraging the sacred bonds of society, and of re-establishing harmony if it has been troubled. In short, if envy is to have less hold over men, it is essential that they be esteemed only in proportion to their virtues and considered great only in proportion to their service, so that there might never be among them any rivalry except for the public good. Then the ambition of enslaving and oppressing men will be regarded as the greatest of crimes and the ultimate disgrace. Thus regard and honors and praise will no longer be shameful tributes offered by fear or misery, and haughty opulence will no longer take pride in homages that are as debasing for the idol as for the idolater.

If Europeans had been better acquainted with the dignity of man, they would have been more virtuous, more opposed to depredations. They would have recognized the Indians as brothers. Far from treating them with indignity, they would have sought the means to make themselves loved, by inspiring them with the desire to unite with them and to form one single people. Wise legislators, instead of opposing laws or departing from them, would have endeavored to conform to them to derive from them the wisdom which would change savages into a gentle, compassionate, wise, and happy people. They would have known that if these Indians, whom we are pleased to call savages, do not reason methodically on the rights of humanity, they nonetheless originally have these principles graven in their hearts. The savages are less removed than we from the principles of good civilization.

Let them be shown the utility of virtues, and they will observe them with more constancy and more strength than we do. For in spite of our proud arrogance, our sophisms and our books, we are forced to admit our own weaknesses in the practice of virtue, and we do not even blush to justify our passions by artificial needs. Wise teachers would begin by teaching them that in addition to means of sustenance provided by hunting and fishing, which can often fail them, there are more certain and less difficult means such as the cultivation of the earth and the keeping of animals, resources capable of providing them with the commodities of life. That is precisely what the Europeans should have done at the time of the discovery of the New World. It is only by adopting these principles that they will increase the blessings they now enjoy, and remedy those ills which spoil their happiness.

### *Conclusion*

The blessings and the evils produced by the discovery of a new hemisphere have not yet reached their limit. Both will continue to grow and even after many centuries man will still not know whether he might finally hope that the sum of the blessings will one day balance that of the evils. In following the course of the human heart, we have more reason to grieve than to rejoice. Our morals become more and more corrupt; our physical constitution deteriorates from generation to generation; each day our requirements grow more numerous and more urgent; our love of relaxation makes labor more difficult for us; it enervates our bodies, weakens the resiliency of our souls. Whatever we might have gained through our arts and sciences, we shall lose through our indolence and frivolity. Such is the sorry picture we must show of our future generations.

It is the New World, formerly our slave, peopled for the most part by our own emigrants, that will come in turn to enslave us. Its industry, its force, and its power will increase as ours diminish. The Old World will be subjugated by the New; and this conquering nation, after having undergone the laws of revolution, will itself perish at the hands perhaps of a people it will have been unfortunate enough to discover. Thus good and evil, perpetuating themselves and never separating, will always constantly exist in seeming disparity, to astonish, to surprise the philosopher in the midst of his meditations, the philosopher desirous of discerning and comparing them, and deciding between them. (pp. 66–88)

IN THE SAME YEAR that Mandrillon published the *Recherches philosophiques*, there also appeared his *Spectateur américain,* which seems to be in direct conflict with the point of view of the *Recherches*. Yet is this really so?

In the first work, Mandrillon was speaking of the whole of the New World, with, in fact, a considerable emphasis upon Spanish America, and this in a historical perspective looking back nearly three centuries. In the *Spectateur*, on the other hand, his subject is the independent colonies of North America. He does consider their history, to be sure, but his main interest is rather an examination of their present state and of their potential—an optimistic view of the future rather than a pessimistic view of the past.

These two works do not seem to us to be in such strong conflict one with the other. It was probably not entirely by chance that Mandrillon caused them to appear together in the same volume, both in the first edition of the *Spectateur américain* in 1784, and again in 1785 when he published a second edition. Indeed, the *Spectateur* might even be considered a continuation of the conclusion of the Lyons prize essay. Did he not say in his *Recherches philosophiques* that the young United States was an exception?—that the American natives are more virtuous than Europeans? And does he not criticize in both works the corruption and avarice of Europeans?

## FROM *The American Spectator*

### *The Population of North America*

NORTH AMERICA OWES ITS large population to the encouragement of agriculture, and to the necessity of having children in order to make agriculture flourish and to increase its productions. It has a population of around three million inhabitants; its Negroes number four hundred thousand if estimates are not exaggerated. In some of the colonies, the number of citizens doubles every fifteen or sixteen years; and in others, every eighteen or twenty years.

According to Dr. Franklin, the population increases by reason of numerous marriages, and the number of marriages increases in proportion to the facilities that can be found for supporting a family. In a society become aged through its own progress, the rich, alarmed by the expenses of women's luxuries, decide as late in life as possible upon a union that is then difficult to form and costly to maintain; and people without fortunes spend their lives in a state of celibacy that often troubles marriages. Masters have few children; servants have none; and artisans fear to have any. This disorder is especially noticeable in large cities where the generations do not even reproduce themselves enough to maintain the level of the population, and where there are continually more deaths than births.

In an agricultural nation, morals are what they should be. Women are gentle, modest, understanding and helpful; they have those virtues that perpetuate the influence of their charms. The men are occupied with their primary duties of caring for and developing their farms, the mainstay of their prosperity. A sentiment of benevolence unites all families. Nothing contributes more to such a union than a certain equality of comfort, the security that comes from proprietorship, the hope and facility for augmenting possessions, and that mutual dependency of all men for their needs, their convenience, and their pleasures. Instead of luxury which brings poverty in its wake, instead of this distressing and hideous contrast, a universal well-being, wisely shared through the original distribution of lands and through the course of industry, as created in all hearts the desire for all to thrive in common—a far more satisfying wish, doubtless, than that secret desire to injure that is inseparable from extreme inequality of fortune and condition. People always meet with pleasure when they are neither so far removed from one another that they become indifferent, nor in that state of rivalry that is so close to hatred. People draw closer to each other; they meet often; indeed, they enjoy in the colonies that pastoral life which was first intended for man, the most favorable to health and fertility.

Perhaps the greatest possible happiness compatible with the frailty of mankind is enjoyed there. We find no evidence there of all those studied graces and talents, those affected pleasures, whose demands and expenses exhaust all resiliency of mind and spirit and induce the vapors of melancholy after the sighs of sensual pleasures. Instead there are domestic pleasures, mutual affection between parents and children, and conjugal love, that love so pure and so delicious for those able to appreciate it. That is the enchanting spectacle North America offers everywhere. There, a first love becomes an eternal love. There, innocence and virtue never allow beauty to perish. The large population of North America must be attributed to the blessings derived from the purity of morals. But it is to be feared that the prodigious number of European emigrants who, with their greed for fortune, bring their vices and the dangerous poison of seduction, might well effect a fatal change in the morals of this virtuous people. The contagion of bad example is no less to be feared for an entire people than for an individual. (pp. 6–9)

### *The Colonies*

The history of societies teaches us that civilization spread from east to west, from Asia to Africa and Europe, and from Europe to America. Thus the founding of the colonies has followed, step by step, the progress of civilization. Authentic accounts of the most remote events indicate that the nations of Asia started to become celebrated through settlements founded on the eastern coasts of the Mediterranean sea, that they extended their colonies over most of the islands and on several coasts of this sea, and finally that they introduced tribes or at least the art of cultivation as far west as Greece. From Greece, colonies extended to Italy or Sicily, and the Romans sent settlers as far as the western borders of their empire. Between the fall of the Roman Empire and the discovery of America and the Indies, the founding of colonies seems to have been interrupted. The barbarism and ignorance that covered all of Europe during this long sequence of centuries, the control of superstition and error over the minds of men, halted all undertakings that might have contributed to perfecting and enlightening mankind. . . .

Of all the colonies the world has seen, Carthage stands apart in its importance and its power; thus the Romans devoted all their glory, employed all their resources and their force, to destroying it. We can assume that Carthage would have been victorious, even over the Roman Empire, if it had not alienated men by exercising a tyrannical despotism over its own colonies.

. . . England now presents to the universe an example of the same progress, the same greatness, the same tyranny, and the same decadence as Carthage. In the case of Carthage, it was a distant nation that came to subdue the capital; in England's case, its own colonies, rebelling against the chains imposed upon them, broke these chains over the heads of their oppressors, and raised their own power over the ruins of the throne. Thus the resemblance between Carthage and Britain consists only in the consequences of abuse of power. In espousing the cause of the North Americans, France could have played, toward England, the role of the Roman Empire toward Carthage, if like Rome France had wished to employ all its resources to subdue its enemy. But times have changed, and the political balance of European nations being opposed to the extension of too great power, France could do no more, in this dispute, than contribute to American independence and thus weaken Great Britain. The outcome justified its hopes; America is free, and England humiliated.

England, like all the powers of Europe that have formed distant colonies, seems to have had the increase of its population and its wealth as its primary object in establishing with these colonies an interchange of trade profitable to both. Wherever the attempt was made, experience proved that the English colonies were completely equal to the first of these aims. It can be presumed that this would be just as true elsewhere if the same principles were followed, for it cannot be denied that without the encouragement of the mother country in all that pertained to agriculture and trade, the American colonies would not have reached that degree of maturity that made them simultaneously so powerful and so redoubtable. . . .

As for the differences in climate between the Old World and the New, this is a common error arising from the ancient belief that there exist uninhabitable zones. It has long since been proved that there is no climate under the heavens the human constitution cannot adapt to if certain precautions are taken. The very necessity of these precautions would cease with the first colonists, and the climate would become natural to all children born there. Accordingly, we must conclude that the establishing of colonies is advantageous for all nations founding them wisely, that it cannot harm population since population always increases rapidly wherever industry is encouraged and becomes an assured means of procuring the comforts of life. Moreover, the establishing of an advantageous commerce between the colonies and the parent state procures infinite resources to both and becomes a permanent source of prosperity, provided the mother country is able to preserve the worth of its services and not set them at too high a price. (pp. 123–129)

### *On Liberty in America*

Among all the peoples of the universe, the love of liberty seems to have prevailed even over the love of country. The first has always produced heroes; more often the second has made victims. Rarely has liberty been sacrificed for the sake of one's country; more often country has been sacrificed to the cause of liberty. This sentiment is so strong and so natural in man, that if it is not suppressed at the very moment it is born under a despotic rule, man would rather die free than live in slavery. This exalted love of independence, however, must not be looked for in our monarchies nor in the majority of our modern republics. The first, alluring because of the opulence surrounding them, contribute to weakening the spirit under the dangerous charms of ease and indolence. The second, themselves slaves to the party spirit dividing them, wrangle over liberty without knowing how to enjoy it.

If a people exists anywhere on earth that has been able to guarantee and preserve its privileges against all attacks, it is doubtless there that we must seek examples of true liberty. And this people, even though it is now beginning to degenerate, is the English people. In peace just as in war, under ferocious kings as under kings who were imbeciles, in moments of servitude as in times of anarchy, the English people have ceaselessly claimed their rights. We have seen them dethrone and decapitate their kings for having tried to violate their rights, or give up their own heads to the executioner's ax rather than to renounce these rights. It was natural that this nation, in founding colonies in North America, should carry its principles beyond the seas, and that the same ideas be transmitted to its children. The English of Europe should therefore have recognized that an attack on the rights and principles of the English of America was an attack on their own rights and an injury to their own principles; for the American English, after having adopted the maxims of their ancestors and having made them the foundation and basis of their constitution, would never permit these maxims to be destroyed.

North America will become the cradle of liberty in the New World, but many jolts will be necessary before the part that remains enslaved can follow such an example. Nothing is more favorable to nourishing successful seeds of liberty in Americans than the land they inhabit. Spread far and wide in an immense continent, free as the nature that surrounds them, among the crags and the mountains, the vast plains and the deserts, at the edge of forests where all is still wild, where nothing reminds them of servitude or man's tyranny, they encounter the lessons of liberty and independence in all the physical objects about them. Not so in Europe, where slavery is found in the midst of vices, wealth, and the arts, where fanaticism and superstition pervert men's hearts, and where base flattery creates and nurtures tyrants. In America everything bears the mark of free and virtuous men. Moreover, these free men continually engaging in agriculture, in commerce and in useful labors, cannot help but preserve their morals and their strengths. . . . (pp. 129–131)

### *Some Reflections on American Independence*

One of the greatest and most memorable events of this century is without doubt the American Revolution. All the powers of Europe have been in a state of ferment, and this explosion has caused a conflagration that is almost universal. War has broken out on all sides; even the most distant ports of Asia have felt the commotion. This astonishing and rapid revolution has changed the political and mercantile structure of Europe. The annals of England attest that since its beginnings it has never experienced a more critical situation. Indeed, nothing more unfortunate could have happened to England than the loss of her American colonies. Almost all aspects of her commerce have suffered, and this division breaks forever the dominion she had usurped over the seas. But at the same time, nothing more favorable could have occurred for the other maritime powers and for the new republic that has just been formed.

If it be noble to raise the flag of liberty and to become free from the plague of tyranny, it is also dangerous to undertake such a feat unless a profound feeling of confidence, based upon justifiable complaints, arouses in the spirit of the people the need for a revolution, secretly prepared by the prudent and thoughtful policy of the leaders who plan it. When this fermentation then becomes general, it would be impossible to destroy its origins and to submit such a people to the laws of the old government it wants to renounce. This is the point of view from which we must consider the American cause and the lack of success of the British armies in that part of the world. Many centuries must yet pass and much devastation occur before the independence of the thirteen United States leads to that of all America, but it appears inevitable. From the conflict between the blessings and the evils of the two hemispheres must be born this general scission that will weaken the thrones of Europe by depriving them of the abundant sources of their wealth. The New World then regaining its original freedom, and reaching a higher degree of civilization, it will perhaps become formidable enough to intimidate us in our own lands.

Doubtless the natives of America are not without vice, but their corruption falls far short of that of Europeans. Their virtues, drawn from nature and from the simplicity of their lives, are not, as ours so often are, the products of hypocrisy or of pride. Theirs is an unsullied virtue, such as flourished in the halcyon time when man's primitive innocence did not need to combat the tyranny of the passions or the seductions of bad examples.

And yet an advantage for the inhabitants of this new hemisphere will arise from the fury and the devastations of Europeans in America: the spirit of sociability, the development of knowledge in the arts and sciences following after ignorance and barbarity. The natives will draw more closely together, will become more communicative, and will lend each other mutual assistance. I am aware that the arts and sciences bring with them many disadvantages, that they are the nutriment of luxury which is the eternal cause of depravity and from which one can never hope to be free. But if advantages must always be balanced by disadvantages, without its being within man's power to upset this fixed and eternal order, we must hope that the Americans, in general more wise than we, will indeed profit by their knowledge and by our example, and will avoid the vices of our constitutions, our laws, and our societies.

Religious tolerance already appears to be the fundamental basis of the laws in the thirteen United States, and this wise policy lays the foundation for the happiness and the populating of this new republic. The people adopting this principle and remaining zealously attached to it will be happy indeed! It is by their hand that the great revolution will come about, to which the independence of North America is now only a prelude. Happy indeed that nation which, impressing the still uncivilized natives with the merits of its government, will cause them to come forth from their retreats, to join with it, and to participate in the increase of the population of the New World and in the glory of having forever broken its chains. All good and intelligent people must hope that Europe will view such a revolution without jealousy and without fear, and considering it an eternal and sacred decree, will hasten to favor it by sacrificing its own fancied pretensions that were obtained by force and that force could easily destroy.

Let us leave to this new nation the right of bringing us its products and its merchandise. Let us allow its commerce and its industry to be free, and let that European nation that treats it best be the only one to have any claim on its favor. Let us hope, finally, that a noble emulation and gentle fraternity remain forever between it and ourselves the indissoluble bonds of our relations and our mutual needs. The treaties of commerce and friendship that the United States propose to make with the European powers are founded upon sublime principles. (pp. 133–136)

# 8.

## The Marquis de Condorcet

*"The example of one great nation where the rights of man are respected is invaluable to all the others."*

ONE OF THE LEADING *philosophes* of the eighteenth century, MARIE JEAN ANTOINE-NICHOLAS DE CARITAT, MARQUIS DE CONDORCET, was equally celebrated in his lifetime as a mathematician and a revolutionary. He was born in Ribemont, in Picardy, on September 17, 1743, into a very old and noble family. Educated first at the Jesuit College in Rheims, then at the Collège de Navarre in Paris, he revealed a great talent for mathematics that attracted to him the patronage and friendship of d'Alembert and the mathematician Fontaine. His first important work, *Essai sur le calcul intégral*, was presented before the Academy of Science in 1764 and published the following year. *Sur le problème des trois corps* followed in 1767, and in 1769 he was elected to membership in the Academy of Sciences. His *Eloges des Académiciens de l'Académie Royale des Sciences morts depuis 1666 jusqu'en 1699* was published in 1775, and in 1777, Condorcet became the perpetual secretary of that Academy. His refusal to write an *Eloge* for a late Minister of the King who had been responsible for issuing the infamous *lettres de cachet* earned for him the enmity of the Minister Maurepos who opposed his election to the French Academy, and in spite of strong support of his candidacy for many years, Condorcet did not become a member until 1782.

D'Alembert's early patronage of Condorcet developed

into a lasting friendship between the two men. They traveled together to Ferney to visit Voltaire in 1770; d'Alembert invited Condorcet to contribute articles to the *Encyclopédie;* and Condorcet was named one of d'Alembert's executors in his will. Condorcet's other friendships included Voltaire and Turgot who had interested Condorcet in political economy. (In 1786, Condorcet published his *Vie de M. Turgot,* and in 1789, his *Vie de Voltaire;* both works enjoyed very great success.) It was during Turgot's ministry that Condorcet was appointed Inspector-general of the Mint and took up residence in the Hôtel des Monnaies. He had married Sophie de Gouchy, a very famous beauty, in 1784, and her salon at the Hôtel des Monnaies was one of the most brilliant of the period. Condorcet remained in this post until 1791, when Louis XVI appointed him Commissioner of the Treasury under the constitutional monarchy.

During the Revolution, Condorcet played a prominent role in the new government. Member, then secretary and president, of the Legislative Assembly, he continued to support the constitutional monarchy until Louis XVI's attempted flight in 1792. Condorcet was frequently called upon when important public statements were to be written or new laws drafted. He drafted plans for the revision of the public education system; it was he also who prepared the statement to the French and to Europe on the suspension of the King, in 1792; and in 1793 he presented to the National Convention his draft of a proposed constitution. His draft, however, was rejected in favor of another, although the accepted constitution was never put into force. When the time came to vote on the sentence of the King, Condorcet stood out against the death penalty, calling instead for "the severest penalty save that of death" (*"la peine la plus grave qui ne soit pas celle de la mort"*).

As a member of the Convention, in which the Jacobins were in the majority, Condorcet frequently voted on the side of the Girondins. Not only did he defend the Girondists, he also opposed the Reign of Terror,[1] and on July 8, 1793, he was denounced before the Convention. His arrest

[1] See Antoine Diannyère, *Notice sur la Vie et les Ouvrages de Condorcet,* Paris, 1796. Diannyère relates that by May of 1793, Condorcet had become convinced of the impossibility of reconciliation between the opposing factions, but still hoped that Robespierre might be restrained through fear. At that time, Condorcet said to the author, *"Personne n'est sûr de vivre six mois."*

and the confiscation of his property were ordered, but he succeeded in escaping. In October 1793, his name appeared with Brissot's on a list of persons condemned to death for the crime of conspiracy.

The last eight months of Condorcet's life were spent in hiding in the Paris house of Madame Vernet. It was during this period that, with the encouragement of his hostess, he wrote his famous *Esquisse d'un tableau historique des progrès de l'esprit humain,* not published, of course, until after his death.

Constantly worried about jeopardizing the safety of Madame Vernet, Condorcet succeeded in escaping from her surveillance on March 5, 1794. Disguised as a poor man, he wandered to Fontenay-aux-Roses, then eventually to the village of Clamart where on March 7 he was recognized as an aristocrat. He was arrested and taken to jail in Bourg-la-Reine. The next morning he was found dead in his cell, and it is believed he took poison to escape being returned to Paris and the guillotine.

Condorcet too had been attracted by the prize contest at Lyons, and had begun an essay on the subject proposed by Raynal. His final product, however, was entitled *De l'Influence de la révolution de l'Amérique sur l'Europe.* It was published in his complete works[2] with an introduction that contains the following statement by Condorcet:

*Le prix proposé par M. l'Abbé Raynal, sur le bien et le mal qui ont résulté pour l'Europe de la découverte du Nouveau Monde, avait excité mon intérêt; j'avais osé entreprendre de résoudre cette question, mais j'ai senti que ce travail était au-dessus de mes forces, et je n'ai sauvé de l'incendie que le chapitre où j'examinais l'influence que l'indépendance de l'Amérique aurait sur l'humanité, sur l'Europe, sur la France en particulier, et l'analyse des principes d'après lesquels j'essayais de trouver une méthode de mesurer les différents degrés du bonheur public.*[3]

[2] *Oeuvres complètes de Condorcet,* ed. Garat & Cabanis, Paris, An IX [1800–1801], Vol. XI, pp. 249–294.

[3] *Ibid.,* pp. 238–239. "The prize offered by the Abbé Raynal on the good and the evil that have ensued for Europe from the discovery of America had aroused my interest. I had begun to prepare a study of the question, but felt that it was beyond my capabilities. Accordingly, I destroyed by burning all but the chapter in which I examine the influence of American independence on humanity, on Europe, on France in particular, and the analysis of principles in which I attempt to find a method for measuring different degrees of public happiness."

This essay does more than just side with those who believed the discovery of America to have been a blessing, and despite its profound admiration for the new United States, it remains more than just an eloquent homage. The essay emphasizes the important advantage of America with respect to foreign trade. Condorcet is an optimist about material benefits; they contribute to progress, and human happiness itself is the result of progress. The essay, by comparing America with France and other European nations, criticizes European institutions and points of view, and indicates abuses in existing governments and practices. The blessings of America are many: it has furthered the progress of human enlightenment; America is bound to insure the preservation of peace in Europe; its example alone will serve the eventual reforms of Europe and the betterment of all mankind.

## ON THE INFLUENCE OF THE AMERICAN REVOLUTION IN EUROPE

### *Part I. Its Influence on the Opinions and Laws of Europe.*

*Le genre humain avait perdu ses titres, Montesquieu les a retrouvés et les lui a rendus.*[1] It is not enough that the rights of man be written in the tomes of philosophers and in the hearts of virtuous men; the ignorant and the weak must also be able to read them in the example of a great nation.

America has given us this example.

The act of declaring its independence is a simple and sublime exposition of these rights that are so sacred and have so long been forgotten. In no other nation have they been so recognized, so preserved in such perfect integrity. . . . This is the only nation where one finds neither Machiavellian maxims established as political principles, nor, among its leaders, the belief, sincere or feigned, in the impossibility of perfecting the social order and of reconciling public prosperity with justice.

The example of one great nation where the rights of man are

[1] Voltaire, "Mankind had lost its rights; Montesquieu found and restored them."

respected is invaluable to all others, despite differences of climate, customs, and constitutions. It demonstrates that these rights are everywhere identical, and that except for one, which the virtuous citizen, in the interests of law and order, must be willing to renounce under certain constitutions, there is no state wherein man cannot enjoy all the others to their full extent.

Such examples bear witness to the influence full enjoyment of these rights has on common prosperity, for they demonstrate that man, who has never feared outrage for his person, acquires a gentler and more noble nature, that he whose property rights are always assured finds probity easier, and that the citizen who is not dependent upon laws has more patriotism and more courage. . . .

As a necessary consequence of the respect American laws have had for the natural rights of humanity, every man, whatever his religion, opinions or principles, is certain to find asylum there. In vain would England offer the same advantage, at least to Protestants. The industry of its inhabitants leaves no resource to the foreigner; its wealth repels the poor man; little room is left in this land where commerce and manufacture have increased population. Even its climate is suited to the people of only a small part of Europe. America, on the contrary, offers tempting hopes to industry; the poor man finds an easy subsistence; assured property, sufficient for his needs, can become the reward of his labors. Its more varied climate is suitable for men of all countries.

But at the same time, America is separated from the nations of Europe by a vast stretch of ocean. Other motives are required to cross it than the simple desire of increasing one's well-being. Only the oppressed can have the will to confront this obstacle. Europe, therefore, without having to fear great emigrations, finds in America a helpful check for ministers who might be tempted to govern badly. Oppression must become mitigated when it knows an asylum exists for its victims and that these victims can both escape from and punish such oppression in forcing it to appear before the tribunal of opinion.

Freedom of the press is established in America, and it has been justly regarded as the right to speak and the right to listen to truth, one of the most sacred rights of humanity. . . . The mere example of all the good freedom of the press has done and will yet do in America is all the more valuable to Europe since it is more likely than the English example to insure against the supposed disadvantages of this freedom. More than once have we seen Americans peacefully submit to laws whose principles or effects they earlier had heatedly attacked, and respectfully obey the trustees of public authority without giving up the right of trying to enlighten them and denounce to the nation at large their faults or their errors. We have seen public discussions destroy prejudice and prepare the support of public opinion for new laws. . . .

In observing that in America the most wide-spread tolerance any nation has ever enjoyed brings about peace and prosperity instead of troubles, is it possible for governments of countries where intolerance still reigns to continue to believe such intolerance necessary for the peace of the state? Will they not learn, at long last, that they can without peril obey the voice of justice and humanity? In the past, fanaticism dared to show itself openly, to demand the blood of men in the name of God. Reason forced it to take cover; it assumed the mask of politics, and it is supposedly for the good of the peace that it still insists upon troubling it. But America has proved that a nation can be happy without persecutors or hypocrites, and politicians who have difficulty believing it only on the authority of wise men, will believe it on the authority of this example.

If we recognize how Americans have founded their peace and happiness on a small number of maxims, which seem to be no more the simple expression of what good sense could have dictated to all men, we will stop praising these complicated machines whose multitude of springs make the functioning violent, irregular and difficult, where so many counterweights, supposedly intended to give stability, combine in reality only to weigh upon the people. Perhaps we will realize the insignificance, or rather the danger, of these political subtleties that have too long been admired, of these systems that want to force laws —and therefore truth, reason, justice, and their immutable bases—to change according to the temperature, to yield to the forms of governments, to customs consecrated by prejudice, and even to the idiocies adopted by each nation, as if it would not have been more humane, just, and noble to try to rid such nations of these dangers by reasonable statutes.

We will see that it is possible to have brave warriors, obedient soldiers, disciplined troops, without having recourse to the harshness of the military administrations of many European nations, where subordinates are judged on the secret reports of their superiors, condemned without having been heard, punished without having been able to defend themselves; where even asking to prove one's innocence becomes an additional crime, and to publish that one is not guilty an even greater one. Yet it must be admitted that it is not to corruption, to deliberate injustice, to tyrannical harshness that one must attribute this system of secret oppression that violates both the rights of citizens and those of nations. Even less is it the result of need, for need is as useless and as dangerous for discipline and for the safety of the state as it can be unjust. What then should we accuse? Alas! nothing but the insuperable ignorance of natural law; and the example of a people, free but willingly subject to military as to civil laws, will surely cure us of it.

The example of the equality that reigns in the United States, assuring peace and prosperity, can also be helpful to Europe. We no longer believe that nature divided the human race into three or four orders, and that one of these orders was condemned to work hard and eat little. We have heard so much about the advantages of commerce and currency that the nobleman is now beginning to regard the banker and the merchant as almost his equals—providing they be rich enough. But our philosophy goes no further, and we were still proclaiming not very long ago that the people of some countries are by nature liable only to tillage labor.

We were saying, not very long ago, that the sentiment of honor cannot exist in all its force except in certain classes, and that it was necessary to degrade the majority of a people in order for the rest to have more pride.

But here is what we can read in the history of America. A young French general, charged with defending Virginia against a superior army and abandoned by the soldiers taken from their own regiments to form troops for him, declared, in order to stop this desertion, that since he wished to keep with him only the best men, he would dismiss from his army all those whose valor, faithfulness, and intelligence he mistrusted. From that moment on, no one had the idea of withdrawing. One soldier to whom he wanted to entrust a particular mission insisted upon his promise that if he were to die while executing this mission, it would be published in his home newspaper that he had left the detachment only on order of the general. Another, unable to walk because of his wounds, hired a wagon at his own expense in order to follow the army. Are we not forced to agree that the sentiment of honor is the same under all constitutions? that it acts with equal strength upon men of all conditions, provided that no conditions be debased by unjust opinion or oppressed by bad laws?

These are the advantages all mankind can expect from America's example, and we would be surprised if these advantages were to be considered chimerical simply because they have no immediate physical influence upon the fate of individuals. That would be ignoring that truth that the happiness of man in society depends almost solely upon good laws, and that if these laws owe their first debt to the legislator, who unites the wisdom of conceiving them with the will to promulgate them, those who, by their teaching show each legislator the laws he must establish, become, after him, the first benefactors of the nation.

### *Part II. Its Advantages with reference to the preservation of peace in Europe*

The Abbé de Saint-Pierre dared to believe that men would one day become so reasonable that nations would renounce the barbarous rights of war, and submit their claims, their interests, or their grievances to the judgment of arbiters. This idea is not chimerical, for it has been clearly proved that war can never be an advantage for the majority of people in a nation. Why should men, who have agreed for so long to indulge in absurd and deadly errors, not agree one day to adopt these simple and salutary truths? This hope is still far from being realized.

Perhaps the Abbé de Saint-Pierre would have been more helpful if instead of proposing the renunciation of the right to make war, he had suggested the preservation of this right, but the establishment at the same time of a tribunal charged with arbitrating the disagreements that arise among nations—the extradition of criminals, the application of the laws of commerce, the seizure of foreign vessels, violations of territorial rights, the interpretation of treaties, etc. The sovereign states would then reserve the right to execute the judgments of this tribunal, or to appeal to force. . . .

Let us come directly to the effects of the American Revolution, and let us see if, even though it cost humanity a war, it has not been an advantage.

If England had been reconciled with her colonies, the British ministers would have felt that a foreign war was the only means of securing taxes, establishing military authority, and in general having some profit from them. Such a war with the house of Bourbon would have entailed the loss of a large part of the islands that France and Spain could have defended against a united America and England. I would not regard in itself the loss of the Sugar Islands as a very great misfortune for France. The produce of these islands, less the expenses of cultivation and the costs of administration and defense, adds only a very small sum to the total products of French territory, and these possessions that are so difficult to defend, diminish rather than augment the national strength. But not so in cases where there is danger that a nation, ignorant of the true interests of its own commerce, might refuse wealthy traders the right to enjoy a monopoly over foreigners, a monopoly which this nation itself would also feel burdensome. In this hypothesis, the interest of each consumer nation would reside in having a means for obtaining, at least in part, essential commodities without having to depend upon the whims of other nations. It is from this point of view that the possession of colonies in the Antilles is so important for European nations. . . . In the hypothesis we are considering, the consequences of the loss of these islands would have been fatal for France. The French navy, destroyed by an unsuccessful war, would have left England mistress of the seas. Before long, England would have tried to invade the commerce of India, of Africa, of both parts of America.

The spirit of monopoly that England carries into commerce would have led her, even at the expense of her own wealth, to take measures most ruinous for other nations, would have exposed them to all that a vexatious and insulting mercantilist policy can devise. But into how many wars would the nations of Europe have been dragged, before this Machiavellian system could have attained its end, before the British Empire could have been divided? For this policy would have been constantly, if unevenly, followed by ministers interested in occupying their nation with conquests, whether in order to retain their own posts, to avoid domestic troubles, or the secession of colonies, or subtlely to destroy the constitution and create an absolute monarchy. Perhaps more than a century of oppression and wars would have preceded the time when the division of this empire would have caused peace and freedom of the seas to be reborn. Thus, humanity can forgive the American war by remembering the evils this war preserved it from.

The same revolution should make European wars more rare. Indeed it cannot be denied that the Americans are almost the absolute masters of making the balance in the American seas incline in favor of the power they favor. They can conquer and protect these seas more easily than can Europeans. Furthermore, the inhabitants of these islands, indifferent about the name of the power to whom they belong because they are not so much real proprietors of the land as simple contractors, would be disposed to unite themselves with a people who, scorning to command subjects, want only fellow citizens, and for whom conquest means only having the conquered share independence and liberty. It may happen that English, French, or Spanish colonials fear the coming of Americans to their countries more than they desire it, if Americans but banish slavery in their own country and if the European powers have the barbarity to preserve it. Then the Americans would be only more certain of success, for upon their arrival on each island, they would find numerous partisans, animated by all the courage that vengeance and the hope of liberty can inspire.

Thus, when the United States has rectified the evils that were the price of its independence, no nation of Europe could prudently undertake a war in seas where it will be in danger of losing all if the United States were her enemy. . . .

By their example, Americans will also serve to maintain peace in Europe. In the Old World, some eloquent philosophers—Voltaire, in particular—protested against the injustice and absurdity of war, but they did not succeed in mitigating martial fury. The immense throng of men who aspire to glory and fortune only through massacre jeered at their protests, and repeated in books, in camps, and in courts, that patriotism and virtue no longer existed since an abominable philosophy wanted to spare human blood.

But in America, these same peaceful opinions are those of a

great and brave people who successfully defended their homes and broke their chains. All idea of war undertaken for ambition and conquest is stigmatized by the calm judgment of a humane and peaceful nation. There the language of humanity and justice cannot be the object of jeers, either for the warlike courtiers of a king, or for the ambitious heads of a republic. There, the honor of defending one's country is supreme, and no military state weighs heavily upon the citizen. What can the warlike prejudices of Europe set against this example?

### *Part III. Its Advantages with reference to the perfectability of mankind.*

We have tried to show how the example of America and the enlightenment born of the freedom to discuss all matters important to man's happiness can be valuable in destroying the prejudices that still prevail in Europe. But there is another kind of usefulness we feel it our duty to consider, even though we are convinced that it will appear chimerical to the majority of our readers.

America is a country of vast extent, with millions of men preserved by their education from prejudice, and disposed toward study and reflection. There exist no social distinctions, no lure of ambition, that can turn them away from their natural desire to improve their minds, to apply themselves to useful studies, to aspire to that glory which rewards great enterprises and discoveries. And nothing there holds down a portion of humanity to that abject condition which condemns it to ignorance and poverty. There is reason, then, to hope that, by producing almost as many men who contribute to knowledge as all Europe, America will, in a few generations, double the progress of Mankind and make that progress doubly swift. That progress will embrace both the useful arts and the speculative sciences.

The good that can result from this must be added to the consequences of the revolution. Dependency upon the mother country would not have extinguished the natural genius of Americans; M. Franklin is proof of this. But it would almost certainly have turned this genius toward other objects. The desire to be important in England would have stifled all other sentiments in an American born with industry and talent, and he would have chosen the surest and most rapid means of succeeding. Those who might not have been able to nourish this ambition would have fallen into discouragement and indolence. . . .

Perhaps you are surprised to see me place discoveries, inventions, and the progress of knowledge alongside such great objectives as the preservation of human rights, the maintenance of peace, and even the advantages that result from commerce. Having been long concerned with the means of ameliorating the lot of humanity, I cannot help believing that there really is only one means: to accelerate the progress of enlightenment. All others have only a limited and momentary effect. Even if we were to admit that error, legend, and laws deriving from local prejudices, have made for the happiness of some nations, we would be forced to admit that in every case this overrated blessing has disappeared within a short time, to make way for evils that reason has not yet been able to cure, even in several centuries. Let man be enlightened, and you will soon see good born, without effort, from the common will.

### *Part IV. On the Good the American Revolution can do for Europe, and for France in particular, through Commerce.*

Up to this point, we have considered mainly the advantages that are by their very nature common to all nations. That of maintaining peace has greater importance for nations that, like France, Spain, England, and Holland, are exposed to wars in the American islands. France will draw more advantage than any other European nation from the sound ideas of Americans on the rights of property and on natural liberty, for having greater need of these than the English nation, she is in that stage of enlightenment which will permit her to profit by them. She also enjoys a constitution whereby beneficial reforms would encounter only few obstacles to overcome, far fewer obstacles than in England.

We will begin by examining the advantages to the commerce of all nations that will result from the American Revolution. We will then consider if, in this matter, France should have some special advantages. But before undertaking this examination, it will be useful to inquire what kind of advantage a nation might derive from foreign commerce.

It finds first that of procuring necessary (or almost necessary) commodities it lacks, or procuring them at advantageous prices, and of having a greater assurance of not being without them. Second, that of increasing, by greater outflow of domestic products or manufactured objects, the interest of cultivators in multiplying their yield, and at the same time, of increasing industry and the activity of manufacturers who can expand without adversely affecting the produce of the land and consequently real wealth.

These two advantages, that of a more favorable or more certain importation of goods, and that of extended export, might seem to be identical, for one can hardly exist without the other. But we differentiate between them, because the direct object of the first is the increase of well-being, and of the second, the increase of wealth. We should also observe that production cannot increase in a country without having this surplus of goods reduce the danger of being without them.

We can also count among the advantages of foreign commerce those that a nation derives from its industry and from its skill in trading. A people who inhabit a barren rock and who have capital could exist and even increase this capital by receiving each year as a reward for its work or its speculations a portion of the territorial revenue of another nation.

This third advantage, the most important for small nations engaged solely in commerce and industry, is almost nonexistent for large nations occupying vast territories.

Commerce is always based on exchange, and on exchange of goods that are consumed each year. Otherwise, it could not last, for a nation that would each year exchange, for a commodity it needs, a commodity that it never consumed, would find itself by the end of a certain period in the impossibility of making such exchanges. . . .

All extension of free trade is good, first, in that it necessarily results in more encouragement for cultivation and more benefits for the same price, and second, in that each nation sooner reaches the point of cultivating or manufacturing only what it can cultivate or manufacture with the most advantage. The increase in wealth and in well-being that can easily result from establishing this natural order is incalculable. Unfortunately, the passion of all nations for cultivating and manufacturing everything possible, with a view toward buying nothing outside the country, proves how much the benefits of extended free trade are unrecognized even today.

Americans, occupying an immense land not yet fully reclaimed, cannot be anything but cultivators for a long time to come. In a free country, all men, whatever their activity, will prefer the condition of proprietor to all others, as long as there is hope of attaining it without sacrificing too much comfort. For a long time to come, America will have only raw material to bring to Europe, and manufactured goods to take from there. She will have little money to invest in commerce, for the large share of her capital will be devoted to the cost of reclaiming land in distant areas. The only commodity she will need from Europe, and will continue for a long time to require, is wine, one of those products whose export is most profitable.

At the same time, France seems to be the European nation for which trade with America is the most important: 1. Because she is obliged to expend money to obtain from the North oils, iron, hemp, and woods that she could procure in America in exchange for her manufactured goods. 2. Because in the years of grain shortages, the wheat and rice of America would be an important resource for her provinces located on the ocean, or connected with the sea by canals and navigable rivers. 3. Because she can establish with America an extended commerce in wines, and having almost a monopoly in this particular commodity at the same time that she can maintain at least relative competition with England in manufactured goods, it must naturally follow that this necessary trade give her the preferences over England for all the others. There is no doubt that France has preference over the rest of the European nations as long as the industry of Portugal and Spain make no progress.

One might suppose that England would on the contrary have this superiority, and certainly, all things being equal, the conformity of language, way of life, and religion, combined with the habit of using English manufactured goods, could have a great influence. But it must be noted that this influence would be strong only at the outset. And at this moment, the remains of well-founded indignation, the liaisons contracted during the last war, must necessarily diminish the effect of reasons which might have led Americans to give their preference to England. France, on the other hand, will have the time to employ means dependent upon her alone to prevent these reasons from counteracting its real advantages. Our mills will soon learn to conform to the taste and the needs of Americans, whom our merchants will learn to know and to provide for.

Communication in the two languages can be facilitated by establishing schools in some of our cities, where Americans would send their children to be educated, where indeed they would even send large numbers of them if all religious instruction were banned.

Religion must not be an obstacle for long. The most important dogma for Americans, the one they cherish most, is the dogma of tolerance, or rather of religious freedom; for in that nation, inspired more than any other by reason alone, the word "tolerance" seems almost an insult to human nature. Indeed, why should we despair of seeing tolerance (forgive my use of this European word) soon established in our own country? Doesn't it already exist in the Old World from Kamchatka to Iceland, from Lapland to the Apennines? The princes of the house of Capet are the only great sovereigns who have not yet admitted it to their states. In France, the unanimous voices of all enlightened men in the clergy, the nobility, the magistracy, in commerce, continue to solicit this revolution. Will these pleas be useless? Should we not hope instead that the government will give in to the reasons of justice and that tolerance will be established in France on a more regular basis, more consistent with natural justice? We would thereby repair the misfortune (or perhaps the shame) of having so long delayed in following the example of other nations. . . .

It is impossible that one more nation added to the small number of those actively and intelligently engaged in commerce, should not increase competition among these nations, and the natural effect of such competition would be the lowering of transport expenses. It is also an advantage for all nations who have no other interest than to procure for themselves, in ample quantity and at the lowest possible price, the goods that need or habit have made essential to them.

In short, we must not believe that commerce with America should be limited to those objects it now furnishes Europe. This immense land contains so many resources barely known today to our naturalists and almost unknown even to its inhabitants, whose use will become familiar to us through trade. Even if this conjecture were not based upon knowledge of several products which it is easy to predict will some day become objects for trade, this hope should not be considered chimerical. It would be absolutely contrary to the established order of nature if this vast continent offered only products valuable or common to Europe.

Austere philosophers will perhaps tell us that this advantage, which would serve only to create new needs for us, should be considered as evil. But we answer that it will instead give us new resources to satisfy those needs nature subjects us to. In all lands and in all ages where a great inequality of fortunes exists, men will always have artificial needs and the contagion of example will cause them to be felt even by those prevented by poverty from satisfying them. Thus to multiply the means for satisfying these artificial needs and to make these means less costly is to do real good, to render inequality of wealth less tangible, less dangerous for mutual accord. If ever the slow but certain influence of a good legislative system can destroy this inequality in Europe, the artificial needs this inequality inspires will disappear with it; or rather, only those that are necessary to preserve the activity, the industry, and the curiosity necessary to human progress, and consequently to human happiness, will remain. . . .

If we examine the history of the administration of the United States since the declaration of its independence, we will not find constitutions equally well devised in all states. There is none wherein some fault cannot be found. All the laws established since the act of independence are not equally just and wise, but no section of political or criminal legislation offers gross errors, or oppressive or ruinous principles. In the operations of finance and commerce, on the other hand, almost everything points to a constant struggle between old European prejudices and the principles of justice and liberty that are so clear to this respectable nation, and often these prejudices have won the victory.

However, after acknowledging these failings, the love of Americans for equality, their respect for liberty, for freedom, and the form of their constitutions, will doubtless always prevent these prohibitions, whether absolute or indirectly prescribed by the establishment of enormous fees, exclusive trade privileges, monopolies on certain commodities, inspections insulting and contrary to the rights of citizens, barbarous laws against fraud, exclusive corporations of goods or workmen, and finally all the absurd vexations that the mercantilist mind and the passion for regulation and oppression have produced in Europe. The example of America will at least teach us to see their uselessness and to recognize their injustice. . . .

# 9.

## The Marquis de Chastellux

*"However important the discovery of America may appear, its most important advantage to Europe has been in expanding and increasing her commerce."*

ANOTHER AUTHOR WHO TURNED his attention to the prize context at Lyons was the MARQUIS FRANÇOIS JEAN DE CHASTELLUX. Chastellux was not only a man of letters; he was also a military man, and seemed perhaps better qualified than many other essayists, for he had spent nearly three years traveling in America, even taking an active part in the American Revolution.

Born into a noble family in 1734 in Paris, Chastellux entered the army at fifteen, and at twenty-one was colonel of his own regiment. He later served as colonel in the Guyenne regiment, and took a distinguished part in all the German campaigns between 1756 and 1763. Other promotions followed, and in 1780 he went to America as an officer in the expedition sent from France to help the colonies in their war against Great Britain. He served as a major general in Rochambeau's army; courageous and intelligent, he earned the respect and friendship of General Washington.

Chastellux's travel experiences in America eventually resulted in the publication of his complete journals, *Voyages dans l'Amérique septentrionale dans les années 1780, 1781 et 1782* (Paris, 2 vols., 1786), but this was only after the journals had first appeared separately and a bad pirated edition from Cassel had published them together. The first part of the journals treated his voyage from Newport to Philadelphia and was first printed in a very small edition on a portable printing press located on a French warship lying off Newport; the second part of the journals concerned travels through Virginia and Pennsylvania, and appeared first in small sections in the *Journal de Gotha.* When the illegal edition of Cassel appeared, entitled *Voyage du Chevalier de Chastellux*, the unfavorable publicity of this edition caused Chastellux to give the authorized combined *Voyages* of 1786.

Among his other publications, the most important is undoubtedly *De la Félicité publique* (Amsterdam, 2 vols., 1772). This work, greatly admired by Voltaire, earned Chastellux his place among the Immortals; he was elected to the French Academy in 1775, and his inaugural address, entitled "Sur le goût," was published under the title of *Discours de Réception à l'Académie française* in 1775. He also published his translations from the Italian of Argarotti's *Essai sur l'Opéra* (Paris and Pisa, 1775) and from the English, Humphreys's *Discours en vers adressé aux officiers et soldats des armées américaines* (Paris, 1786).

His *Discours sur les avantages et les désavantages qui résultent pour l'Europe de la découverte de l'Amérique* appeared in both London and Paris in 1787. The main point of Chastellux's essay is simple: The discovery of America brought about an extraordinary expansion of commerce for Europe, and since foreign commerce seems to be the remedy for most of the ills now plaguing the Old World, the discovery of America was clearly a great blessing. The essay, however. was never submitted to the Lyons Academy. In a preface to this edition, the editor explains that no prize was awarded by the Academy, and that he, the editor, thought it well to present the essay in this form to the public.

The *Discours* was published just one year before Chastellux's death. Toward the end of 1787, Chastellux married an Irish woman, a Miss Plunkett, whom he had met at Spa. The marriage appears not to have been a very happy one, though it was short-lived. Chastellux died in Paris on October 28, 1788.

## ON THE ADVANTAGES AND DISADVANTAGES RESULTING FOR EUROPE FROM THE DISCOVERY OF AMERICA

. . . LET US start with an admission which does not seem difficult and which will perhaps lead us to discussions whose result will serve as basis for our opinion. However important the discovery of America may appear, whatever luster it may have given to the age that brought it about, whatever light it may have shed on succeeding centuries, we cannot doubt that its most important advantage to Europe has been in expanding and increasing her commerce. If commerce were not the very source of prosperity for nations; if, on the contrary, it tended to cause disorder in society, to upset the balance of wealth and possessions, to diminish populations, to stir up rivalries and eternal hatreds among nations, it would be useless to go any further in considering the subject we have proposed. A sterile admiration would be the sole reward for the accomplishment of the immortal Columbus, and the laurel that grows on his grave would be watered only by our tears. Thus our subject, already vast in itself, expands and this new question arises: *Is commerce favorable or adverse to the prosperity of nations?*

There are those whose imaginations, more capricious than enlightened, evoke countries sufficiently protected by seas and rivers, where a fertile terrain, always ready to respond to the slightest solicitations, furnishes ample food for those who work it in common or who continue to share it equally as they increase in number, for those populations who even as they increase never need fear famine or the caprice of the elements. Let those who believe these fancies cast doubt upon the advantages of commerce. Let them even violently disparage it and consider it to be the perdition of nations. Gladly will I forgive them, and I am even disposed to subscribe to their opinion providing they can put into effect these dreams produced by their illusions. But as long as history and observation continue to show, in the regions of the east and south, the fertility of terrain offset by inclemency of weather or the languor of its inhabitants, the increase in population offset by the cowardliness of men or the oppression they are subject to; and in the regions of the west and north, the most refractory land and elements conquered solely by man's ingenuity, and this ingenuity aroused by love of property and desire for wealth, I will conclude that commerce is advantageous to nations. . . .

But why resort to vain speculations? We need only look about us and consider things as they are. Doubtless what has happened up to now was unavoidable, nor are we able to remake the world. Looking about us, what do we see? Except for nomads or races that thrive on hunting alone, the right of property is universally established. Property is considered the basis of all society, the safeguard of nations and the source of public welfare. And what limitations are there to the right of property? None, other than the contribution required for the defense of the state, and it can be easily proved that this is less a limitation upon property than an expense necessary for its preservation. This natural and precious right is not limited to the possession of a piece of land or of chattels; it extends to one's work, to one's trade or activity. It consists not only in the right of preservation, but also in that of expansion and acquisition. Would that individual who, by his talents or his labors, has accumulated some capital, whatever its nature, be in reality the master of this capital if he were unable to use it to acquire whatever he pleased? And the man who possesses a field, would he in truth be its owner if he were forbidden to sell it or to convert it into other assets?

On the other hand, all that man's labor brings him in excess of bare essentials becomes capital which, by different progressions, leads him to barter or to commerce, and from there, to wealth. If his harvest exceeds his normal consumption, the wheat in his granary can be considered capital, for the following year, not having to sow more in order to meet his needs, he can cultivate a vineyard. If the vineyard produces more than his needs, the work he had devoted to it can then be turned to cultivating hemp or anything else, until the rewards of this labor, no longer necessary to satisfy his needs and to provide him with possessions, can be used to pay for those of others and thus enable him to enjoy what he could not have obtained by his own labor. Free use of property and industry, then, leads to the formation of capital, this capital to the need for exchange, and this exchange is nothing but commerce.

Thus, since the use of property cannot be limited, since capital of any size can come from all possessions and any kind of labor, and since wealth that continually increases is born of this capital, it has been demonstrated that inequality in fortunes necessarily arises from property. It has also been proved that, just as means exist for augmenting fortunes, so are there ways of diminishing them. It has been proved that if prosperity invites one to buy, poverty and distress oblige another to sell; that it is in fact desirable that capital constantly be reinvested in agriculture and that, as much as possible, wealth be allied with ownership of land. Moreover, observation, which is always preferable to mere speculation, teaches us that the majority of nations have followed a course opposite to that which several philosophers have supposed. According to them, advances in agriculture have preceded those of commerce, whereas on the contrary, it happens that they came about only after the latter. Everything depends upon capital. Experience proves that whatever its sources, the success of all enterprise is due to its expenditure. . . .

Those European nations possessing colonies in America have gained from them the appreciable advantage of having expanded their commerce, of having brought into it preferential merchandise that is certain to stimulate all exchanges and, while filling in many respects the functions of gold and silver, still has the property of not being able to be accumulated, of not depreciating (for it is quickly consumed and its demand is constantly renewed). On the other hand, the nations that have no colonies, in experiencing new desires and new pleasures, owe the increase in their agriculture and their domestic activity to these desires.

Let us return to the first principles that have already served, and always should serve, as the basis for our opinions. I should like to speak of the necessity of supporting the poor at the expense of the proprietor. You will see at a glance that the needs and the passions of the proprietor cannot be underestimated. You who protest against luxury, would you banish all refinement in food and drink? Then you should banish refinement in all other pleasures as well. Banish the arts whose object is always to encourage new expenditures—the fine arts in particular, which serve to relieve the proprietor of the burden of his riches and which, in perfecting his faculties, so closely ally his desires with his thoughts that he soon loses all sense of his power and indeed becomes dependent upon them.

It is a fond illusion to rely upon the nature of man, to believe it good in itself. But who can have faith in the rich man? The powerful man who lives without luxury, without taste, without pleasures, is the vilest, the most abject of tyrants. But if this great lord who rules over an entire region becomes a sensitive man, refined in his pleasures, he will soon find good use for his wealth. He will no longer have an excess of riches, and it is just that excess which gives the sense of independence whose consequences are oppression and tyranny. He will no longer amass the products of his land just to let them rot, or distribute them according to his whims; instead he will be eager to exchange them for goods from the colonies, those noble children of commerce and industry who know no other master and who are proud not to have been born under the scourge of feudalism. . . .

You guilty conquerors of this hemisphere discovered by genius, and that commerce alone should have governed, why do you force me to a painful reckoning of your atrocities? Why should I find myself reduced to enumerating all the means of prosperity that you have involuntarily caused, in order to compensate, if possible, for all the ills you make me deplore? . . .

But was it really necessary for Europeans to cross the seas to become unjust and bloodthirsty? Should we blame the discovery of America for all the vices of its age? Are not the Moors and Jews of Spain experiencing the bloodiest persecutions even in our own wretched times? When Italy was being ravaged by domestic tyrants and foreign brigands, was not the noble and ancient empire of the Germans bowed under the iron yoke of despotism and intolerance? Were not scaffolds raised in England and in Holland? And did not the blood of both foreigner and citizen inundate France? Did not fanaticism and superstition reign over all Europe? If we were to see cruel wolves come down from the mountains to devour innocent flocks of sheep, would we say it was these timid sheep that made the wolves greedy and bloodthirsty? . . .

Already I hear other objections, no longer to all the misfortunes of the New World, but rather to the depopulation of the Old. To unnecessary possessions that were long unknown, these objectives oppose a cruel plague, a malady that is all the more dangerous for having sensual pleasure as its minister, and for attacking men at the very moment they fulfill the first wish of nature, that of reproduction. And finally, against all the undisputed advantages of extensive commerce, I see opposed the dangers of long and difficult navigation.

I have hidden nothing, and I hope to give answer to all. To begin with, the depopulation of Spain, the only nation this objection can concern, was not due to the discovery of America, but rather to the expulsion of Moors and Jews, to the terrors inspired by a fanatical Tribunal, to superstition which increased the number of monks and celibates, to ignorance, to the weakness of the last Austrian monarchs, to expensive foreign wars, to the frequent sacrifices the Spanish branch of this ruling house was obliged to make to the Germanic branch. . . .

I wish it were as easy to absolve America of the second objection, which seems to me only too well-grounded, for I will not try to avail myself of the opinion of a few modern authors who claim that the discovery of the New World was not the origin of a dreadful malady which was nevertheless unknown until that time. . . . I continue to believe that the island of Santo Domingo was the home of this terrible disease, and that it was brought to Europe from there. But I would ask that we at least concede that this fatal event could have happened even if Europeans had established no colonies in America. Pure accident could have led a vessel to one of the islands found at the entrance of the Gulf of Mexico. . . . If then a simple call at one of these islands could have sufficed to produce so many disorders, we might well complain of nature herself who surrounds us everywhere with snares, and not of the discovery of America which not only taught us to cure the malady it caused, but also gave us quinine, the most efficacious remedy for other ailments that the Old World was only too justified in considering its own heritage.

But even if it were true that the delights of certain products of America, and the utility of others, compensated for the deadly acquisition upon which we have already too long fixed our attention, what can compensate for the dangers of the long and perilous voyage? Up to now, only the land was avid to devour its own children; and now also the sea, which did not give them birth, offers them a vast tomb. . . . But then! Was the daring art of navigation born only at the moment of the discovery of America? Until that time, navigation was timid and cautious. If men left the land where nature had ordained their habitation, their glance at least remained attached to it and did not yet turn upward except to beseech the heavens and not to study them. Yet it was precisely this timid ignorance that caused their destruction. It is near the coast that shipwrecks are the most frequent. How many fleets have been sunk in full view of the shore! History offers a thousand examples, especially in that time when need had not yet obliged industry to develop all its resources. There is no doubt that there were far more dangers for the vessels *Drusus* and *Germanicus* sailing along the coasts of Germany than there are for the *Cook* and the *Peyrouse* sailing around the world. Peter the First used to say that the victories of his greatest rival would teach him to be victorious in turn. Our modern navies can apply this clever thought to themselves, for if commerce with America did at first cause some loss of life, it is this very commerce that by perfecting navigation removed almost all the dangers that existed earlier. Far from destroying more and more men, commerce in fact favors their increase everywhere. . . .

Up to this point we have considered America only as a producer of luxury goods that are intended merely to give pleasure. Europeans, consider it henceforth as insurance against the famines that only too often afflict you. Differences in latitude influence only the nature of produce; longitudinal differences have the particular advantage of favoring produce similar to our own, but that grows under different conditions. A north or south wind, if it blows long enough, can bring destructive drought or injurious rains from St. Petersburg to Madrid. But either the prevailing winds of North America are different from those we know, or they produce different effects. The northwest winds which here announce rain and storms, there bring calm; and the east winds that bring our good weather, the zephyrs so celebrated by our poets, in America carry snow and hail and storms. Thus one hemisphere can always come to the help of the other. Will not so many combined advantages prevail over the momentary disadvantages whose effect is lessening daily?

. . . Yet a new duty is now imposed upon me. That friend and benefactor of humanity who wished to encourage our efforts, doubtless foreseeing the results, has asked that if the discovery of America is recognized to be beneficial to Europe, we should develop means of multiplying these benefits, as well as for mitigating whatever disadvantages might also result; for where on this earth can good exist that is not mixed with evil?

To have fulfilled the first part of this task is to be far advanced in the second. Such is the happy union of the principles of reason and humanity with those of enlightened self-interest, that the results of both must always be identical. Only the motive for actions distinguishes the good man from the clever speculator.

One part of the American continent and almost all of the islands are unhealthy for habitation; one part of the American continent and almost all the islands are cultivated by slaves, and these slaves are even more miserable than their state of servitude should of itself cause them to be. Let us see how the light of reason and self-interest will eventually succeed in remedying this disadvantage.

Let us first of all establish as a principle that if any place in particular can be unhealthy for its inhabitants, no region in general can be so for the races native to it, or for those it has assimilated over a period of years. When Europeans settled in the American islands, the first colonists, for the most part made up of adventurers and people committed to vice and debauchery, found themselves as badly prepared for inhabiting these new climates as they were unaccustomed to their effects. For a long time, on the other hand, ignorance and greed prevented them from choosing, for cultivation, those regions where the air was least harmful. Whether the terrain was dry or marshy, exposed to harmful winds or to refreshing breezes, the place most adapted to the production of sugar cane, closest to the sea and its loading docks, was always preferred. If fatal epidemics came to carry off the masters and slaves, greed immediately replaced them with other imprudent men and other unfortunates. Why should anyone expect greed to follow a different course in the New World from the Old? . . . In the islands, when all the most desirable regions were occupied, new adventurers were obliged to undertake more arduous reclamations, and the need for water, almost general in all regions, necessitated opening up canals and providing new drainage. By degrees, cultivation of the land extended into those places that had at first been neglected, even into those marshes whose dangerous effluvia were borne far and wide by the winds. A general rule, in America as in Europe: all uncultivated land is unhealthy to live on; all land that has been well-reclaimed and cultivated is free of this disadvantage. Thus, advances in agriculture, as has already been proved in Martinique, Guadaloupe, and Santo Domingo, and will be one day in Santa Lucia and Puerto Rico, are the best means for making countries healthy.

But what is the best means of advancing agriculture—multiplying the workmen who are almost its sole instruments. If avarice has for a long time preferred to demand more work of these men rather than to increase their number, we should deplore this iniquity, just as we deplore all those men are guilty of. . . . Again it is here that the advances made in commerce will serve to remedy the harm it has caused. The more commerce flourishes, the more capital it creates, and this is the capital to be used for increasing the number of Negroes and thus advancing agriculture. Note that the salubriousness of the climate is not the only advantage we can envisage in this amelioration; for if on one hand the increase in Negroes produces an increase in land reclamation, on the other hand it cannot help, sooner or later, to bring about some relief in the lot of these miserable victims of our greed, for often it is the disproportion between the nature of the work required and the number of available workers that necessitates overtaxing them. . . . Furthermore, the vast sums used for the purchase of Negroes will soon make their acquisition most difficult. The markets will no longer be so well supplied. Africa itself will no longer be able to fulfill this demand. Alas! must we be obliged, to the great shame of humanity, to wait until that time before we can see the colonist turn all his efforts and attention to the preservation of his slaves? Indeed, must slavery itself continue to degrade commerce and corrupt the source of public prosperity? . . .

Yet legislation has not been able—and perhaps will not for a long time be able—to banish slavery. It is nevertheless starting to relieve its miseries, and relieving them implies working toward destroying them. Let me explain what I mean. Everyone who has known the colonies and fathomed the details of their workings knows that on one hand the Negro raised on the plantation is better treated than the Negro brought in from the outside; and on the other hand, that this slave is more attached, more faithful, and more capable of improving himself. It will therefore be a great step forward when the good treatment of Negroes has favored their multiplying, and continued importations will no longer be necessary. Nor is that all: these domiciled Negroes, brought up with our customs and our principles, will soon form on the plantation a sort of family in which the relations between master and slave will be more gentle and more humane. The white man will lose some of his pride, the Negro some of his abjectness. When a certain lapse of time shall have improved this foreign population, what is to prevent its being granted a share, an interest in the profits of its own work? The Negro should not, at least not at the outset, be made a totally free farmer or day laborer, but rather a serf attached to the land. Moreover—for I do not want to impose any limits to my hopes—what will prevent the black serf from becoming free one day just as the European serf became free? . . .

We have thus far considered the colonies only in terms of their relation to commerce in general and to the public prosperity which is its effect. Let us admit now that they are essential to every nation that is already old, and by this word *old* I mean a nation whose population is large, where wealth is considerable and unevenly distributed, where the subsistence of the majority of its people is difficult and precarious—in short, a nation such as France or England. In those nations, a sort of wheel of fortune continually spins and exerts not only a central force which condenses and restrains, but also a centrifugal force that repulses and disperses. The large majority of individuals closely follow its revolutions, but others are thrown out of this sphere of activity. Often the poor man's hands cannot hold on to the support they have grasped; often the rich man falls from the comfortable chair he is seated upon. Around this fatal wheel, one can see unfortunates ceaselessly wandering, some deprived of their fortunes, others of their illusions. All are badly pressed; all try to climb back upon it, and if crime is the only step they have, they might well resort to it. But Hope, whom they no longer believe in after having so often been deceived, appears here in another form. Dressed in foreign clothes, surrounded by unfamiliar products, she calls them to the shore and shows them a vessel about to set sail. Crowds of them come running; they depart, and often their expectations are not disappointed. But always, the nation is freed of their troubled activity or of their despair that is as dangerous for their compatriots as it is for themselves.

Just consider this spring whose gentle waters trace among the pebbles an oblique and arduous path. Wherever you draw water, you will find it fresh and healthful; but if its slope should carry it toward some large basin, the inevitable end of its course, it will soon lose its purity. Thus if you wish the ornament of your garden not to become infected, you must arrange for this confined water to have a hidden drain which will still give it some appearance of movement and liberty. The European population is like this water surrounded by obstacles and always ready to become corrupt or to overflow. The colonies are the release, the necessary drain by which the excess must run out. . . .

Thus the discovery of America has been advantageous for the European nations:

1. Because in giving greater impulse to commerce, in introducing a preferential commodity that has all the advantages of coined metals with none of the disadvantages, it has expanded trade, increased the needs of the rich, and contributed to the means by which industry succeeds in recovering its share in property.

2. Because in creating new wealth on the face of the earth, it has increased the circulation of this wealth, and more evenly distributed it, for the more differing weights one puts on the scales, the easier it is to strike a balance.

3. Because in the age in which this discovery took place, in those disastrous times when military despotism had assumed empire over the land, when war was the only recourse open to greed and conquest its sole objective, it was necessary to look elsewhere and to substitute the balance of wealth for that of power.

4. Because America opened up a vast asylum to persecuted virtue, to frustrated ambition, to crime hesitating between despair and repentance, so that to this discovery we owe the preservation of the good, the exile of the evil, and the rehabilitation of the depraved.

5. Because while its commerce and its particular produce increase labor and redouble activity in the Old World, the abundance of those products common to both hemispheres but which grow under different conditions and at great distances apart, insures the Old World against inclement seasons and the famines that are their consequence.

And if we still fear we have paid too dearly for such great advantages, if we deplore on the one hand the many victims of the burning climate and the rash emigrations, and on the other the revival of a barbarous practice that our religion and our morals had proscribed, we can now recognize that these evils attached to property itself are due less to the discovery of America than to the age in which this discovery took place. Medicine, instructed by experiments and new objects of study, is now starting to cure the maladies that came to us from that hemisphere while it also finds powerful relief against those maladies that have always been our lot. We can now be persuaded that progress in agriculture will mitigate the heat and prevent the malignant influence of a torrid climate, and that the progress of reason and humanity will soon relieve the burden of slavery and finally eradicate it. . . .

# 10.

## Friedrich von Gentz

*"The discovery of America is a decisive gain for mankind in every possible way."*

THE GERMAN PUBLICIST AND statesman, FRIEDRICH VON GENTZ, born in Breslau, Silesia in 1764, spent his successful career almost entirely in the service of Austria. In 1778, his father, a general director of the Mint, moved his family to Berlin where Gentz attended the Joachimsthal Gymnasium; later he attended the University of Koenigsberg where the philosopher Kant was one of his teachers.

Returning to Berlin from the university, Gentz was employed in the Department of Finance, in an ordinary functionary's situation in which he remained until he went to Austria in 1802. During this early period he was an articulate liberal. Enthusiastic over the early reforms of the French Revolution which curbed absolute power, he expressed himself in pamphlets attacking the Prussian abuses in the court of the aging Frederick William II. When this autocrat died in 1797 and was succeeded by Frederick William III, Gentz addressed a memorandum to the new king, urging him to found his reign on liberal ideas, social reforms, freedom of commerce, and notably freedom of the press. In later years, when from a secure position of influence, Gentz just as emphatically supported repression in the universities and suppression of the press, his enemies reprinted the 1797 pamphlet and used it in attacks against him.

It is from this liberal period that his essay on the results of the discovery of America is dated (1795). The essay reflects many of the same liberal ideas found in the missive to the king. Not only was the discovery of America a blessing, it was to be counted above such events as the Reformation and the invention of printing in the order of things advancing man's enlightenment and well-being. The benefits already obtained by Europe have been remarkable, and the greatness of America and its new Republic would only be continually enhanced by free trade and freedom of the press.

Around the turn of the century, Gentz's political ideas changed in a rather dramatic way, and it is this evolution which has made him such a controversial figure. This transformation from liberal to conservative was not a sudden thing, however. Undoubtedly Gentz was already sympathetic to more conservative views when in 1794 he published his translation into German of Burke's *Essay on the French Revolution.* In 1799, he founded his *Historisches Journal* in which he published articles hostile to the French Republic, articles which also found favor with British policy toward France. The journal was discontinued after only a year, and Gentz published instead a number of essays on European politics, these, too, having particular reference to France and its affairs. In his *Über den Unsprung und Charakter des Krieges gegen die französische Revolution* (On the Origins and Character of the War against France), 1801, he is critical of the German government for having made peace with France. In the same year, his *Essay on the Administration of Finance in Great Britain* praised the British system, criticized the French, and put him in even greater favor with England.

Dissatisfied with his mediocre post in Germany, in need of more and more money for the stylish life he had come to lead, and critical of German thought and politics—indeed, his hatred of German nationalism and of Prussia remained constant all his life—he went to Vienna and entered the service of the Austrian government as publicist with the title of imperial councilor and a large income. In the same year (1802) he also traveled to England where he was warmly received, and there granted another pension for his services as publicist to England. His most notable writings in the next several years were almost all directed against Napoleon and his aggressions; *Fragments on the Balance of Power in Europe* (Leipsig, 1805; London, 1806) is perhaps the most important of these. Napoleon is reputed to have referred to him as "a wretched scribe named Gentz, one of those men without honor who sell themselves for money," although it has been recognized that in reality Gentz wrote nothing that was in conflict with his own beliefs or principles.

In a position of increasing influence, Gentz strove for an alliance among Austria and Prussia and England to resist Napoleon, but his efforts were unsuccessful. In 1812, he met Metternich and became his close friend and adviser. After the downfall of Napoleon, Gentz served as secretary to all of the important congresses in Europe from the Congress of Vienna in 1814 to that of Verona in 1822, being in a real sense the "Secretary of Europe." [1] By 1820, the Austrian government was in such a supremely sound position in Europe, both in internal and external affairs, that Gentz's services as publicist were no longer required, though he continued to receive a large pension for the rest of his life. Weary, cynical, and at the end of his life apathetic, he died in Vienna on June 9, 1832.

## ON THE INFLUENCE OF THE DISCOVERY OF AMERICA ON THE PROSPERITY AND CULTURE OF THE HUMAN RACE

PLACING THE DISCOVERY of the fourth part of the world and the concurrent discovery of the passage to the East Indies around the Cape of Good Hope on the same level of importance with the invention of printing, the Reformation of Luther, the emigration of learned Greeks from Constantinople, and other great events of the fifteenth and sixteenth centuries, does not do them justice. Not only did these two events bring about greater changes and revolutions in the physical and intellectual condition of the human race than did even the most fruitful of those other things with which they are compared; they also invested all other great events with their full power and their true dimensions. Even more, by their very nature alone, they sooner or later had to affect not only what actually had happened but, of necessity, all the great advances of mankind toward happiness and culture. . . .

If the discovery of America had had no other effect than that

[1] Golo Mann, *Secretary of Europe: The Life of Friedrich von Gentz, Enemy of Napoleon,* New Haven, 1946.

envisaged by the first adventurers to travel to that part of the world—that is, covering Europe with a flood of gold and silver obtained without effort from the surface of the earth—it would have been of less consequence for the welfare of mankind than the least improvement in the most insignificant mechanical art. If the route to the East and West Indies had had no other result than the enrichment of a half-million European merchants, it would have been epoch-making in the history of trade, but not in world history. Finally, if the occupation of those distant lands had raised two or three European powers to the highest pinnacle of splendor and political importance without having any salutary influence upon other states and upon humanity in general, this occupation would certainly be important in the history of those powers, and in any case in the history of the balance of power, but never would it attain a significant position in a general picture of human progress.

Since the genius of an enlightened generation has combated and dispelled so many misleading phantoms of national wealth, national strength, and national prosperity; since gold and silver are no longer considered the greatest treasure of a state, nor trade monopolies and advantageous trade balances the critical point of orientation of a wise administration, nor the weakening or destruction of neighboring powers the greatest triumph of its policies, we must look elsewhere for an explanation of the unmistakable connection between communication with the East and West Indies and the continually increasing progress of civilization and human prosperity despite political blunders, national enmities, and violent, bloody wars.

If we can forget for a moment the misery and oppression suffered at the hands of Europeans by the greatest part of America and all provinces of the East Indies; if we can forget the shortsighted and fanatical despotism enthroned in Brazil, Peru, and Mexico, and the rule that a merchant society on the Thames, protected by a free and liberal constitution, exerts over the former slaves of the Moguls; if we direct our view toward North America alone, we are impelled to consider the condition of this country as the final and greatest result, the single important gain, of the crossing of the Atlantic by Europeans and their efforts to explore new parts of the world.

Actually, if European navigation and the good fortune which crowned it at the close of the fifteenth century had itself been without importance in terms of European culture; if it had had no other result than the foundation of a new state raised by European emigrants to a level of freedom and prosperity unequaled anywhere in the Old World, a state wherein six million people enjoy all the pleasures of civilized life and know but a few of its burdens, wherein the original spring of wealth flows in abundance and the happy father looks forward without fear to future generations for whom the spring will flow only with increased riches, wherein simplicity of customs, equity of goods, and peaceful opinion give promise of permanent good fortune, a state which will remain the comfort of the unfortunate and persecuted of Europe, the hope of friends of humanity, and possibly even the source of wisdom and strength for our old continent; if European navigation had done no more than cause this state to exist, those skillful spirits who first crossed the uncharted seas, directed by their theories and inspired by their living faith, would not have worked in vain for the well-being of the world and their fellow Europeans.

Great and brilliant as this result may be, it is neither the sole nor the most significant of that extraordinary undertaking. That Europe itself, from Lisbon to the Volga, has become what it is at this moment; that it has climbed for three centuries from art to art, from science to science, from one plateau of enlightenment, refinement, and freedom to another; that it could send America its new citizens and in them the germs of an immeasurable prosperity; and that it surpassed in breadth and diversity the most prized states of antiquity—all that is due to America and to renewed and strengthened ties with the East Indies more than to any other cause; more, possibly, than to all other causes taken together.

The way by which this great, educative process was started and completed is, in brief, the following: *The discovery of America and a new route to the East Indies opened the greatest market, the greatest inducement to human industry, that had ever existed since the human race emerged from barbarism.* A closer consideration of this fact shows that such a development in the sphere of human efficacy must benefit Europe in three ways. First, it encourages the wealth, the activity, and the mutual contact of individuals, and the greater and lesser civil societies.

I. Everything that mankind counts as material goods, in the

broadest meaning of the term, is composed of two parts. Nature provides the first, i.e., material in the most general sense, and man supplies the other, i.e., his labor. . . . There is no other means for increasing the amount of wealth than through multiplication of labor, for even the discovery of new material is possible only through voluntary and persistent activity. Everything that encourages man to be more active, everything that makes his activity easier, more flourishing, worthwhile and general, fertilizes the field from which new pleasures and possessions unceasingly grow, provides new treasures for humanity, and stimulates and raises the capacity to achieve still greater harvests through still greater efforts.

That which spurs individuals and nations to increase the amount of labor over their needs of the moment is the hope of sale or the intent to exchange the surplus of their production for the surplus of others' and thereby to gain new pleasures. Nothing has so dramatically and so rapidly stimulated the excitement engendered by this exchange as the discovery of the two Indies.

Before this great discovery, the nations of Europe had not suffered any lack of impetus to industry and remuneration. But the most telling characteristic of its impact is that it began to operate so suddenly and so powerfully. Earlier, the products of European industry had improved bit by bit, new products were derived only slowly from nature, the efforts and artistry of manufacturers only gradually developed new methods and produced new forms, and the hope to enrich oneself was only very slowly developed and satisfied. Now suddenly a world full of treasures appeared before acquisitive eyes, and the impetus that this sight stimulated in all active powers had inevitably to effect a great revolution in the whole area of human industry, awaken the most lethargic from his slumbers and draw forward even the most indifferent.

Further, the goods offered by this new world were exactly those which have held the most powerful excitement for civilized man since time immemorial. On the one hand, the great variety of spices, roots, aromatic foods, powerful medicines and costly dyes, which had made the route to the Indies so important to the European even in the earliest times of his civilized existence; and on the other, gold and silver, the two goods which for millennia had fixed the worth of all others, whose possession exerted a curious and omnipotent magic, and of which America unexpectedly exhibited such great provision that within a century the relationship of these to all other goods and the price of every purchasable item underwent a great revolution.

As soon as reports spread over Europe of so many new means for the enjoyment of life, and especially of the limitless gold and silver supply, the inhabitants of those lands from which the voyages of discovery originated were feverishly aroused to obtain a part of the new treasures for themselves. Somewhat later the same was true of more distant places of trade with which these lands had contact, and, finally, of the most remote regions of our climes.

Industry in both city and country, all arts and enterprises, took on new wings. Since one could participate in this immeasurable booty only on an equal basis with others, could gain stock in this new enterprise only through labor, all physical and intellectual forces that had lain slumbering up to then were awakened and all activity doubly renewed. In order to have limitless objects ready for exchange against the new treasures, the products of European labor, and consequently the amount of European wealth, were limitlessly multiplied. The merchant spurred the manufacturer to new inventions; the manufacturer encouraged the farmer to exploit his fields, to extend his domain over the land, and to improve the produce he obtained from it. The stream from the East Indies and America which tempted Spanish, Portuguese, Dutch, French, and English ships did not allow itself to be confined to the narrow limits of ten or twelve harbors; it went further and irrigated the farthest extremities of the cultivated continent. In the heart of Germany, the desire for profit and pleasure, supported by diligence and artistry, brought more than one city to a brilliant flowering. In the fairy-tale mountains between Bohemia and Silesia, a splendid industry grew up and shared with the conquerors of Peru and Mexico the yield of their gold mines. Even where coarseness and poverty had earlier ruled, even among half-barbaric nations, there fell a spark from the fire. The slave, attached to the soil of Poland or Russia, felt a desire to collect some crumbs from the richly set table, and could not do so without increasing the prosperity of his fatherland through his increased labor. For those who had no direct contact with the East Indies and with American metals, the desire for products obtained by their more intelligent and adventurous neighbor was just as effective a spur as the sight of costly objects across the ocean had been to the latter.

In time, a new urge associated itself with the older one that had developed for knowledge of this New World's existence, and this new impulse was generated by the population of the New World. Next to the great market for European products, which nature had prepared and merchant industry had cultivated, the colonization of America provided a second and no less important one. The millions of Europeans who in the course of some centuries had settled on almost all the coasts and islands of America, and who had convinced the world that the soil of this new continent was far more important than its gold and diamonds, took with them not only a great number of needs, but also created new ones daily through their increasing culture and prosperity. A part of these needs was and is still of a kind that only Europe could satisfy. While colonists obtained from the earth itself all the costly products which at first constitute only the amenities of life and then gradually become necessities, Europeans worked incessantly to provide the ingenious manufactures which blossom more easily and more fully in the older nations. . . .

II. Up to this point, we have considered industry as the mother of wealth, and only that which enhances industry as beneficial to society. Industry lends itself, however, to observation from another point of view: it is a symbol or synonym for the activity of the human spirit.

Man could not all at once fulfill his destiny; the most sublime aspects of his nature had to develop gradually. The power which shows the stars their course and an intelligible world its laws, had first to exercise itself upon the cultivation of a clod and the coarsest demands of raw sensuality. However, everything that increases activity on the one hand, and refines pleasures on the other, leads man closer to his goal. Even if at first the wheel does no more than roll, it will soon roll in a more pleasing path. Once internal activity is aroused, it will soon see before it the small circle of its first objectives. For a long time, it must be encouraged by the lure of external reward, before it evolves to the point of being its own and greatest reward. . . .

We may not arbitrarily dismiss what has happened on this shining road since the beginning of the sixteenth century. In one and a half millennia, our race had not taken such giant steps as in this period. Many powerful causes united to bring forth this extraordinary effect; however, none of them is comparable in energy and creative influence to the discovery of America. The invention of printing merely provided an instrument which enabled an awakening spirit to lighten some of its operations. This invention created nothing; it was important only because it sprouted up in the middle of other great creations. The Reformation was a powerful and fruitful work; however, the one-sided impetus it gave to the spirit could be decisive only in an age when the urge for change and improvement was fermenting on all sides. The first shout of joy brought forth by the sighting of the promised land by Columbus' doubt-ridden ships, was the true signal of a new era for the European nations. We search in vain through the whole of human history for a greater and more constant spur to human activity than the revelation of a continent of unknown size, full of excitement and promise.

III. It is an eternal principle of human progress that man's strength can be developed only insofar as it comes in contact with other forces of the same nature. Expressed in everyday terms, this is the well-known maxim that "man is a social animal." . . .

If one single event multiplied the points of contact between men, it was certainly the discovery of America. It did this in two ways; first through its direct effects, and then through its mighty influence on European trade.

The savages Europeans encountered on their first explorations of America were still close to barbarism, or so deeply sunk in this primitive condition that acquaintance with them could contribute little or nothing to the education and improvement of their more civilized brothers. The relationship between the original inhabitants and the new arrivals soon became one of the most unfortunate and notorious ever to exist among men. The European, himself a semi-barbarian, saw the American primitive as an animal, created by nature for servitude. He bound him to work the field he had stolen from him; he killed him to get an ounce of gold which he believed he had hidden. The insatiability of one blinded by greed to his own advantage, the savage desire of a dark and superstitious religion to convert, the iron hard-heartedness of blatant disrespect of humanity—all these human traits combined plunged the first conquerors of America into the darkest of all wars and almost obliterated the original inhabitants from all the areas explored by Europeans. Yet, even this could not restrain the benefits which mere knowledge of the New World exerted on the people of the Old. Even if the rude Americans offered no advantageous point of contact to Europeans, the European found such a relationship among his compatriots who explored, cultivated, or plundered those far regions. Surrounded by an endless variety of new objects, he became a citizen of another world and instilled in other Europeans, insofar as they came into contact, thousands of new ideas, feelings, wishes and desires, and so served as a bridge between the curiosities of one hemisphere and those of the other.

Far more important and extensive, however, was the influence exerted by the Americas and the East Indies on general human culture through the exceptional expansion of European trade. It is well known that trade emerged from its infancy only when shipping dared to cross the great oceans. From the sixteenth century on, it grew from year to year and forged an indestructible bond among all civilized nations. Of all human occupations, activities and relations, none has been so valuable for the cultivation of the entire race as trade. Since the spirit of this activity comprises a varied and ever new interest as common ground between diverse men, it is therefore more closely related than any other principle to the great concept of sociability on which rests all of man's education. Although it appears to work only for the enrichment of man, it constantly teaches and refines him. Through the immeasurable community which it opens among all peoples, the insights, inventions, deep understanding, the finest flowers of feeling and imagination are borne immediately on the wings of the wind from land to land and from sea to sea, until like all pleasures and products of the spirit no matter where they originate, they become common property in which the whole civilized world can find nourishment. . . .

The philosophers of political economy have made the just remark that it would have been advantageous for the prosperity and flowering of states if the three great wellsprings of production and profit—farming, manufacture, and trade—could have been developed in their natural order so that the highest possible perfection in agriculture could have brought about the greatest expansion of manufacture possible, and in turn the increase in trade. It is well known that this development occurred in reverse order: trade stimulated manufacture and the latter aroused agriculture; and the great neglect of this last main branch of human industry, the imperfections and limitations to which the cultivation of the earth has been confined in most civilized lands, is our fault as well as that of the one-sided mercantile system, in that we were so late in discovering the simple processes of nature. As a result, it seems as if chance or fate had opposed this system and had intended nothing less than harm for our culture. No human endeavor affects the general education of nations more than trade, and none less than agriculture. Agricultural peoples remain isolated, coarse, ignorant, and limited. Urban industry and its companion, trade, have made Europe into what it is at this moment. If it had been possible to acquire all that we now have and will have by the method above, which is essentially the most natural one; if it is true that the excess of farm produce could have brought about manufacture and trade, and that the benefits which accrue from them would eventually have flowed to us in greater proportion than at present and without the inconveniences under which we now suffer, we would nevertheless have eventually reached the point at which we now stand; and it is questionable that, even with all our present capabilities and insights, we could have as completely and quickly arrived at the great goal to which that simple and direct way would surely have led us. If this is the case, the discovery of America (among all world events which have contributed to the pre-eminence of trade over agriculture) is a decisive gain for mankind in every possible way, even when a more comprehensive examination seems to show that it worked disadvantageously for mankind.

If the discovery of America prepared all these benefits and wonders, it is obvious that it has greatly affected the civil and political existence of man and that the state too, as a state, had to feel its advantageous and powerful influence. Accordingly, it is best to show, in times when all minds are occupied with the political relationships of man and the principles of constitutionality, how the discovery of America affected the transition from individual to collective improvement of European humanity, and thus to present the connection between the direct, distant, and ultimate consequences of that great event. . . .

The highest possible degree of civil freedom, insured by a constitution which fits it best, is the highest purpose and ideal of any political association. The more a state approaches this ideal, the more perfectly are all purposes of civil society attained.

Freedom in the European state was encouraged by the discovery of America in two ways. First, the wealth of these states was increased, and, second, their degree of enlightenment was increased.

IV. Europe's condition in the Middle Ages was approximately the following: All public power was concentrated in the hands of the great landowners; the remaining classes were either slaves, peasants, or semi-slaves, inhabitants of those places first provided with city privileges, or finally, the poor, ignored and constantly plundered citizens of cities. This remained the case in most of Europe into the seventeenth century. All political rights were bound to ownership of land, and he who enjoyed no political rights could hardly count himself as worthy of humanity. There was no alternative between domination and servility. Rulers possessed only enough power to commit single oppressions. They were much too weak to affect the whole structure permanently, especially in a beneficial sense. At every step, they encountered jealous, bellicose, and rigid powers which would never concede that the benefit of the state could emerge from the rubble of their dissipating power. In the bloody wars between despotism and aristocracy, between spiritual and temporal tyranny, the oppressed nations could only tremblingly ask which form their yoke would assume. The feudal system prevented the emergence of a true system of government. The coarseness, the brutality, the barbarism of customs made the practice of lawless rule even more revolting than its nature and origins necessitated, and the gross ignorance blanketing Europe denied to millions of oppressed all hope that from their suffering, perhaps, a way could be found to a better future.

Let us examine how the increase in wealth, promoted by the discovery of America, gradually washed away the lamentable characteristics of feudalism.

1. Wealth gradually brought about greater equality among the classes of society, in that it transformed into independent proprietors those who had previously lived by the grace of others, deprived the former lords of the earth of part of their force, and led the rest into other channels, for it created a counterweight to the oppressive superiority of immovable fortune in the tremendous and ever-increasing amount of movable fortune. . . .

The wealth and industry which followed upon the discovery

of America and spread over the whole of Europe brought forth a large class of men who had previously been of little note and no political influence. Through its ever-increasing wealth, through the mass of active, skilled, and inventive men it embraced, through the interesting undertakings which sprang from its bosom, through the point of unification it offered to the scattered inhabitants of the nation for all kinds of business affairs and contacts, and, finally, through all coarse and refined pleasures for which it became the exclusive gathering place, the city quickly rose to a position of great wealth and dominance in all European nations.

Once the citizens of these cities had experienced the glories of life and mastered the attendant arts; once they had come so far that the higher classes had to seek their services and their associations; once they had finally acquired through their wealth some of the appearance of the upper class and even the titles of its dignity, overpowered its influence through theirs, humbled its pride through their brilliance, bound themselves through their sons and daughters to its families; once kings sought their favors and state officials recognized them as the source of their power and the most effective tool for great undertakings; once the learned of the earth had striven for their approval, all possibility for treating them with disrespect or indifference disappeared. Those means which had won them the honorable position they now occupied also put them in a position to maintain it. Gradually a portion of their fortunes and political independence flowed over to the farmer, who slowly rose from his humiliating position of savagery and slavery. As soon as the farmer was assured of sustenance and a bearable existence, he could no longer tolerate the iron yoke imposed by the greed and haughtiness of his masters. The inequality of strengths daily narrowed on all sides, and the equality of rights became daily more applicable, necessary, and natural.

At the same time and in the same way that the lower classes increased their wealth and influence, the higher classes saw theirs reduced or lost. Nothing is more understandable than that the desire for the new treasures dispersed over Europe by trade and manufacture should be even more strongly awakened in the higher classes than in the lower. But they had no desire to gain these treasures through their own labors, and even if they did, their own labors would never have been enough to acquire a share commensurate with their position. Nothing remained to them, therefore, than to sell a part of their prerogatives, usurpations, and power. They ceased to rule because they found it more pleasurable to enjoy life. They exchanged true power for its exterior trappings. They let men go free in order to acquire some new toys, and they renounced their greatness to satisfy their greed and vanity. The proud lord who had fed thousands from his abundance and who had been regarded by those thousands as the only source of their existence and honored by them as their master and father, who could have ordered them into danger and death with a nod of the head, this lord let go his impressive retinue and satisfied himself with a moderate house staffed by paid servants because he found it more pleasant to fill his table with delicacies from distant lands, to put jewels from Brazil on his fingers or in the hair of his wife, and to let his house be adorned with gold and silver from Peru, clothes from the East Indies and China, and thousands of products of European industry. The brightly garbed master gradually freed his underlings, enriched them intentionally and improved their lives through a momentary sacrifice in order to improve the yield of his lands and thereby insure the means for life's pleasures that could now be acquired only through money. Now the wasteful or bored landowner sold a great part of his lands, delivered them into the hands of his servants or the slaves of his father, and in return received treasures that his grandchildren would perhaps never see. Through the impoverishment of his own family, he founded or increased the prosperity of hundreds of others. . . .

It would not be proper to examine here how the relationship of landowner to the monied classes should be formed or ordered, or how the freedom of all and the security of the state should be secured. It would be just as improper for us to develop and present the injurious consequences which could result from a too great preponderance of the monied classes and which could arise very easily from an unenlightened use of their powers. For our purposes, it is enough to indicate that through the origin and education of this class of proprietors, which has increased in size and influence so greatly since the discovery of America, the freedom of all citizens has visibly benefited, and perhaps benefited more by this than by any other means.

2. Through the increase in wealth, the governments of all

European nations became more orderly than they had previously been, and for this reason, they approached perfection. . . .

That time when most European states exchanged the feudal constitution for the monarchical was, to be sure, somewhat earlier than the discovery of America. However, that the wealth which this discovery brought about weakened the power of the great and encouraged the equality of classes, contributed to completing this great change and to giving unity, dignity, and power to governments, is clear not only through a reasonable analogy, but also through the actual teachings of history. More obviously and decisively, the growing wealth of Europe affected the order and perfection of governments in that it multiplied and improved their tools. Great undertakings were now possible for princes in their efforts to improve civilization in their nations, an undertaking even the most active and well-meaning rulers could not have attempted without the means given them by the new prosperity of their subjects. What did the wiser and more active rulers do with these means? Look at what even less attentive and enlightened rulers have done for agriculture, trade, industry, and education in the last century. Even if more could have been accomplished in some cases, even if the natural course toward betterment has at times been hindered instead of accelerated, still much has happened on the whole for the happiness, culture, and freedom of nations.

3. More gentle customs, refined sociability, the more lenient maxims and axioms which accompanied the general prosperity could not remain without influence on rulers and necessarily made them more gentle, more humane and more attentive to the rights of their subjects and their freedom.

It is unnecessary to explain in detail this entirely natural result or to prove its reality. The best commentary on the foregoing is what has happened in the last hundred, even in the last ten or twenty years. In fact, one could point to what is happening daily around us. We can observe the gentle but unmistaken path along which humanity has been led from dark recesses to safe and airy heights. It is unthinkable that a crude and reactionary ruler could arise in a nation refined almost to the point of softness, and that, were his power unlimited, he could commit singularly brutal, tyrannical and repulsive acts. Reason and experience combine to declare this development impossible, that a barbaric system of government could arise in such a nation accompanied by tyranny and lust for blood. The general character of all individuals within a state unavoidably determines the character of the government and of the men who implement it. In the long run, only reasonable and liberal methods can rule reasonable men, just as only absolute power can rule coarse and barbarous peoples. It is an old but true commonplace that kings and their servants will always remain the same, even if heaven and earth themselves were to change. . . .

3. The enlightenment of a nation is the result of a long, continued education of the spirit. We have seen that the discovery of America affected directly and indirectly the activity of the human spirit and the utilitarian direction if its strengths. It cannot therefore be doubted that this great event contributed a great deal to the enlightenment Europe now enjoys.

It is indisputable that enlightenment is connected with freedom. To be free, one must know what freedom is, and it is one of the ultimate purposes of enlightenment to instruct nations in this important point. An obscure longing for liberation from chains, a feeling shared by all oppressed people, is not a true desire for freedom. One must think long about man and his condition before a true idea of the greatest and most artificial of all man's relationships can gain ascendancy. Enlightenment leads gradually but infallibly to this conclusion. In that it raises all classes to power in its silent progress, it leads the prince to a realization of his duties and his true advantage, at the same time that the subject becomes aware of his true rights. While the latter strives for greater freedom, the former feels more inclined to grant it. Even when the inclination of the prince lags behind the demands of his subjects, it is enough that they continually approach one another. Sooner or later the enlightenment fulfills its purpose, great as the obstacles may be, and it does this as inevitably as in other areas, in spite of all obstruction.

It would be repetitious to show what the enlightenment has done for Europe's political relations since the last century. The harshest critics of slavery in our age, the loudest defamers of our generation, the most one-sided apologists of the past, provide in one way or another the best witness to this fact. Never has the humanity of all people been so respected, never have their rights and prosperity enjoyed so much attention and effort from individual governments, as is now the case in most European states. We are reminded that the greatest event of our century, the French Revolution, was the consequence of extraordinary pressure, but we tend to forget all too easily that this was only one side of the coin. This Revolution, viewed from the other side, was also the result of the greatest indulgence and the greatest liberality ever to rule since thrones have existed.

. . . A penetrating look at the history of the past three centuries, and in particular at our present century, must console everyone as to the future of the race. Obstacles and disturbances there will continue to be, perhaps for all time, but the prospects are on the whole heartening. As we approach the third millennium, we can look forward with reassurance to a radiant condition for mankind on the path towards ultimate perfection if there is no interruption to the progress which began with the discovery of America.

# Sources and Bibliography

WE HAVE NOT ATTEMPTED here a comprehensive or critical bibliography for the subjects discussed in this volume. The excellent bibliography in Antonello Gerbi's *La Disputa del Nuevo Mundo* (Mexico City, 1960) is exhaustive and comprehensive. See, in addition, the admirable bibliography in *French Travellers in the United States* by Frank Monaghan (New York, 1933) and the comprehensive bibliography to be published in Commager, *America and the Enlightenment* (New York, 1967).

We have limited ourselves to giving here bibliographical data for the material we have presented, and what appear to be the most important critical commentaries.

## I. SOURCE MATERIALS


1. Buffon, Georges-Louis Leclerc, Comte de. *Natural History, General and Particular*. Translated by William Smellie. 20 vols., London, 1812. Vol. VI, pp. 224–272.
   ———. *Histoire naturelle*. 17 vols., Paris, 1774–79. "Des Américains" in Vol. V, *L'Histoire naturelle de l'Homme*, 1778, pp. 525–538.
2. De Pauw, Corneille. *Recherches philosophiques sur les Américains, ou Mémoires intéressants pour servir à l'Histoire de l'Espèce humaine*. 3 vols., London, 1774.
3. Pernety, Dom Antoine-Joseph. *Dissertation sur l'Amérique et les Américains, contre les Recherches philosophiques de Mr. de P.* Berlin, 1770.
4. Raynal, Guillaume Thomas. *A Philosophical and Political History of the Settlements and Trade of the Europeans in the East and West Indies*. Translated by J. Justamond, M.A. 4 vols., London, 1776.
5. Robertson, William, Jr. *The History of America*. 2 vols., London, 1777.
6. Roubaud, Pierre-Joseph. *Histoire générale de l'Asie, de l'Afrique, et de l'Amérique*. 5 vols., Paris, 1775.

7. Mandrillon, Joseph. *Recherches philosophiques sur la découverte de l'Amérique.* Amsterdam, 1784.

———. *Spectateur américain,* Amsterdam, 1784.

8. Condorcet, Antoine-Nicholas, Marquis de. "De l'Influence de la Révolution de l'Amérique sur l'Europe," in *Oeuvres complètes de Condorcet,* ed. Garat & Cabanis, Paris, An IX [1800–1801], Vol. XI, pp. 249–294.

9. Chastellux, François Jean, Marquis de. *Discours sur les avantages et les désavantages qui résultent pour l'Europe de la découverte de l'Amérique.* London and Paris, 1787.

10. Gentz, Friedrich von. "Ueber den Einfluss der Entdeckung von Amerika auf den Wohlstand und die Kultur des menschlichen Geschlechts" in *Ausgewählte Schriften von Friedrich von Gentz.* 5 vols., Stuttgart & Leipsig, 1838. Vol. V, pp. 173-216.

II. GENERAL

Bain, R. N. *Gustavus III and his Contemporaries, 1746–1792.* 2 vols., London, 1904.

Bell, Whitfield J. *Science and Humanity in Philadelphia, 1775–1790.* Unpublished Ph.D. dissertation, University of Pennsylvania, 1947.

Cailliet, Emile. *La Tradition littéraire des Idéologues.* Philadelphia, 1943.

Casas, D. J. J. *El Dorado Fantasma.* Madrid, 1930.

Chinard, Gilbert. *L'Amérique et le Rêve exotique dans la littérature française au XVIIe et XVIIIe siècles.* Paris, 1913.

———. *Correspondence of Jefferson and DuPont, with an Introduction on Jefferson and the Physiocrats.* Baltimore, 1931.

———. "Eighteenth Century Theories on America as a Human Habitat," in XCI *American Philosophical Society Proceedings* (1947), pp. 27 ff.

———. *L'Homme contre la nature. Essais d'histoire de l'Amérique.* Paris, 1949.

———. *Jefferson et les Idéologues.* Baltimore, 1925.

———. *Volney et l'Amérique.* Baltimore, 1923.

Crome, A. F. W. *Über die Grösse, Clima und Fruchtbarkeit des nordamerikanischen Freystaats.* Dessau, Leipzig, 1783.

Ducros, Louis. *Les Encyclopédistes.* Paris, 1900.

Dumas, J.-B. *Histoire de l'Académie de Lyon.* Lyon, 1839.

Echeverria, Durand. *Mirage in the West: A History of the French Image of American Society to 1815.* Princeton, 1957.

Faÿ, Bernard. *The Revolutionary Spirit in France and America in the Second Half of the Eighteenth Century.* New York, 1927.

Gerbi, Antonello. *La Disputa del Nuevo Mundo: Historia de una Polemica, 1750–1900.* Mexico City, 1960.

———. *Viejas polemicas sobre el Nuevo Mundo. En el umbral de una concencia americana.* 3rd ed., Lima, 1946.

Hawkins, Richard. *Madame de Staël and the United States.* Cambridge, 1930.

Jones, Howard Mumford. *America and French Culture.* London, 1927.

———. *O Strange New World.* New York, 1964.

Miller, Ralph N. "American Nationalism as a Theory of Nature," in *William and Mary Quarterly,* Vol. XII, January 1955, pp. 74 ff.

———. *The Historians Discover America: A Study of American Historical Writing in the Eighteenth Century.* PhD. Thesis Northwestern University, 1946 (unpublished).

Monaghan, Frank. *French Travellers in the United States, 1765–1932: A Bibliography.* New York, 1933.

Morley, John Viscount. *Diderot and the Encyclopaedists* (Vol. I). London, 1921.

Sherill, Charles H. *French Memoirs of Eighteenth Century America.* New York, 1915.

Stark, Werner. *America: Ideal and Reality.* London, 1947.

Tilley, Winthrop. *The Literature of Natural and Physical Science in the American Colonies.* Brown University Ph.D. dissertation, 1933 (unpublished).

Tuckerman, Henry T. *America and Her Commentators.* New York, 1864.

Zavala, Silvio. *America en el Espiritu Frances del Siglo XVIII.* Mexico City, 1949.

## III. ESSAYS ON THE SUBJECT

Anon. *Discours sur les avantages ou les désavantages qui résultent, pour l'Europe, de la découverte de l'Amérique. Objet du prix proposé par M. l'Abbé Raynal.* Par M. P. . . . , Vice-Consul, à E. . . . London, Paris, 1787.

Anon. *Dissertation sur les suites de la découverte de l'Amérique, qui a obtenu en 1785 une mention honorable de l'Académie des Sciences et Belles-Lettres de Lyon. Revue et corrigée pour le concours de l'année 1787, sous l'embleme d'un navire avec ces mots: Orbem conjugit utrumque.* Par un Citoyen, ancien Syndic de la Chambre du Commerce de Lyon, 1787.

Benson, Adolph B., ed. *Peter Kalm's Travels in North America.* New York, 1937.

Blanchard, Claude. *Guerre d'Amérique (1780–1783): Journal de campagne de Claude Blanchard.* Paris, 1881.

Bonnet, J. E. *Réponse aux principales questions qui peuvent être faites sur les Etats-Unis d'Amérique.* Lausanne, 1795.

Bonsal, Stephen. *When the French Were Here.* New York, 1945.

Brissot (de Warville), Jacques-Pierre. *Nouveau Voyage dans les Etats-Unis de l'Amérique.* 3 vols., Paris, 1791.

Brun, Jean-André. *Le Triomphe du Nouveau Monde.* Paris, 1785.

Buffon, Georges Louis Leclerc, Comte de. *Les Epoques de la Nature.* Edition critique par Jacques Roger. Paris, 1962.

Carle, Henri. *Discours sur la question proposée par M. l'Abbé Raynal: La Découverte de l'Amérique a-t-elle été utile ou nuisible au genre humain?* Paris, 1790.

Carli, Gian-Rinaldo. *Delle lettere americane.* 2 vols., Florence, 1780.

Cerisier, Antoine-Marie. *Le Destin de l'Amérique.* London, 1780.

Chase, Eugene Parker, ed. *Our Revolutionary Forefathers: The Letters of François, Marquis de Barbe-Marbois, during his Residence in the United States as Secretary of the French Legation, 1779–1785.* New York, 1929.

Chastellux, François Jean, Marquis de. *Travels in North America.* Ed. by Howard C. Rice, Jr. 2 vols., North Carolina, 1963.

Condorcet, Antoine Nicholas, Marquis de. *Dissertation sur les suites de la découverte de l'Amérique*. Paris, 1787.

———. *L'Influence de la Révolution de l'Amérique sur les opinions et la législation de l'Europe*. Paris, 1786.

———. *Sketch for a Historical Picture of the Progress of the Human Mind*. Translated by June Barraclough with an introduction by Stuart Hampshire. London, 1955.

Currie, William. *An Historical Account of the Climates and Diseases of the United States of America*. Philadelphia, 1792.

Démeunier, Jean-Nicolas. *Essai sur les Etats-Unis*. Paris, 1786. For Jefferson's contribution to this *Essai*, see Boyd, ed., *Jefferson Papers;* VIII, 678; IX, 155–6, 192–3, 382–3; X, 3–65.

Deslandes, le Chevalier. *Discours sur la grandeur et l'importance de la Révolution qui vient de s'opérer dans l'Amérique septentrionale*. Paris, 1785.

Engel, Samuel. *Essai sur cette question: Quand et comment l'Amérique a-t-elle été peuplée d'hommes et d'animaux?* Par E.B.d'E. Amsterdam, 1767. [Engel's name does not appear on the edition at all, but he is known to be the author.]

Genty, Louis. *L'Influence de la découverte de l'Amérique sur le bonheur du genre humain*. Paris, 1787.

Gentz, Friedrich von. *The Origin and Principles of the American Revolution, compared with the Origin and Principles of the French Revolution*. Translated by John Q. Adams. Philadelphia, 1800.

Girod-Chantrans, Justin. *Voyage d'un Suisse dans différentes colonies d'Amérique*. Neuchâtel, 1785.

Linguet, Simon. *Political and Philosophical Speculations on the Distinguishing Characteristics of the Present Century, and on the State of Legislation, Military Establishments, Finances and Commerce in Europe, with Occasional Reflections on the Probable Effects of American Independence*. London, 1778.

Mailhé, J.-B. *Discours qui a remporté le prix à l'Académie des Jeux-Floraux en 1784 sur la Grandeur et l'importance de la révolution qui vient de s'opérer dans l'Amérique septentrionale*. Toulouse, 1784.

Mazzei, Filippo. *Recherches sur les Etats-Unis de l'Amérique septentrionale, avec quatre lettres d'un bourgeois de New-Haven sur l'unité de la législation*. Paris, 1788.

Pastoret, M. de. *Tributs offerts à l'Académie de Marseille*. Paris, 1782.

Pernety, Dom Antoine-Joseph. *Examen des Recherches philosophiques sur l'Amérique et les Américains et de la Défense de cet ouvrage*. 2 vols., Berlin, 1771.

Poivre, Pierre. *De l'Amérique et des Américains, ou Observations curieuses du philosophe LaDouceur, qui a parcouru cet Hemisphère pendant la dernière Guerre, en faisant le noble métier de tuer des Hommes sans les manger*. Berlin, 1772.

Robin, Claude C. *New Travels through North America*. Translated by Philip Freneau. Philadelphia, 1783.

Scherer, Jean-Benoit. *Recherches historiques et géographiques sur le Nouveau Monde*. Paris, 1777.

Van der Kemp, Francis Adrian. *An Autobiography, together with Extracts from his Correspondence*. Ed. by Helen Lincklaen Fairchild. New York, 1903.

Volney, Constantin-François. *Tableau du climat et du sol des Etats-Unis*. Paris, 1803.

Whitridge, Arnold. "Two Aristocrats in Rochambeau's Army," in *Virginia Quarterly Review*, Vol LX. No. 1, 1964, pp. 114–128.

## IV. CRITICAL WORKS ON AUTHORS OR GROUPS OF AUTHORS

Ariès, P. *Histoire des populations françaises et de leur attitude devant la vie depuis le XVIIIe siècle*. Paris, 1949.

Beyerhaus, Gilbert. "Abbé de Pauw und Friedrich der Grosse, eine Abrechnung mit Voltaire," in *Historische Zeitschrift*, Munich, Vol. CXXXLV (1926), pp. 465–493.

Bridenbaugh, Carl and Jessica. *Rebels and Gentlemen. Philadelphia in the Age of Franklin*. New York, 1942.

Church, Henry W. "Corneille de Pauw and the Controversy over his *Recherches philosophiques*," in *PMLA*, Vol. LI (1936), p. 178 ff.

Crocker, Lester G. "Linguet's Prognostication for the American Colonies," in *The French American Review*, II (1949), pp. 45–52.

Cruppi, J. *Un avocat journaliste au XVIIIe siècle: Linguet*. Paris, 1895.

Diannyère, Antoine. *Notice sur la Vie et les Ouvrages de Condorcet.* Paris, 1796.

Echeverria, Durand. "Roubaud and the Theory of American Degeneration," in *The French American Review* (January-March 1950), III, pp. 24–33.

Ellery, E. *Brissot.* Cambridge, Mass., 1915.

Feugère, Anatole. *Un Précurseur de la Révolution: l'abbé Raynal (1713–1796).* Angoulême, 1922.

Garlick, Richard Cecil, Jr. *Philip Mazzei, Friend of Jefferson: His Life and Letters.* Baltimore, 1933.

Gidney, Lucy. *L'Influence des Etats-Unis d'Amérique sur Brissot, Condorcet, et Mme. Roland.* Paris, 1930.

Gooch, G. P. *Germany and the French Revolution.* London, 1920.

Hindle, Brooke. *The Pursuit of Science in Revolutionary America, 1735–1789.* North Carolina, 1956.

Humphreys, R. A. *William Robertson and his History of America.* London, 1954.

Liedtke, Kurt. *Die Darstellung Amerikas durch den Abbé Raynal und damit verbundene Zeitproblem.* Erlangen, 1954.

Mann, Golo. *Secretary of Europe: The Life of Friedrich Gentz, Enemy of Napoleon.* Translated by William H. Woglom. New Haven, 1946.

Marraro, H. R., ed. *Memoirs of the Life and Peregrinations of the Florentine, Philip Mazzei.* New York, 1942.

Rice, H. *Le Cultivateur américain.* Paris, 1933.

Ronan, Charles S. I. *Francisco Xavier Mariano Clavigero: A Study in Mexican Historiography.* University of Texas Ph.D. dissertation (unpublished).

Rush, Benjamin. "The Influence of Physical Causes on the Moral Faculty," Address before the American Philosophical Society, 1786; reprinted in Blau, Joseph L., *American Philosophical Addresses,* New York, 1946, pp. 312 ff.

Sicot, Lucien. *The Marquis de Chastellux.* Paris, 1902.

Sweet, Paul. *Friedrich von Gentz, Defender of the Old Order.* Madison, 1941.

Thiébault, Dieudonné. *Mes Souvenirs de vingt ans de séjour à Berlin.* Paris, 1804.

Varnum, Fanny. *Un philosophe cosmopolite du XVIIIe siècle: Le Chevalier de Chastellux.* Paris, 1936.

Wolpe, Hans. *Raynal et sa machine de guerre.* Stanford, 1957.

www.ingramcontent.com/pod-product-compliance
Lightning Source LLC
LaVergne TN
LVHW091045080826
845145LV00002B/624

* 9 7 8 1 6 2 8 2 0 0 9 4 2 *